ICC Guide to Incoterms® 2010

Understanding and practical use

By Jan Ramberg

International Chamber of Commerce
The world business organization

M·A·

ICC Services
Publications
38 Cours Albert 1er
75008 Paris
France

ICC Publication No. 720E
ISBN: 978-92-842-0082-5

www.iccbooks.com

Contents

Going through the 11 Incoterms rules   83

Role of the Incoterms rules in an international contract of sale   205

Annexes   209

INTRODUCTION

The Evolution of the Incoterms rules from 1936 to 2010

After their initial introduction in 1936, the Incoterms rules were revised for the first time in 1957 and thereafter in 1967, 1976, 1980, 1990 and 2000. This appears to suggest that, in recent times, the Incoterms rules have been revised at 10-year intervals. This, however, is a false impression. It is merely a coincidence that the last three revisions are separated by 10-year periods. Indeed, the main purpose of the Incoterms rules is to reflect international commercial practice. Needless to say, commercial practice does not change at a set interval.

It is a common misunderstanding that the Incoterms rules represent nothing more than standard contract terms that could be revised at any time. In fact, the value of the Incoterms rules as an expression of international commercial practice would be endangered by frequent changes for some purpose or other, such as to make them more reader-friendly or to clarify a few points of minor importance. A revision of the Incoterms rules therefore requires that something important has taken place in commercial practice.

The first version of the Incoterms rules was clearly focused on commodity trading and fixed the important delivery points at the ship's side or at the moment when the goods are taken on board the ship. The risk transfer point in the latter case was deemed to be the moment when the goods passed the ship's rail. This point was relevant in the important and well-known trade terms FOB, CFR and CIF. In cases where the goods were to be delivered alongside the ship rather than across the ship's rail, the trade term FAS was available. The Incoterms 1936 rules also contained a trade term representing the minimum obligation of the seller, namely EXW ("Ex-Works").

After the Second World War, work on the revision of the Incoterms rules was resumed. Carriage of goods by rail had now increased, and it was necessary to introduce appropriate terms. In railway traffic, the seller frequently undertakes to arrange for the carriage in the same manner as under FOB. In 1957, two trade terms were added for this purpose, namely FOR and FOT ("Free on Rail" and "Free on Truck"). In 1976, a specific term for air transport was added, namely FOB Airport. All these trade terms, which applied to a specific mode of transport, were removed from the 1990 version of the Incoterms rules, as it was deemed unnecessary at that time to have specific terms for different modes of non-maritime transport. It was sufficient to use the general term FCA signifying "Free Carrier named point". This term was first introduced in the 1980 version of the Incoterms rules, as by this time the carriage of goods in containers had increased to such an extent that it was necessary to introduce a new trade term (then with the acronym FCR). This was all the more necessary because the existence of various container terms could, at worst, lead to a chaotic proliferation of variants to the detriment of international trade. Nevertheless, the innovation represented by FCA was regarded as an experiment, which explains why it was introduced as an additional trade term at the very end of the relevant ICC publication. However, in the 1990 version, FCA became one of the more important Incoterms rules. Nevertheless, it took a considerable amount of time before merchants realized that it was no good using trade terms such as FOB when, in practice, the goods were not handed over to the carrier on board the ship but at earlier reception points in the country of shipment: so-called container yards or container freight stations. It was difficult for merchants to understand that a seller should not remain at risk after the goods had been handed over to a carrier nominated by the buyer.

In the 1980 revision of the Incoterms rules, it was necessary to add CIP for non-maritime transport as an equivalent to CIF, under which the seller undertakes to arrange and pay for the carriage and insurance. As a result, the terms CPT and CIP, corresponding to CFR and CIF for maritime transport, were both added to the Incoterms rules. The transport document used for maritime transport – the bill of lading – is not used for non-maritime transport, the reason being that, except when carried by ship, goods are normally not sold in transit. Therefore, there is no need for a specific document like a bill of lading, which enables the holder to sell the goods by transferring the document to a new buyer. Consequently, CPT and CIP only make reference to the "usual transport document".

In 1967, it was necessary to add terms for cases in which the seller undertakes to deliver the goods at destination. In such cases, the seller concludes a contract of carriage in order to fulfil his obligation to deliver the goods to the buyer at destination. Although he also pays for the freight under CFR and CIF, he actually fulfils his obligation upon the shipment of the goods. Under these trade terms, his obligation is reduced to arranging and paying for the transport and tendering a document that enables the buyer to receive the goods from the carrier at destination. However, the seller assumes no risk for loss of or damage to the goods after they have passed the ship's rail in the country of shipment.

It is sometimes difficult for merchants to understand that a contract in which the point at destination is named – such as "CIF New York" – nevertheless signifies that the risk is transferred from the seller to the buyer before the indicated point, namely the point in the country of shipment where the goods are taken on board the ship. Indeed, all terms starting with the letter C signify that there are two critical points: one concerning the transfer of risk at the port of shipment and the other being the point up to which the seller has the obligation to arrange and pay for transport.

In the 1990 revision of the Incoterms rules, it was deemed unnecessary to retain the earlier trade terms relating to specific modes of transport (FOR, FOT and FOB Airport). The revision was also triggered by the shift from paper documents to electronic communication. As a result, a paragraph was added in the clauses dealing with the seller's obligation to tender documents to the buyer stating that paper documents could be replaced by electronic messages if the parties had agreed to communicate electronically.

What then is the reason for the revision of the Incoterms rules resulting in the Incoterms® 2010 rules? It appears that the main problem with the Incoterms 2000 rules was not so much what they contained but rather that it was not sufficiently clear how they should be used in practice. In addition, it is important to expand the use of the Incoterms rules, particularly in the United States, where a possibility to do so has arisen as a result of the removal of the 1941 definitions of trade terms from the Uniform Commercial Code. Indeed, the key trade term FOB is understood differently in the United States than in the Incoterms rules. In the United States, FOB merely represents a point that could be anywhere. In order to achieve an equivalent to FOB under the Incoterms rules, it would be necessary to add the word "vessel" after the term FOB. A new trade term – DAP ("Delivered at Place")- has therefore been added. When using this term, it is possible to indicate any appropriate place. However, DAP is inappropriate in cases where the goods should be made available to the buyer unloaded from the means of transport. Another new term – DAT ("Delivered at Terminal") – has therefore been added for use when the unloading of the goods from the means of transport should be performed at the seller's cost and risk. This means that the maritime terms DES and DEQ in the Incoterms 2000 rules have been replaced, respectively, by DAP and DAT, since the "terminal" in DAT corresponds to the "quay" in DEQ where the goods are unloaded from a ship. In the event that parties continue to use DES or DEQ under the Incoterms 2000 rules, the result will be the same as under DAP and DAT in the Incoterms® 2010 rules.

There are limits to what can be done to increase the understanding of the Incoterms rules. In particular, merchants retain old habits and are not easily persuaded to depart from the traditional maritime terms, although this is clearly necessary when contemplating non-maritime transport. In order to promote a better understanding of the Incoterms rules, the 2010 version starts by presenting trade terms that can be used for any mode or modes of transport and only then presents trade terms that can be used for sea and inland waterway transport. Hopefully, this will induce merchants to first consider the use of the "all modes terms". Nevertheless, it is important to consider the different needs of trading in commodities as compared to manufactured goods. Commodity trading will continue to focus on carriage of goods by ship, and it remains to be seen whether merchants will choose to use the new terms. Be that as it may, merchants need to understand that trading in manufactured goods – which frequently involves containerization – requires a range of trade terms that are tailored to contemporary commercial practice.

Another frequent misunderstanding concerns the very purpose of the Incoterms rules. Although they are needed to determine key obligations of sellers and buyers with respect to the different modalities of delivery, transfer of risk and cost, the terms do not represent the whole contract. It is also necessary to determine what rules apply when the contract is not performed as expected, owing to various circumstances, and how disputes between the parties should be resolved. While the Incoterms rules tell the parties what to do, they do not explain what happens if they do not do so! For this purpose, the parties need to lay down applicable rules in a contract or by using a standard form contract as a supplement. In practice, disputes might nevertheless arise owing to unexpected events that the parties have failed to consider in their contract in a clear and conclusive manner. In such cases, the applicable law may provide a solution. Fortunately, the 1980 UN Convention on Contracts for the International Sale of Goods (CISG) has now become recognized worldwide, thus contributing significantly to transparency and effective dispute resolution in international trade.

The ICC Model International Sale Contract (ICC pub. 556)

Although the applicable law may provide the necessary solutions when parties have not expressly agreed on certain issues in their contract, this is sometimes undesirable or the applicable law is not sufficiently precise to solve the matter. It is therefore necessary to deal with these issues in the individual contract or by reference to a standard form contract. ICC provides assistance to the parties in this respect by means of various standard forms. In the context of the international sale of goods, the ICC Model International Sale Contract (the "ICC Sale Form") is particularly important. Section A of the ICC Sale Form invites the parties to select appropriate solutions themselves. First of all, it is essential to identify the parties and to specify the goods, the price and how the buyer should pay. It is also essential to choose the appropriate term for the delivery of the goods.

It is here that, for the first time, we see a distinction between terms appropriate for the delivery of manufactured goods as opposed to commodities. It is this distinction between the various categories that now appears in the Incoterms® 2010 rules .

Payment conditions can be chosen by ticking the appropriate boxes for payment on open account, payment in advance, documentary collection or the use of a documentary credit. The various documents required for a documentary credit are also specified.

Section B of the ICC Sale Form lists general conditions with respect to liability for non-conforming goods and the consequences of late delivery (payment of liquidated damages and termination when the maximum amount has been reached). There is also a provision relating to default interest in case of delayed payment. The interest rate refers to the average bank lending rate to prime borrowers with an increment of 2%.

In some cases, a party may fail to perform its obligation under a contract. If this failure is due to a certain type of event, it is not reasonable to hold that party liable for its failure to perform. Such events appear under the heading Force Majeure.

Even though parties are able to settle their disputes amicably in most cases, there is a need to provide for the unfortunate event in which they fail to do so. Consequently, there is a provision in Section B referring to arbitration according to the ICC Arbitration Rules.

The parties may depart from the provisions in Section B by completing boxes in Section A. They may wish to insert a particular cancellation date, given the difficulty of determining when cancellation of the contract is possible under the applicable law. In addition, they may wish to depart from the provisions on termination in the case of the late delivery or non-conformity of the goods in Section B. Alternatively, they may wish to provide for a form of compensation other than liquidated damages, for instance a fixed amount, in the case of delay.

The general conditions in Section B provide for a deadline for the institution of an action against the seller for non-conformity of the goods, namely a period of two years from the date of the arrival of the goods. In the specific conditions of Section A, however, the parties may wish to provide for another time period.

With respect to choice of law, the parties may specify in Section A that a domestic sale of goods act should apply instead of the CISG or that the CISG should be supplemented by the law of a specific country or by generally recognized principles of law, such as the UNIDROIT Principles of International Commercial Contracts. They may also choose a form of arbitration other than arbitration according to the ICC Arbitration Rules or litigation before a court of law rather than arbitration.

The ICC Sale Form thus contains highly flexible and important guidelines for parties that wish to draft a contract. They may use the ICC Sale Form "as is" and complete it in the above-mentioned manner or they may use it as a model when drafting their own individual contract. In this context, it should be noted that the ICC Sale Form is designed for the sale of manufactured goods intended for resale, in cases where substitute goods are normally available if the goods delivered do not conform to the relevant specifications. Thus, the ICC Sale Form may be inappropriate in cases where the goods are manufactured specifically for the buyer as end-user.

In any event, with the introduction of the ICC Sale Form, ICC has provided a useful service to the international trading community.

Additional Contracts

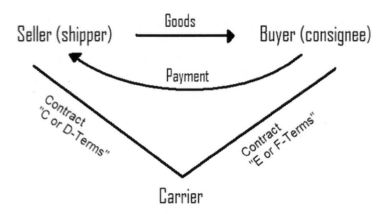

An international trade transaction requires not only a contract of sale but also additional contracts. In the first place, the goods will have to be moved from the seller's location to the location selected by the buyer. Therefore, it is necessary to arrange and pay for their transport. This means that three parties are now involved: the seller, the buyer and the carrier. This can lead to complications. One of the main purposes of the Incoterms rules is to define the different roles of the parties in relation to the contract of carriage.

Under the terms starting with the letter C or D, it is for the seller to conclude the contract with the carrier. In contrast, under the terms starting with the letter E or F, it is for the buyer to do so. When the seller contracts for carriage, it is important to ensure that the buyer is able to receive the goods from the carrier at destination. This is particularly important with respect to shipment contracts. The buyer must then receive a document from the seller – such as a bill of lading – that will enable him to receive the goods from the carrier by tendering an original of the document in return for the goods. If the seller has concluded a contract of carriage under one of the D terms, he must be in control of the goods during the entire transit to the place where they are to be delivered to the buyer. It is the seller's obligation to ensure that the goods can be delivered to the buyer at the indicated place of destination. If something goes wrong during the carriage, the seller bears the risk. This is different in situations involving terms starting with the letter C, where the seller merely has to arrange and pay for the carriage. If something goes wrong during the carriage, the risk is on the buyer.

It is common for the seller to want to escape the risk of loss of or damage to the goods while they are in transit, even in cases where he undertakes to deliver the goods at destination. This is not only a matter of insurance. The fact that the seller may be protected by insurance in the case of loss of or damage to the goods in transit does not relieve him of his obligation under the contract of sale to deliver the goods to the buyer. If the goods have been lost, it is for the seller to provide substitute goods wherever possible. If this is impossible, he may escape liability under the applicable law or according to the individual contract terms. The standard expression "no arrival, no sale" signifies that the parties are relieved from the contract of sale if the goods fail to arrive at their destination. Nevertheless, it is better not to use such expressions but to clearly specify the consequences in the individual contract of sale or by using standard form contracts with elaborate relief clauses that apply in specified circumstances. ICC has provided solutions in its 2003 Force Majeure and Hardship Clause (ICC Pub. No. 650).

With respect to the buyer's obligations, it is important to use appropriate services by commercial banks for payment. When the parties have established a continuing relationship, the seller normally trusts the buyer and sells the goods on open credit. In other cases, it is important for sellers to protect themselves. They can do so by various means. Either party may, of course, arrange for bank guarantees to be opened in its favour, so that money can be collected from the guarantee in the case of non-performance. The most important type of guarantee that is provided in a standard form is described in the ICC Uniform Rules for Demand Guarantees (URDG 758). It is possible to call upon this type of guarantee by means of a so-called simple demand. There are various options to reduce the danger of an abuse of the guarantee ("unfair calling").

In cases where the parties do not know each other well from previous dealings, it is quite common that the buyer is required to open a documentary credit with the seller as beneficiary. ICC has for a long time provided rules for such documentary credits, which are currently known as UCP 600. It is particularly important for the seller to present the correct documents in order to get paid. These documents are specified by the buyer in the instructions to the bank opening the credit. It is therefore essential that the seller is given sufficient time to check whether these instructions conform to the terms of the contract of sale. If they do not, the buyer has committed a breach of contract that, at worst, entitles the seller to cancel the contract. The seller must take care to ensure that the documents presented to the bank comply with the buyer's instructions.

With respect to the terms of the contract of carriage, the Incoterms rules merely state that the seller should provide "the usual transport document". The liability of carriers for loss of or damage to the goods in transit is rather limited. They are not liable for so-called "nautical fault" (errors in the navigation or management of the ship). This exception was abolished by the 1978 UN Convention on the Carriage of Goods by Sea, also known as the Hamburg Rules. However, these rules have only entered into force on a limited scale. A new convention, also known as the Rotterdam Rules, was concluded in September 2009, but it remains to be seen whether it will come into force. In addition to this rather lenient liability regime, maritime carriers are entitled to limit their liability to specific amounts, which may sometimes prove insufficient for compensating shippers and consignees for their losses. The seller or buyer, as the case may be, is usually protected by cargo insurance, which under the Incoterms rules CIF or CIP is arranged and paid for by the seller with the buyer as beneficiary. CIF and CIP only require the seller to provide insurance with minimum cover, the reason being that the insurance terms in so-called "string sales" involving commodities must be standardized to take account of the fact that the insurance requirements of prospective buyers down the string are not known. However, the buyer may ask for additional cover, which will be provided by the seller if procurable. When paying the insured party, the cargo insurer obtains the right to hold the carrier liable under a so-called letter of subrogation, whereby the insured party assigns his right to claim damages from the carrier to the insurer. The carrier's liability is covered by liability insurance. In practice, the loss of or damage to the goods in transit therefore results in a battle between these various types of insurers.

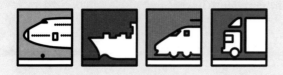

UNDERSTANDING THE INCOTERMS RULES

What are the Incoterms rules, and what can they do for you?

The word "Incoterms" is an abbreviation of International commercial terms, and the chosen Incoterms rule is a term of the contract of sale (N.B. not of the contract of carriage). Although the Incoterms rules are primarily intended for international sales they can be applied to domestic contracts by reference. Trade terms are, in fact, key elements of international contracts of sale, since they tell the parties what to do with respect to

■ carriage of the goods from seller to buyer; and

■ export, import and security-related clearance.

They also explain the division of costs and risks between the parties.

Merchants tend to use short abbreviations – such as FOB and CIF – to clarify the distribution of functions, costs and risks relating to the transfer of goods from seller to buyer. But misunderstandings frequently arise concerning the proper interpretation of these and similar expressions.

For this reason, it was considered important to develop rules for the interpretation of the trade terms that the parties to a contract of sale could agree to apply. The Incoterms rules, first published by the International Chamber of Commerce in 1936, constitute such rules of interpretation.

Referencing the Incoterms rules in a contract of sale

Although the Incoterms rules, in so far as they reflect generally recognized principles and practices, may become part of the contract of sale without express reference, the parties are strongly advised to

■ include in their contract in conjunction with the trade term the words "the Incoterms® 2010 rules"; and

■ check whether a standard contract used in their contract of sale contains such a reference, and, if not, superimpose the standardized reference "the Incoterms® 2010 rules" to avoid the application of any previous version of the Incoterms rules.

In recent years, the Incoterms rules have been revised at 10-year intervals (Incoterms 1980, 1990, 2000 and 2010). These revisions are necessary to ensure that the Incoterms rules represent contemporary commercial practice. It is a mere coincidence that revisions have taken place at 10 year intervals and there is no reason to expect that this will be repeated in the future. Confusion may arise in the marketplace when merchants either fail to observe that there has been a change in the rules of interpretation or fail to clarify which version of the Incoterms rules should apply to their contract. In addition, fundamental changes to the rules, if not properly introduced, could endanger the status of the Incoterms rules as a generally recognized international custom of the trade. Indeed, the reason the 1980 UN

Convention on Contracts for the International Sale of Goods (CISG) did not deal with interpretation of trade terms was a belief that this task could be more efficiently taken care of by the International Chamber of Commerce in cooperation with its national committees worldwide.

To avoid confusion and difficulties in applying the Incoterms rules, a reference to the current version should always be made in the contract of sale. When parties negotiate their contract individually, they should take care not only to refer to the Incoterms rules but also to add the year 2010. If they use a standard contract they should check whether it has been updated to include reference to "the Incoterms® 2010 rules". If not, the previous year should be replaced by the year 2010.

The differences between the Incoterms 2000 rules and the Incoterms® 2010 rules

The studies which were made before the revision was initiated clearly demonstrated that merchants had difficulties in choosing the correct term. The first efforts by ICC to assist merchants appear in the ICC Sale Form, where a distinction is made between "recommended terms" and "other terms". The recommended terms correpond to terms which now appear in the Incoterms® 2010 rules Group I for any mode or modes of transport, while the other terms correspond to the terms in Group II for sea and inland waterway transport.

What the Incoterms rules cannot do for you

The Incoterms rules do not deal with

■ transfer of property rights in the goods;

■ relief from obligations and exemptions from liability in case of unexpected or unforeseeable events; or

■ consequences of various breaches of contract, except those relating to the passing of risks and costs when the buyer is in breach of his obligation to accept the goods or to nominate the carrier under an F-term.

Merchants often believe that the Incoterms rules can solve most of the problems which may arise in practice. Indeed, most of the questions put forward to the ICC Panel of Experts on the Incoterms rules concerned matters other than the interpretation of the Incoterms rules themselves. Frequently, the questions referred to contractual relations other than the contract of sale, such as the obligations of the parties under documentary credits, contracts of carriage and storage. Many questions concerned obligations of the parties other than those connected with the delivery of the goods. Therefore, it is necessary to emphasize that the Incoterms rules are only rules for the interpretation of terms of delivery and not of other terms of the contract of sale. This explains why – apart from the seller's fundamental obligation to make the goods available for the buyer or to hand them over for carriage or deliver them at destination, and apart from the buyer's obligation to take delivery – the Incoterms rules deal only with obligations in connection therewith, such as the obligations to give notice, provide documents, procure insurance, and pack the goods properly and clear them for export and import.

Transfer of property rights

In many jurisdictions, the transfer of property rights in the goods requires that the party take possession of the goods either directly or indirectly through the transfer of documents, such as the maritime bill of lading, controlling the disposition of the goods. However, in some jurisdictions, the transfer of property rights in the goods – the so-called transfer of title – may depend solely on the intention of the contracting parties.

Frequently, the contract of sale determines whether the buyer has become the owner of the goods. In some cases, the buyer may not become the owner when the seller, under a so-called retention of title clause, may have decided to retain title to them until he has been paid. The applicable law will decide the extent to which such clauses are effective in protecting the seller when he has surrendered possession of the goods to the buyer. The ICC Model International Sale Contract (hereinafter referred to as the ICC Sale Form; see ICC publication No. 556) underlines that retention of title clauses are not always effective and that the seller should carefully check the relevant law, normally the law of the country where the goods are situated, to determine if and to what extent he may rely on Article 7 of Part B of the Sale Form (see p. 9 of ICC publication No. 556).

Unforeseeable and unavoidable events

Even though, according to the Incoterms rules, the parties undertake obligations to perform various matters to the benefit of the other party – such as procuring carriage and clearing the goods for export and import – they may be relieved from such obligations, or from the consequences of non-performance, if they can benefit from exemptions under the applicable law or terms of their contract other than those concerning the Incoterms rules. Thus, according to the CISG, the parties may be relieved from their obligations if they are prevented from performing due to reasonably unforeseeable and unavoidable "impediments beyond control". Standard contracts frequently contain explicit force majeure, relief or exemption clauses more or less corresponding to the main principle of CISG Article 79 and in the 2003 ICC Force Majeure and Hardship Clauses (ICC Publication No.650). Such a clause appears in the ICC Sale Form, Part B, Article 13.

Consequently, if a seller or a buyer is prevented from exporting or importing the goods due to an unforeseen export or import prohibition, his obligation under the contract of sale may be suspended, or, if the prohibition lasts for a long period of time, avoided altogether. In the aforementioned Article 13, a period of six months is required in these cases before a party is entitled to terminate the contract with notice. Although the Incoterms rules do not deal with the circumstances in which an obligation undertaken in connection with delivery of the goods may be avoided or modified, it is important to remember that any type of obligation – whether covered by the Incoterms rules or not – is subject to the applicable law or other terms of the contract.

Breaches of contract

The Incoterms rules – in the A5, B5 and A6, B6 clauses – deal with the transfer of risks and the division of costs. It follows from the A5 and B5 clauses that the risk may be transferred from the seller to the buyer before the goods have been delivered, if the buyer has failed to fulfil his obligation to take delivery as agreed or to give appropriate notice to the seller when the buyer is to nominate the carrier under the F-terms. In these cases, costs arising because of the buyer's failure to fulfil his obligation would also fall upon him under the B6 clauses of the Incoterms rules.

However, apart from these specific cases involving the buyer's breach, the Incoterms rules do not deal at all with consequences following from breaches of the obligations under the contract of sale. These consequences follow from the applicable law or other terms of the contract. To note a few examples: if the buyer does not pay for the goods in time, he has to pay so-called default interest (see the ICC Sale Form, Part B, Article 6). If the seller does not deliver the goods in time, he has to pay so-called liquidated damages to the buyer. These damages are calculated by charging certain percentages of the price of the goods for each period of delay (according to the ICC Sale Form, Part B, Article 10.1, this would amount to 0.5% of the price for each complete week of delay). When the maximum of liquidated damages has been reached (5% of the price of the delayed goods), the buyer may terminate the contract by notification to the seller after having given notice to the latter allowing him a further five days for the delivery.

If the goods do not conform with the requirements of the contract, the consequences are set forth in Article 11 of the ICC Sale Form. The Article says that the seller should either replace the goods with conforming goods, repair them or reimburse the price to the buyer. If the contract is terminated, the buyer may be entitled to damages not exceeding 10% of the price of the non-conforming goods. If the buyer retains the non-conforming goods, he may obtain a discount not exceeding 15% of the price.

Agreeing on modifications to the standard terms

In Part A of the ICC Sale Form, the parties are asked to consider whether the standardized terms in Part B are suitable, and, if not, to agree on modifications. In some cases, where time is of the essence, it may be appropriate to insert a fixed cancellation date, so that if goods are not delivered by that date the buyer could immediately cancel the contract by notification to the seller (Part A, clause 9 of the Sale Form). In addition, the percentages of the price payable in case of delay according to the standardized terms in Part B may be replaced by higher percentages or a fixed amount, depending on an agreement by the parties.

Summary: limits of the Incoterms rules

In summary, as far as the seller's obligation to deliver conforming goods is concerned, the Incoterms rules determine when the seller has fulfilled his obligation to deliver the goods on time but no more. The consequences following from the seller's non-performance must be found elsewhere. Ideally, the simultaneous use of the Incoterms rules and the ICC Sale Form should provide most of the answers required. (see introduction p.7)

The Incoterms rules and contracting practice

The Incoterms rules standardize contract practice by enabling the parties to

- use generally recognized key words;

- agree on the most common understanding of such key words; and

- avoid misunderstandings in the use of them.

Problems remain because

- commercial practice is inconsistent;

- variations of the basic key word may be not appropriate or sufficiently clear;

- the Incoterms rule is not sufficiently precise; and/or

- the parties inadvertently choose the wrong term.

The need for interpretation of "key words"

Short abbreviations, such as FCA, FOB and CIF, can be regarded as "key words", which, when used, unlock a number of rights and obligations. But these key words cannot be understood unless they are given a specific meaning through rules of interpretation. It is only through interpretation that the Incoterms rules are indispensable. In the absence of an authoritative interpretation, merchants may suffer from great confusion.

It can be debated whether the key words included in the Incoterms rules represent consistent commercial practice. Ever since the first version of the Incoterms rules in 1936, every effort has been made to ensure that this is the case. But a number of short expressions used by merchants do not correspond to the Incoterms rules. To note a few examples, the term CFR frequently appears in contracts of sale as C&F. In some cases, CFR appears as C+F. One can generally assume that the parties in these cases intended that the abbreviations mean the same as CFR, but it is far better, for the sake of clarity, to use the term as written in the official text.

In other cases, however, the parties may choose an expression which is not consistent with any of the terms represented by the Incoterms rules. One example is FOB+I. Here it is apparent that the parties intended to add an insurance obligation for the seller. But it is not clear whether it is of the same kind of obligation as one finds under CIF and CIP. Consequently, disputes can arise as to the extent of the seller's insurance obligation when it appears in another term.

In the Guidance notes to the various Incoterms rules, strong warnings have been inserted to the effect that merchants should explain as precisely as possible what they mean when they use a variation or an addition to the Incoterms rule.

The most common practice

Unfortunately, commercial practice is not the same in all parts of the world. Therefore, the Incoterms rules can do no more than reflect the most common practice. In many cases, it is impossible to reflect in the Incoterms rules what actually happens in connection with the loading and unloading of the goods to and from the means of transport. Nonetheless, as noted, in the Incoterms® 2010 rules further efforts have been made to assist the users of the Incoterms rules in this regard. In particular, under the term FCA when the goods are picked up, it is clarified that the seller has to load the goods on to the buyer's collecting vehicle, and the buyer has to unload the goods when they are delivered for on-carriage on the seller's arriving vehicle.

However, it has not been possible to find such a consistent commercial practice with respect to the loading of ships under FOB and the unloading from ships under CFR and CIF. Here, the type of cargo and the loading and unloading facilities available in the seaports will determine the extent of the seller's obligations under FOB and the type of contract he has to procure to the benefit of the buyer under CFR and CIF.

Before the contract of sale is concluded, therefore, the parties are advised to ascertain if there are any particular customs of the port where the goods are to be loaded under FOB, because these customs are quite different in different ports and may create surprises for the uninformed party. If, for example, the goods are to be loaded on board a ship in the seller's home port, and under FOB the buyer has to nominate a ship, he should ascertain the extent to which costs will be included in the FOB freight and whether there will be some additionals debited to him in connection with the loading of the goods on board.

The FOB point

The traditional FOB point – meaning that risks shift from the seller to the buyer when the goods pass the ship's rail at the named port of shipment – has been criticized for not reflecting what actually takes place in seaports. Nevertheless, ever since the 1700s many customs of the port and commercial practices have been developed around the notion of the ship's rail. This has been changed in the Incoterms® 2010 rules in order to achieve better consistency between the division of risks and costs, with the expression "on board". As before, problems still remain with respect to the exact point for the division of the risk, which depends on the type of goods and the method used to bring the goods on board the ship.

EXW and the seller's assistance

Under the term EXW, it is a fairly consistent commercial practice that the seller assists the buyer in connection with the loading of the goods on to the buyer's collecting vehicle, either by bringing the goods on to a ramp for loading or by loading the goods on to the vehicle. However, under EXW the seller has no obligation to assist; he only has to make the goods available for the buyer and no more. If the buyer wants to ensure that the seller's obligation is extended, he has to agree with him at the time the contract is concluded. This is sometimes done by adding the word "loaded" after the term EXW ("EXW loaded"). However, such an addition does not clarify whether the seller's risk of loss of or damage to the goods should be extended to include the loading operations. The parties should make clear whether the addition of the word "loaded" means "loaded at seller's risk" or "loaded at buyer's risk".

If it is intended that the seller bear the risk during the loading operations, the parties could preferably contract using the trade term FCA, since in the Incoterms® 2010 rules it is clear that under FCA the seller has to load the goods on to the buyer's collecting vehicle. The choice of FCA instead of adding "loaded" after EXW would bring the parties entirely within the authoritative interpretation of the trade term, whereas any self-made addition means that they contract at their own peril. However, using FCA instead of EXW also shifts the obligation to clear the goods for export from the buyer to the seller, which may or may not be what the parties intend.

Containerization

Trading patterns are usually difficult to change, even if the reasons for the choice of the trade term have changed and call for quite another choice. As an example, consider the changed routines for cargo handling. Since the late 1960s, particular difficulties have arisen in maritime trade where containerization (which occurs when the goods are prepared and stowed in containers before the arrival of the ship) has made the traditional FOB point wholly inappropriate. It bears repeating that FOB, CFR and CIF are appropriate only when there is delivery to the carrier by handing over the goods to the ship which simply does not take place when the goods are containerized.

When containerization takes place, the goods are either collected at the seller's premises (a common practice when homogenous cargo is stowed by the seller in containers constituting a full load, i.e., so-called FCL-containers) or delivered to a cargo terminal where the goods are stowed in containers for later lifting on board the container vessel (the normal case when heterogeneous goods do not constitute a full load, i.e., so-called LCL-containers).

The parties may think the differences really do not matter and may believe that things will sort themselves out in any case. This is incorrect. The seller should take care not to remain at risk after the goods have been handed over to the carrier that the buyer nominates. This is particularly important when the seller has no possibility to give instructions with respect to the care and custody of the goods, which occurs, for example, when the carrier is obliged only to take instructions from his own contracting party, the buyer.

Continued use of terms which do not appear in the Incoterms® 2010 rules

Although the traditional maritime terms DES and DEQ no longer appear in the Incoterms® 2010 rules, it is expected that they will continue to be used in commodity trading. If there is no reference to the Incoterms rules at all, some guidance for the interpretation of these trade terms may, as before, be found in the earlier versions of the Incoterms rules. Ideally, the parties should refer to DES and DEQ of the Incoterms 2000 rules. If by mistake they refer to these terms with the addition "the Incoterms® 2010 rules", it is reasonable to assume that they meant "the Incoterms® 2000 rules". In any event, no problem would seem to arise, as the substance of DAP and DAT corresponds to DES and DEQ respectively.

Checking how the goods are handed over for carriage

It also happens that the parties may choose a trade term intended for maritime carriage when they contemplate using other modes of transport. They believe, quite wrongly, that if a trade term has served well for maritime carriage it must also be appropriate for other modes of transport. As has been said, great efforts have been made in the Incoterms® 2010 rules to avoid an incorrect choice by presenting the terms in two groups, one for any or all or modes of transport (Group I) and one for transport by sea and inland waterways (Group II).

FCA, FOB, CPT, CFR, CIP and CIF compared

However, the parties are always strongly advised to check how the goods are, in fact, handed over for carriage, thereby avoiding the choice of a term which keeps the seller at risk after the goods have left his direct or indirect control. The choice of FOB should be restricted to cases in which the goods are actually intended to be (a) lifted across the ship's rail, or (b) tendered to the ship in hoses for liquid cargo, or (c) filled from silos when the cargo is to be carried loose in bulk. In all other cases, FOB should not be used. Instead FCA, indicating the actual place where the goods are handed over for carriage, is the appropriate term.

Under the C-terms, since the seller makes the contract of carriage, it may seem irrelevant whether the risk passes when the goods are placed on board or earlier when they are received by the carrier in his terminal. Nevertheless, if the seller wishes to avoid being at risk after handing over the goods for carriage until loading on board the ship, he should refrain from using CFR or CIF and instead use CPT or CIP, where the risk passes upon the handing over to the carrier. With regard to container traffic, such handing over will normally take place in the carrier's terminal before the arrival of the ship. If loss of or damage to the goods occurs during the carrier's period of responsibility, it may, in practice, become impossible to ascertain whether it has occurred before or after the delivery to the ship. This is another reason for choosing a trade term, such as FCA, CPT or CIP, where the risk of loss of damage to the goods passes from the seller to the buyer when the goods are handed over to the carrier.

The seller's duty to provide substitute goods

It should also be noted that the seller's possibility to recover from his insurer in case of loss of or damage to the goods does not relieve him from his duty to perform as he is still required to provide goods in substitution for the goods which might have been lost or damaged while he was still at risk, for example, during the period from handing over the goods for carriage until they were placed on board.

Cargo handling costs

Buyers are often concerned that their agreement to accept delivery at an inland point, rather than when the goods are placed on board, could result in an obligation for them to pay additional costs charged by cargo handling facilities, terminals or the carriers themselves (terminal handling charges, THC). However, this can easily be taken care of by an agreement between the parties either to split these costs or to place them entirely on the seller (for example, by inserting clauses to read "50% of THC to be paid by the seller" or "THC for seller's account").

Checking availability of documents required under the Incoterms rule

It happens that the parties fail to take into account that the maritime terms call for particular documents – namely a negotiable bill of lading or a so-called sea waybill – which are simply not available when other modes of transport are used. Negotiable bills of lading are not used for other modes of transport because sale of the goods in transit – which traditionally requires a bill of lading for title of the goods to be transferred to the next buyer – does not occur when the goods are carried by road, rail or air. This means that if a seller in London, for example, undertakes to sell goods CIF Yokohama when the goods are to be carried by air from London to Yokohama, he will find himself in the unfortunate position of not being able to fulfil his obligations under CIF to present an on board bill of lading to his buyer. Moreover, he would be the victim of his indifference or ignorance in that he has given the buyer the possibility of escaping a bad bargain by invoking the seller's breach of contract in not presenting the correct document under CIF.

Why are as many as 11 Incoterms rules required?

The purpose of the Incoterms rules is to reflect contemporary commercial practice and to offer the parties the choice among

■ the seller's minimum obligation only to make the goods available for the buyer at the seller's premises (EXW);

■ the seller's extended obligation to hand over the goods for carriage either to a carrier nominated by the buyer (FCA, FAS, FOB), or to a carrier chosen and paid for by the seller (CFR, CPT) together with insurance against risks in transit (CIF, CIP);

■ the seller's maximum obligation to deliver the goods at destination (DAT, DAP, DDP).

The Incoterms rules are sometimes criticized for offering an abundance of different terms. Would it not be possible to restrict the number of terms so that the parties would be invited either to choose delivery at the seller's place or at the buyer's place? The answer is that commercial practice involves different trading patterns for different types of cargo. With respect to commodities, such as oil, iron, ore and grain, the goods are frequently carried in chartered ships accepting the cargo as a full load. In this type of trade, the ultimate buyer may not be known, since the goods may be sold in transit. This, in turn, explains the need for a negotiable transport document, the bill of lading. Moreover, even if the ultimate buyer is known, he is usually not prepared to accept costs and risks which occur in the seller's country. This explains the need for the maritime terms, which are still used for the largest volume of world trade.

With respect to manufactured cargo, however, maritime terms are inappropriate. Here, in most cases, the parties are well advised to use one of the Incoterms rules appropriate for delivery at the seller's place (EXW or possibly FCA) or delivery at the buyer's place, i.e., the destination terms, DAT, DAP and DDP. In many cases, carriage of manufactured goods is entrusted to logistics service providers, which should preferably be able to communicate continuously with their original contracting party. It is therefore impracticable to use terms such as CPT or CIP, where the seller makes the contract and leaves the rest to the buyer.

With respect to insurance, it is only when the goods are intended to be sold in transit that it is appropriate to let the seller undertake an insurance obligation to the buyer. In other cases, the buyer should preferably arrange his own insurance so that the insurance cover can be adapted to his particular needs. However, this is not possible when sale of goods in transit is contemplated, as the ultimate buyer is not yet known. This explains the frequent use of CIF in such cases.

Which Incoterms rule should be chosen?

Commercial practice and the type of goods will dictate whether

- the seller should refrain from undertaking any additional obligation;

- the seller is prepared to do more than to make the goods available to the buyer at the seller's premises;

- the buyer's bargaining position allows him to require the seller to undertake extended obligations;

- the seller is able to undertake additional obligations and, in particular, to quote a more competitive price by extending his obligations;

- it is necessary to use the maritime terms FAS, FOB, CFR or CIF when the goods are intended to be resold by the buyer before they reach the destination.

The ICC Model International Sale Contract

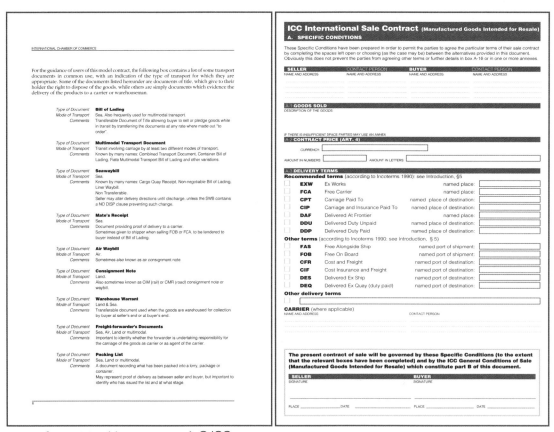

Extract from ICC Publication No 556. © ICC

Terms and business strategies

Sellers and buyers seldom reflect on the choice of an Incoterms rule for every transaction. Normally, the choice is determined by their business strategy. As noted, the choice of the maritime terms in most cases depends on the type of the cargo and the buyer's intention to sell the goods in transit. Here, the choice between any of the F-terms rather than the C-terms depends on the ability of sellers and buyers to obtain the most favourable contract of carriage.

In countries where the seller has good possibilities of procuring maritime transport, or where he is induced to use a national shipping line, he may prefer to use CFR or CIF. Where the buyer for the same reasons has good possibilities to procure the transport, he is likely to insist on the choice of FAS or FOB. In the same manner, the choice between CFR and CIF depends on the seller's and the buyer's insurance arrangements and their possibilities to arrange insurance at the most competitive rate.

In principle, the same considerations apply with respect to the sale of manufactured goods. In this case, however, sellers, in order to remain competitive, frequently have to sell on extended terms using either DAT, DAP or DDP. But when a small exporter sells goods to a sizeable wholesaler or department store, these buyers may find it more advantageous to arrange for transport in order to ensure just-in-time deliveries at the most competitive price. In such cases, the buyer may prefer to use EXW or FCA.

CPT or CIP may be appropriate when the buyer prefers that the seller procure carriage (CPT), or carriage as well as insurance (CIP), but nevertheless agrees to bear the risk of loss of or damage to the goods when in transit. It should be added that the term CIP, if unamended is inappropriate with respect to manufactured goods, since the insurance cover is then far too restrictive and additional insurance is required. Normally, the most extended cover available (e.g., Clause A of the Institute Cargo Clauses LMA/IUA) is appropriate.

The Incoterms rules and the contract of carriage

The relation between the Incoterms rules and the contract of carriage creates particular problems, because

- some of the Incoterms rules can be used only when the goods are intended to be carried by sea (FAS, FOB, CFR, CIF);

- the same terms are often used in both contracts of sale and contracts of carriage;

- commercial practice under contracts of carriage changes from time to time and varies in different places, ports and regions;

- the contract of sale is sometimes difficult to match with the contract of carriage;

- under contracts of sale and the applicable law, such as CISG, the seller has to tender goods or documents representing them and the buyer has to pay for them;

- unless otherwise agreed, goods should be exchanged for money simultaneously; this principle also applies when a carrier is used by the parties and acts on behalf of the seller or the buyer, depending upon the chosen Incoterms rule;

- the parties may continue to use a traditional Incoterms rule when it has become inappropriate because of changed commercial practice (for example, they may continue to use FOB instead of FCA when there is delivery not to the ship, but to a carrier's terminal in or outside the port area);

- the seller under the C-terms enters into the contract of carriage with the buyer as beneficiary; this makes it necessary to give the buyer the possibility of claiming the goods from the carrier, even though the buyer did not make the contract with him;

- the parties do not understand the exceptions from, and limitations of, the carrier's liability (particularly with respect to carriage of goods by sea).

Charter parties

As noted, the maritime terms FAS, FOB, CFR and CIF can be used only when the goods are intended to be carried by sea, and a wrongful use of these terms may cause serious problems. Moreover, even a correct use of the maritime terms may cause problems in practice. As one example, the terms FAS and FOB are used as terms in charter parties as well, but as such they do not necessarily correspond to their use in the Incoterms rules. Instead, the exact terms of the charter party will decide what they mean. This is particularly important with respect to the time under the charter party that is offered the charterer for bringing the goods alongside the ship (FAS) or for loading them onboard (FOB). If that time is exceeded, the charterer will have to pay compensation to the shipowner (so-called demurrage). If the charterer uses less time, thereby saving time for the shipowner, he may be paid for this in the form of so-called dispatch money. The terms of the charter party will not concern the FAS or FOB seller, since he is not a party to the contract with the shipowner. It is therefore necessary to match the conditions of the charter party with the terms of the contract of sale so that the FAS or FOB buyer, in his capacity as charterer in the charter party, does not have to pay demurrage without recourse against the seller when the latter fails to bring the goods to the ship within the time needed for avoiding payment of demurrage to the shipowner.

Under CFR and CIF, the seller will charter the ship, and it will be in his self-interest to speed up the loading operations to avoid demurrage payments to the shipowner and possibly to earn some dispatch money. However, the problem now appears at destination. Under B4 of CFR and CIF, the buyer must not only accept delivery at the point where the goods according to A4 have been loaded on board the vessel at the port of shipment, but he must also "receive them from the carrier at the named port of destination". Here again, the terms of the charter party might not match the terms of the contract of sale.

Therefore, even if according to the charter party the shipowner has no obligation with respect to the discharging operations (as under the charter party term "free out"), this does not necessarily mean the seller has the right under CFR and CIF to procure a contract of carriage which does not include the discharge of the goods from the ship. In order to clarify that discharging costs are included, the parties sometimes add the words "liner terms" to CFR and CIF. Although this normally means that the discharging operations are included, there is no authoritative interpretation of "liner terms". The parties are therefore advised to clarify in the contract of sale to what extent the cost of discharging operations is included.

When the discharging operations are for the buyer's account under the contract of sale, it is necessary to specify how much time he is allowed before he has to pay demurrage for keeping the ship in port. The buyer must be prepared to discharge the ship as soon as so-called notice of readiness has been given. If time starts to run before he is ready to undertake the discharge, he assumes the risk. In addition, he will assume the risk for various hindrances preventing the discharging operations unless the hindrances are excepted under the terms of the contract of sale. Again, it is necessary to match the terms of the contract of sale with the terms of the charter party.

Normally, the buyer does not risk having to pay the seller demurrage when the goods are carried by liner shipping companies. In this case, the goods are normally discharged by these companies and stored in cargo terminals until they are received by the buyers. This is particularly true with respect to containerized cargo. But the problem of matching the terms of the charter party with those of the contract of sale is particularly important with respect to commodities carried in bulk. Because commercial practice differs in different ports and changes from time to time, a failure to match the terms of the contract of sale with the terms of the charter party may result in unpleasant and expensive surprises for the contracting parties.

Usual, normal and suitable carriage

Under the C-terms (A3(a)), it is for the seller to procure carriage "on usual terms". Furthermore, the contract should provide for carriage by the usual route in a seagoing vessel (or inland waterway vessel) of the type normally used for the transport of goods of the type sold. The reference to what is "usual" and "normal" does not necessarily mean that the seagoing vessel is, in fact, "suitable" or that it minimizes the risk of loss of or damage to the goods. But if the seller knowingly selects a substandard vessel, which is therefore not "normal", the buyer may hold him responsible if there is damage to or loss of the cargo.

Risk distribution under CIF

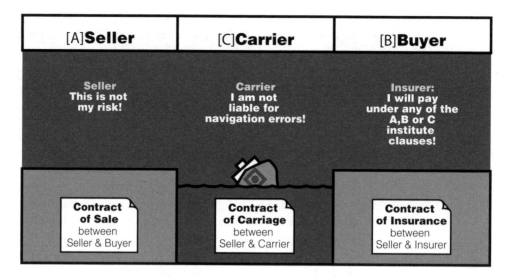

The maritime carrier's responsibility is traditionally limited to the exercise of due diligence in ensuring that the vessel is seaworthy when it leaves port. He is exempt from liability for fire or for loss of or damage to the cargo resulting from errors in the navigation and management of the vessel. This limited liability explains the need for sellers and buyers to take out marine insurance to protect themselves against risks they have to bear under the contract of carriage. If the goods are sold under any of the C-terms, the buyer can obtain protection, either by the obligation of the seller to take out insurance under CIF or through his own insurance arrangements. The traditional carrier defence of nautical fault has disappeared in the 1978 Hamburg Rules and the 2009 Rotterdam Rules. But the former has only been ratified by states representing a rather limited section of the international maritime trade and the future of the Rotterdam Rules is uncertain.

The bill of lading

The fact that under the C-terms the seller procures the contract of carriage for the benefit of the buyer puts the buyer in a position where he has to exercise rights against someone with whom he has not made the contract. This, indeed, explains the development of the bill of lading used for maritime carriage. Possession of the bill of lading controls the right to claim delivery of the goods from the carrier at destination. It is a fundamental obligation of the seller under CFR and CIF A8 to provide the buyer with such a document, which enables him to claim the goods from the carrier at the port of destination and, unless otherwise agreed, to sell the goods in transit by the transfer of the document to a subsequent buyer.

Traditionally, only the negotiable bill of lading could fulfil both of these functions. But in recent years other maritime documents have also been used. Now, even without a bill of lading, the buyer is entitled to claim the goods from the carrier at destination. So-called sea waybills (liner waybills, cargo quay receipts) contain instructions from the shipper to the carrier to deliver the goods to a named person at destination. These instructions can also be made irrevocable, with the result that the shipper is prevented from giving further instructions to the carrier. The instructions can also be given by an electronic data interchange message, as discussed in later sections.

Sale of goods in transit

The Incoterms rules do not contain a term for sale of goods in transit. In practice, CFR or CIF are frequently used. When the seller has concluded a contract of carriage with the carrier, he will obtain a bill of lading which may be used for the first contract of sale, as foreseen in article A8 of the Incoterms rules. But the buyer may then, in a second contract, appear as seller and hand over the same bill of lading to the second buyer. Subsequent sales may be implemented to transfer the risk from the seller to the buyer at the time the contract is concluded, when the goods may be in mid-ocean and nothing can be ascertained regarding their condition. CISG, in Article 68, therefore provides that it may follow from the transport document that the parties have intended the risk to pass at the time the goods were handed over to the carrier. If so, the buyer is protected by his right of action against the issuer of the transport document. In this manner, CFR and CIF are also appropriate to use for the sale of goods in transit. The wording of CFR and CIF A3 (a) has been changed in order to clarify what happens when multiple sales down a chain ("string sales") are intended. The seller then undertakes to "procure" goods delivered for the destination agreed in the contract of sale.

Unlawful rejection of Bill of Lading by Buyer under CFR/CIF

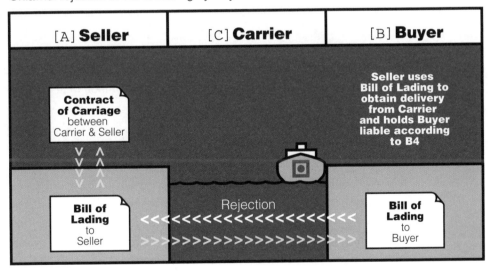

The duties under the Incoterms rules to load and unload the goods

In practice, the seller generally loads the goods whenever the buyer sends a vehicle to collect them, while the buyer unloads the goods from a vehicle sent by the seller to deliver the goods at a place named by the buyer. This is frequently what occurs also under the D-terms: the seller loads the goods on a collecting vehicle sent by the buyer to pick up the goods, while the buyer generally unloads the goods from the seller's arriving vehicle. This is now explicitly stated in DAP A4 ("... placing them at the disposal of the buyer on the arriving means of transport ready for unloading at the agreed point"). If the parties agree that the seller should unload the goods from the arriving means of transport, DAT should be chosen. Here it is stated in A4 that the "seller must unload the goods from the arriving means of transport and must then deliver them by placing them at the disposal of the buyer at the named terminal".

The duties connected to export and import clearance

The Incoterms rules are based on the main principle that the party best positioned to undertake the function to clear the goods and to pay duties and other costs in connection with export and import should do so. Thus,

- under all F-terms the seller should do what is necessary to clear the goods for export;

- under all C-terms the seller assumes the obligation with respect to export, and the buyer assumes the obligations with respect to import;

- under all D-terms, except DDP, the buyer should do what is necessary to clear the goods for import;

- under EXW the buyer has to assume the obligations with respect to export as well as import (this is an exception to the main principle that the exporter clears the goods for export, and follows from the nature of EXW to express the seller's minimum obligation); and

- when there are no customs requirements, all of the Incoterms rules can be used without variations, since the obligations relating to export and import clearance are relevant only "where applicable".

The obligation to clear the goods for export and import respectively is not only a matter of functions and costs. It is also essential to know whether the seller or the buyer will be at risk when difficulties arise. Normally, difficulties result in delays only as a consequence of inadequate or incorrect information provided to the customs authorities or because of inappropriate customs procedures. But in some cases, wrong information may result in customs fines, or an unforeseen export or import prohibition may prevent the goods from leaving or entering the country and thus prevent the performance of the contract of sale.

The Incoterms rules do not resolve the question whether the party obliged to perform the export or import clearance obligation is liable to the other party for breach of contract, or whether such breach would be excused at law or under the terms of the contract of sale (see Article 79 of the CISG).

Normally, it is appropriate that the party domiciled in the country of export or import undertake to clear the goods for export or import, as the case may be. First, it is easier for him to determine any costs, difficulties or risks connected with the clearance of the goods. Second, customs and tax regulations in a country may have been made on the assumption that the exporter and the importer respectively would assume costs in connection with the clearance; this would permit a tax deduction by a party domiciled in the country without according the same benefits to foreigners. The parties are reminded in the Guidance note to DDP that it may be appropriate to exclude from the seller's obligations some of the costs, such as VAT, payable upon import of the goods.

EXW and export formalities

Whenever the term EXW is used for an intended export sale, in order to be consistent with the policy chosen for the F-terms it might seem appropriate to place the clearance for export obligation on the seller. However, this would have meant a departure from the main principle that the term EXW should represent the seller's minimum obligation only to make the goods available for the buyer at the seller's premises. In cases where no immediate export is intended by the buyer, or perhaps no export at all but a resale to another party in the country is intended, a change of EXW with respect to the clearance obligation would have left the parties without the possibility of choosing an appropriate Incoterms rule. Therefore, it was decided to leave EXW unamended in this respect, but with a warning in the preamble that the buyer should ensure that he can carry out the export formalities directly or indirectly. If he cannot, he should abstain from using the term EXW unamended.

Since all C-terms, like the F-terms, represent shipment contracts, it follows that the seller must clear the goods for export while the buyer must clear them for import.

Customs-free regions

There has been some confusion with respect to the use of the Incoterms rules in intra-European Union trade. The parties often looked for an Incoterms rule which did not deal with customs clearance at all, since it was no longer required, at least not in the traditional sense. This problem arises, of course, not only in intra-European Union trade, but also in other regions where customs procedures are not required. Although it goes without saying that an Incoterms rule may be used even if some of the obligations falling upon the seller or buyer have become redundant, it is now made clear that stipulations with respect to clearing of the goods for export or import only take effect "where applicable".

Even in customs-free regions, specific requirements may well be stipulated for a certain type of goods, for example, for alcohol and tobacco (so-called bonded cargo).

Responsibility for charges

In practice, charges of different kinds may be levied in connection with the discharge of the goods. To avoid placing the liability on the seller to pay for all these charges, the word "official" was used in some places in the Incoterms 1990 rules. This word does not appear in the Incoterms® 2010 rules, but it should be observed that under clause A2 the seller is obliged only to "carry out all customs formalities" and that under clause A6 he is relieved from paying additional costs after he has fulfilled his delivery obligation under clause A4. Consequently, such additional costs unrelated to "customs formalities" shall not be for his account.

Security-related clearance

As a result of the terrorist attacks on 11 September 2001 in the United States (the so-called "9/11 attacks") security measures have intensified. In order to comply with such measures, exporters and importers have to give information about the goods in advance and, in some cases, accept scanning and inspection of the goods. Mutual assistance of sellers and buyers is required and this is now explicitly stated in the A10/B10 clauses of the Incoterms rules (see further on this p.68).

The Incoterms rules and insurance

The Incoterms rules deal only with the seller's obligation to take out insurance to the benefit of the buyer under CIF and CIP. Under all other terms, it is for the parties themselves to arrange insurance as they see fit.

The seller's insurance obligation to the benefit of the buyer

■ stems from the nature of the C-term, which requires the seller to contract for carriage – without assuming the risk of loss of or damage to the goods in transit;

■ requires the seller only to take out insurance on minimum terms (the C clause of the Institute Cargo Clauses (LMA/IUA) or any similar set of clauses); and

■ invites the buyer to agree with the seller to arrange additional insurance or to arrange it himself.

Whenever the goods are not intended to be sold in transit, it is natural for the contracting parties to arrange their own insurance in order that the seller can protect himself against risks of loss of or damage to the goods up to the point he is at risk. For the seller, this will require transport insurance up to the point of delivery according to the F-, C- and D-terms, and, conversely, there is no need for him to procure transport insurance when the goods are sold EXW.

Insurance when the parties use FOB instead of FCA

Problems arise when the transportation risk is split between the seller and the buyer at some intermediate point. In this case, the seller has no insurable interest after he has reached the point noted in the A4 clauses of the Incoterms rules, while the buyer has no insurable interest before that point. This means that an FOB-buyer has no insurable interest before the goods have been placed on board and that, accordingly, the FOB seller remains at risk until that point has been reached.

If the parties use FOB when FCA should have been used instead, the seller remains at risk even after the goods have been handed over to the carrier nominated by the buyer at the carrier's terminal or at a place other than the ship itself. Normally, sellers have general insurance arrangements (so-called open cover) which protect them in such cases. However, a seller who fails to cover himself adequately in these situations will not normally benefit from the buyer's insurance, even if that insurance contains a so-called transit clause to the effect that the insurance protection lasts from warehouse to warehouse, thereby covering the period before loading the goods on board. There are two reasons for this: first, the FOB-seller is not a contracting party to the FOB-buyer's insurance contract; and second, the FOB-buyer has no insurable interest before the goods have been placed on board.

Insurance under CIF and CIP

CIF and CIP are the only two Incoterms rules dealing with insurance. The former is an addition to the maritime term CFR and the latter to CPT, which relates to all modes of transport. Since goods are normally not resold in transit except when they are carried by sea, CIF is the most common Incoterms rule containing an insurance obligation for the seller to the benefit of the buyer. This explains why the seller's obligation is limited to take out only minimum insurance, because if the goods are intended to be resold in transit, one does not know beforehand the insurance arrangements of the subsequent buyers.

Nevertheless, minimum cover is often inappropriate even with respect to goods intended for sale in transit. The goods may become damaged because of contamination, breakage or penetration of seawater into the vessel. Such risks are not included in the minimum cover under clauses C of the Cargo Clauses (LMA/IUA).

When insurance is excluded

Note, however, that there is no insurance protection under any customary insurance clauses for loss, damage or expense caused by the nature of the goods, inadequate packing of the goods or such loss or damage or expense which is proximately caused by delay. There is also a general exclusion of coverage for loss, damage or expense arising from insolvency or financial default of the owners, managers, charterers or operators of the vessel. This may expose the buyer to uninsured risks, since the seller under CFR and CIF may escape liability, provided he can prove he has fulfilled his obligation under A3(a) to "contract ...on usual terms ... for carriage by the usual route in a seagoing vessel ... of the type normally used ...". If loss or damage occurs because of inadequate packing, the seller may be liable under the A9 clauses of the Incoterms rules, but neither of the parties can obtain protection from insurers.

Risks of war and labour disturbances

The standard insurance cover excludes war risks as well as loss, damage or expense caused by strikes, other labour disturbances, riots and other civil commotion. If insurance against such risks is requested, the A3(b) clauses of CIF and CIP require the seller to arrange coverage against them, but only if the coverage is procurable.

The Incoterms rules and documentary credits

The relationship between the Incoterms rules and documentary credits concerns the seller's obligation to deliver documents to the buyer in order to prove that the seller has fulfilled his obligations under the Incoterms rule and the contract of sale and that, consequently, the buyer is obliged to pay him. In this context the parties should ensure that

- the instructions given by the buyer to the bank undertaking the documentary credit (the issuing or opening bank) are fully compatible with the requirements under the contract of sale;

- the seller is offered the opportunity in advance, and well before the handing over of the goods for carriage, to check the terms of the documentary credit;

- inconsistency between the requirements under the documentary credit and the requirements under the contract of sale is avoided, since the buyer may be in breach of his payment obligation if the seller cannot get paid under the documentary credit when his documents conform with the contract of sale; and

- the buyer does not instruct the bank to pay against a transport document which does not control the disposition of the goods and which would therefore not prevent the seller from sending the goods to someone else after he has been paid.

Documentary Credits and the Contract of Sale

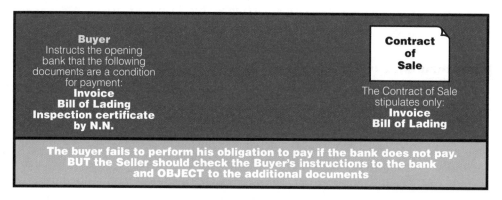

In practice, problems frequently arise because sellers and buyers fail to ensure that the instructions given to the issuing or opening bank conform with the terms of the contract of sale. To assist sellers and buyers in understanding the documents required in different situations under the contract of sale – and to enable the seller to check that the documents required under the contract conform to the documents he has to present under the documentary credit – the ICC Model Contract in the Introduction, Article 8, lists the most common documents as follows:

Type of Document	**Bill of Lading**
Mode of Transport	Sea. Also frequently used for multimodal transport.
Comments	Transferable Document of Title allowing buyer to sell or pledge goods while in transit by transferring the documents at any rate where made out "to order".

Type of Document	**Multimodal Transport Document**
Mode of Transport	Transit involving carriage by at least two different modes of transport.
Comments	Known by many names: Combined Transport Document, Container Bill of Lading, FIATA Multimodal Transport Bill of Lading and other variations.

Type of Document	**Seawaybill (SWB)**
Mode of Transport	Sea.
Comments	Known by many names: Cargo Quay Receipt, Non-negotiable Bill of Lading, Liner Waybill. Non-Transferable. Seller may alter delivery directions until discharge, unless the SWB contains a NO DISP clause preventing such change.

Type of Document	**Mate's Receipt**
Mode of Transport	Sea.
Comments	Document providing proof of delivery to a carrier. Sometimes given to shipper when selling FOB or FCA, to be tendered to buyer instead of Bill of Lading.

Type of Document	**Air Waybill**
Mode of Transport	Air.
Comments	Sometimes also known as air consignment note.

Type of Document	**Consignment Note**
Mode of Transport	Land.
Comments	Sometimes also known as CIM (rail) or CMR (road) consignment note or waybill.

Type of Document	**Warehouse Warrant**
Mode of Transport	Land and Sea.
Comments	Transferable document used when the goods are warehoused for collection by buyer at seller's end or at buyer's end.

Type of Document	**Freight-forwarder's Documents**
Mode of Transport	Sea, Air, Land or Multimodal.
Comments	Important to identify whether the forwarder is undertaking responsibility for the carriage of the goods as carrier or as agent of the carrier.

Type of Document	**Packing List**
Mode of Transport	Sea, Land or Multimodal.
Comments	A document recording what has been packed into a lorry, package or container. May represent proof of delivery as between seller and buyer, but important to identify who has issued the list and at what stage.

In Article 7 of Section A: Specific Conditions of the ICC Model Contract, the parties are invited to insert a date on which the documentary credit must be notified to the seller a certain number of days before the date of delivery. The parties should ensure that the time period is sufficient for the seller to check that the documents mentioned in the instructions to the bank conform with the documents required under the contract of sale.

Note that only the bill of lading is a transferable document of title that can be used when the buyer intends to sell or pledge the goods while they are in transit. This sale or pledge is completed by the transfer of the paper document or its electronic equivalent. Note further that the "sea waybill" is not transferable and that the seller can alter the delivery directions unless the document contains a clause preventing this (irrevocable instructions to the carrier to deliver the goods to a named person, or a so-called NO DISP-clause).

The Sea Carrier's release of the goods to the Buyer

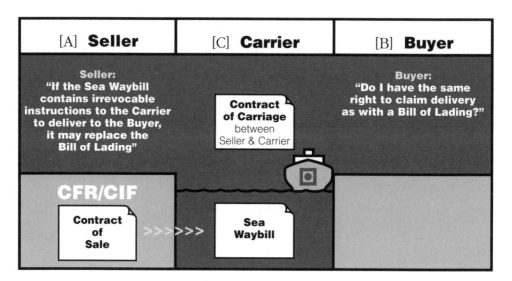

The Incoterms rules and electronic commerce

In the Incoterms® 2010 rules, the replacement of paper communication by EDI applies generally and not only to transport documents. Furthermore, an express agreement to accept EDI is no longer necessary if it is customary to use it. If so, an agreement between the parties is implied. As a consequence, the text referring to EDI in Incoterms 2000 rules clauses A8 has now been moved to clause A1/B1.

- The buyer may still insist on paper documentation unless there is an express or implied agreement to communicate electronically (an EDI agreement);

- any EDI system replacing paper documentation should provide for electronic equivalents to paper documents and must for such purpose be sufficiently secure and well developed.

Early attempts to take account of electronic commerce

In the late 1980s, it was already anticipated that electronic commerce would grow to such an extent that traditional requirements with respect to paper documentation under the Incoterms rules would have to be supplemented with options for the parties to provide electronic equivalents to paper documents. Thus, at the end of every A8 clause (except in EXW, where there are no documentary requirements), both the Incoterms 1990 rules and the Incoterms 2000 rules referred to situations where seller and buyer had agreed to communicate electronically.

At the same time that the Incoterms 1990 rules were developed, the Comité Maritime International (CMI) presented its Rules for Electronic Bills of Lading. Under these Rules, the right to control the goods and to transfer that right to someone else required possession of a "Private Key", which was to be made available to the shipper by the carrier upon his receipt of the goods. The Private Key could be construed in any technically appropriate form the parties could agree upon for securing the authenticity and integrity of an electronic transmission. The transfer of the Private Key to a subsequent party was to be effected by a notification to the carrier that the current Holder intended to transfer its right of control and transfer to a proposed new Holder. If the latter accepted to become a new Holder, the carrier was to cancel the current Private Key and issue a new one to him.

EDI agreement

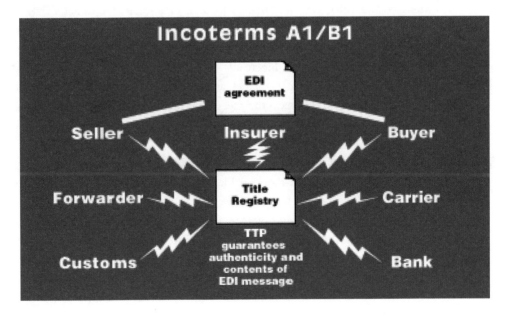

The system was based on the principle that the Private Key was at all times unique to the Holder and could not be transferred to a new Holder. The Private Key was separate and distinct from any means used to identify the contract of carriage and from any security password or identification used to access the computer network. If a proposed new Holder did not wish to participate in the electronic system, the rules gave the current Holder the option to demand a paper bill of lading from the carrier, which could then be transferred to the new Holder. Such a paper bill of lading would then have to contain a statement to the effect that the paper bill of lading was issued upon the termination of the EDI procedures. Upon issuance of the paper bill of lading, the Private Key would be cancelled and the EDI procedures terminated.

Under the CMI Rules, there were, in effect, three players – the carrier, the shipper (acting as the first Holder) and the consignee (acting as the second or subsequent Holder). Provided they all wanted to participate in the EDI procedures according to the Rules, no major problems were expected. However, the market was not prepared to accept the system. Instead, the CMI Rules inspired further moves by international bodies. UNCITRAL developed the 1996 Model Law for Electronic Commerce, containing two important Articles on transport documents (Articles 16-17). The Model Law was based mainly on the system under the CMI Rules for Electronic Bills of Lading. Generally, the Model Law recognizes that a paper document is no more than a medium representing certain functions, the first to evidence an agreement, and the second to give a party the legal right to claim the goods from the carrier at destination and to transfer rights to the goods in transit. If these functions of a paper document can be obtained by another medium, such as the electronic exchange of messages, this should, according to the Model Law, be recognized worldwide. Electronic communication is further enhanced by the 2007 UN Convention on the use of electronic communication in international contracts, as well as by the provisions on the electronic record of the Rotterdam Rules (see www. uncitral.org).

Reliability of electronic v. paper systems: BOLERO and others

Rightly or wrongly, the market considers that a paper document still represents the most reliable method of providing evidence and securing the authenticity of the document's contents. To be generally accepted, an electronic system must be equally reliable as paper documentation. Presumably, the slow development of electronic systems for transport results from the erroneous assumption that they are not sufficiently reliable.

A system called BOLERO, sponsored by the Society for Worldwide Interbank Financial Telecommunication (SWIFT) and the Through Transport Club (TTC), has been developed. BOLERO differs from the system under the CMI Rules in that the electronic messages are received and sent through a Trusted Third Party (TTP). The authenticity and integrity of the electronic message is secured by digital signatures which identify the senders and receivers and exclude the possibility that the parties will change the contents of the message once it has been sent. Consequently, the party managing the system can, as BOLERO does, guarantee the correct delivery of the EDI message.

The BOLERO system offers an added value to all those participating by requiring them to subscribe to a Rule Book that provides an "electronic agreement". The system is not limited to participation by carriers, shippers and consignees, but is also open to other parties, such as freight forwarders, insurers, customs authorities, banks and governmental bodies issuing licenses or certificates of origin.

Variations of the Incoterms rules

Since the Incoterms rules reflect only the commercial practice most commonly used, the parties may wish to either depart from the Incoterms rules or add provisions in order to obtain further precision. It must then be observed that

- the parties operate outside the scope of the Incoterms rules and contract at their own peril;

- they should therefore carefully consider whether a departure from the Incoterms rules is appropriate;

- an amended or added term should be carefully worded to avoid unintended consequences; and

- an added obligation does not necessarily change the risk distribution under the Incoterms rules; risks do not necessarily follow from functions and costs, as evidenced by the C-terms under which the seller has to pay for the freight up to the indicated destination but does not have to assume the risks of loss of or damage to the goods after dispatch from the country of export.

In the Guidance note to several terms, the need to adapt an Incoterms rule has been recognized. In some cases, such as under EXW, commercial practice frequently differs from the rules of interpretation under the rules. As noted, EXW has nevertheless been retained in its traditional wording because of the need to include a term available to the parties when they do not wish to place any obligation on the seller in addition to his simply placing the goods at the buyer's disposal at his premises.

Normally, it is not necessary to transform what the seller does into a legal obligation. Consequently, when an EXW-seller, for example, assists the buyer in moving the goods on to a ramp for subsequent loading on the buyer's collecting vehicle – or even assists the buyer in loading the goods on to that vehicle – it is rare that the parties see a need to use a contract term to ensure that the seller, if he does not assist the buyer, is held liable for non-performance.

Additions to EXW

If the parties wish to put additional obligations on the seller, they should make clear exactly what these imply. If, for instance, the parties merely add the word "loaded" after EXW, it is reasonable to assume that the seller is obliged to load the goods on the buyer's collecting vehicle. But it is not clear whether they also wish the seller to be at risk until the goods have been so loaded. It is also unclear what would happen to the risk of loss of or damage to the goods if the buyer's collecting vehicle did not arrive in time. Should the seller nevertheless remain at risk?

If the parties do not want any change in the risk allocation under EXW, but only want to add an obligation for the seller to load the goods on the buyer's collecting vehicle, they may add after the word "loaded" the words "at buyer's risk", or, even more precisely, "at buyer's risk subsequent to the seller's notice that the goods have been placed at the disposal of the buyer".

Additions to FOB

In some cases, the trade term will not assist the parties in determining exactly how the costs of loading or discharge should be distributed between them. This is the case with the maritime terms FOB, CFR and CIF. Therefore, the parties frequently seek further precision by adding after FOB words such as "stowed" or "stowed and trimmed". Here again, it is not clear whether they refer not only to functions and costs, but also to risks, and intend that the latter go along with the former. Clarifications similar to those suggested for EXW would then be appropriate: for example, "stowed and trimmed but at buyer's risk after the goods have been placed on board".

The danger of unspecified variants of the Incoterms rules

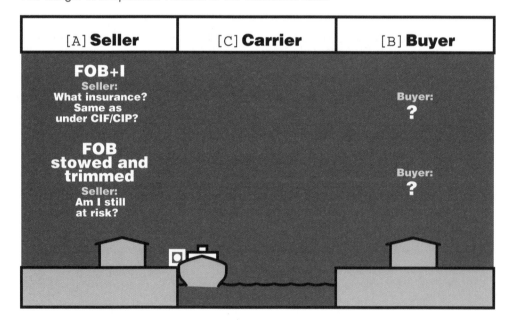

Additions to FCA

When the parties use FCA instead of FOB, the point of delivery is shifted from the ship to an inland point in or outside the port area in the country of shipment. Consequently, a number of costs may arise from the FCA point until the goods have been placed on board the ship. In particular, difficulties arise with respect to various costs debited in connection with the handling and storage of the goods in cargo terminals, so-called Terminal Handling Charges (THC). The buyers' reluctance to accept payment of THC may explain why the parties continue to use FOB, even though FOB reflects an incorrect reception point. However, if the parties wish the seller to pay the THC, it would be better to say this explicitly: "FCA Bremen Incoterms® 2010, THC for seller's account". Alternatively, the parties can divide the THC into percentages: "50% of THC for seller's account".

Additions to the C-terms

Additions to the C-terms are particularly cumbersome, since these terms represent so-called shipment contracts, under which the seller fulfils his obligations by procuring a contract of carriage and handing over the goods to the carrier. If obligations referring to the destination are added, this may be interpreted to change the basic nature of the term – from a shipment term to an arrival term – with the result that the seller would be at risk until the goods have actually arrived at the destination.

However, when expressions such as "CIF landed" or "CIF outturn weights" are used, these are normally not intended to change the basic nature of the term. The word "landed" is usually understood as referring only to the costs of discharge, and the term "outturn weights" merely signifies that the buyer should pay according to the weight ascertained after discharge, so that, for instance, condensation of the goods during the transport should be disregarded when fixing the price. However, this does not mean that the seller would bear the risk of fortuitous loss of or damage to the goods during the carriage. Nevertheless, if the parties merely intend to clarify the extent to which the seller should pay for the discharge of the goods at the port of destination, it would be preferable to say this explicitly (for example: "discharging costs until placing the goods on the quay for seller's account").

The Incoterms rules and other terms in the contract of sale

Since it is obviously related to the price, the reference to the Incoterms rules is usually made in the seller's offer: the more obligations for the seller, the more expensive his offer becomes. If there is a contract in writing, or a standard contract such as the ICC Sale Form, the reference to the chosen the Incoterms rule is in the part of the contract dealing with delivery. It should be noted, in particular, that

- even in the absence of specific relief clauses, exemptions at law are available to the benefit of both parties (for example under the CISG Article 79);

- the Incoterms rules do not deal with property rights in the goods; and

- the Incoterms rules require the seller to deliver goods conforming with the contract of sale but do not deal with the consequences if they are non-conforming.

A quick glance at the ICC Sale Form, Part B General Conditions shows the relative importance of an Incoterms rule compared with other terms of the contract. Reference is made to EXW in Article 7, but there is a reminder that another term might also be appropriate, signalled by the introductory words "Unless otherwise agreed". No reference is made to the Incoterms rules version current at the time when the ICC Sale Form was published (1998), since it was already known at that time that a new version, the Incoterms 2000 rules, was forthcoming. Instead, Article 1.4 states that any reference made to a publication of the ICC is deemed to be made to the version current at the date the contract is concluded.

Delivery terms are indispensable for the implementation of the contract of sale. In the absence of a delivery term, the parties would simply not know what to do. Most of the other terms concern problems arising when the contract is not performed as contemplated (various breaches of contract, such as delayed or non-conforming good. In other words: the Incoterms rules tell you what to do and other contract terms, as supplied by the applicable law, tell you what happens if you do not do it.

Increase of costs after the contract is concluded

As noted, the Incoterms rules contain specific provisions for the transfer of costs and risks from seller to buyer, but the risks referred to are limited to the risk of loss of or damage to the goods. Thus, the Incoterms rules do not deal with the problems caused by an increase of costs between the time of the conclusion of the contract and the performance. For example, consider the case in which a seller in Sudan quoted a CIF price for delivery of the goods in Hamburg, but because of the war between Egypt and Israel, the Suez Canal was closed. The seller, at the time, had not yet arranged contracts of carriage and insurance. He had to make a contract for the carriage of the goods around the Cape of Good Hope, and, apart from the cost increase resulting from the considerably longer distance, the freight rates rose sharply as a result of the war. The seller sought unsuccessfully to avoid the contract because of the considerable cost increase, but the UK House of Lords, in an oft-quoted decision, ruled against him. If the seller had quoted an FOB price, the risk of the cost increase would have been borne by the buyer instead.

Risk of performance if goods are lost or damaged

Another important question concerns the risk of performance in case the goods become lost or damaged. The Incoterms rules can resolve who has to bear the risk of the loss of or damage to the goods, but they do not determine whether the affected party is relieved from his obligation to perform. Consequently, if the seller has undertaken to deliver the goods under any of the D-terms and the goods are lost in transit, he is still obliged to perform by finding substitute goods as quickly as possible. If unforeseen and fortuitous events have caused the loss or damage, he may avoid having to pay damages caused to his buyer by the delay. But he cannot avoid the duty to perform the contract, unless he can be relieved under a term of the contract or, exceptionally, under the applicable law.

Non-conforming goods

When non-conforming goods are delivered to the buyer, the non-conformity may or may not be cured by the seller. If the seller fails to cure the non-conformity or to provide substitute goods in time, the buyer may be entitled to avoid the contract. Here again, the conclusions which may be drawn from the Incoterms rules are limited to the question of whether or not the goods have been delivered and whether any non-conformity has resulted after the time the risk of loss of or damage to the goods has been transferred from the seller to the buyer.

Transfer of risk v. transfer of property rights

In practice, merchants often confuse the transfer of the risk with the transfer of property rights in the goods. This is understandable, since a change of possession of the goods often also implies a change of ownership. However, a transfer of the risk may well occur before the change of possession or ownership – namely, if the buyer fails to take delivery as agreed or if the seller has agreed with the buyer that the former will remain the owner until he has been paid ("retention of title").

Unfortunately, the method of determining whether title to the goods has passed differs among jurisdictions, and the matter is outside the scope of the CISG. Whether some international unification of the law will be reached in the future remains to be seen. In the meantime, the parties are advised to take appropriate measures to protect themselves whenever there is a risk the other party may become insolvent or incapable of fulfilling his obligations. The ICC publication *Transfer of Ownership in International Trade* (N°546) is indispensable in providing first-hand information. In practice, parties often protect themselves by contractual guarantees, for example, in the form of demand guarantees, or by documentary credits, whereby the seller may be paid in connection with the shipment of the goods provided he is able to present the proper documents to the bank.

The Incoterms rules and dispute resolution

International contracts of sale usually contain terms dealing with resolution of disputes which determine

- where disputes, in the absence of amicable settlement, should be litigated;

- how disputes should be resolved (by courts of law or by arbitration); and

- which law or rules of law should be applied.

The choice of arbitration

Contracting parties seldom reckon with the risk that conflicts between them will arise and that they will fail to settle their differences amicably in case something unexpected occurs. However, when they contract by incorporating standardized terms, these terms frequently contain clauses dealing with the resolution of disputes. In some cases, the clauses stipulate that the parties should first try to settle their disputes amicably. This, of course, goes without saying. Fortunately, the parties can usually settle either between themselves or with the assistance of lawyers. But there may be situations where, for one reason or another, they will require the assistance of a neutral, third person in their settlement negotiations (so-called conciliation). If this does not result in a settlement, the parties may have no other alternative than to have their dispute resolved by arbitration or by litigation before courts of law. The 1998 ICC Rules of Arbitration offer well-designed rules, and, in case of arbitration, the procedure is supervised by the ICC International Court of Arbitration, ensuring equality and fairness and resulting in an enforceable arbitration award (see ICC publication N° 581).

Jurisdiction of the arbitral tribunal

When negotiating a contract, parties with equal bargaining positions normally prefer not to give the other party any advantage by agreeing to a dispute resolution in the latter's country, or to the choice of the law of that country. When the parties choose arbitration they can avoid such choices simply by allowing disputes to be resolved under rules of various arbitration institutions, such as the ICC Court of Arbitration. If the parties have not stipulated the place of arbitration, it will be fixed by the ICC Court (Article 14 of the ICC Rules), and if the parties have not chosen the applicable law, the arbitral tribunal will apply the rules of law which it determines to be appropriate (Article 17.1). Although Part B Article 14 of the General Conditions in the ICC Sale Form refers to ICC Arbitration, Part A of the Specific Conditions Article 15 also offers the parties the opportunity to specify another kind of arbitration, or, alternatively, litigation before a named court of law.

Alternatives to arbitration and litigation

Arbitration and litigation before courts of law should be regarded as methods to resolve disputes when all other efforts have failed. Even though arbitration provides a smoother system by offering secrecy during the proceedings and a quicker, and sometimes more reliable, way to obtain an award than litigation – where a decision by a lower court may be appealed to higher courts – arbitration can be a costly and cumbersome exercise. In recent years, alternative methods for dispute resolution have expanded (so-called ADR procedures), enabling the parties to obtain an award in a simpler way at a reduced cost.

It is true that any simplification of the dispute resolution process which limits a party's opportunity to present his case in full, using all appropriate evidence, may create uncertainty regarding the correctness of the award. But in practice a losing party seldom understands why he lost in any event, so the choice between maximum certainty and optimal simplification frequently results in opting for the latter.

Need for specificity in referencing arbitration

An arbitration agreement should be in writing and a reference to arbitration rules must be clear and specific. The following arbitration clause is recommended by ICC: "All disputes arising out of or in connection with the present contract shall be finally settled under the Rules of Arbitration of the International Chamber of Commerce by one or more arbitrators appointed in accordance with the said Rules."

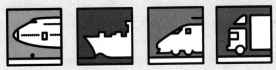

THE FOUR CATEGORIES OF INCOTERMS RULES: MAIN COMPONENTS

Important differences between shipment and arrival contracts

There is an important distinction between the delivered-terms ("D-terms") and the other trade terms with respect to determining the critical point when the seller has performed his delivery obligation. Only with the D-terms (DAT, DAP and DDP) is the seller's delivery obligation extended to the country of destination. Under the other trade terms he fulfils the delivery obligation usually in his own country, either by placing the goods at the disposal of the buyer at his (the seller's) premises (EXW), or by handing over the goods to the carrier for shipment (FCA, FAS, FOB, CFR, CIF, CPT and CIP).

To make the important distinction between this fundamentally different nature of the "groups" of trade terms, contracts of sale are often classified accordingly, as, for example, when the D-terms would turn the contract of sale into arrival contracts. Contracts using F-terms or C-terms would fall into the category of shipment contracts.

It is important to note that the seller's obligation to arrange and pay for the carriage does not in itself extend his delivery obligation up to the point of destination. On the contrary, the risk of loss of or damage to the goods will pass at the point of delivery, and the insurance which the seller has to take out under the trade terms CIF and CIP will be for the benefit of the buyer, who has to assume the risk after the delivery point.

The C-terms, by extending the seller's obligation with respect to costs of carriage and insurance respectively to the destination, make it necessary to consider not one but two critical points: one for the division of risks and another for the division of costs. Because this is not always easily understood, the C-terms are frequently misunderstood by merchants, who believe them to be more or less equivalent to D-terms. This, of course, is completely incorrect.

A seller having sold his goods on C-terms is considered to have fulfilled his delivery obligation even if something happens to the goods after the point of shipment, while a seller having sold the goods on D-terms has not fulfilled his obligation in similar circumstances.

Consequently, if the goods are lost or accidentally become damaged after shipment but before the goods have arrived at the agreed destination point, a seller having sold the goods upon D-terms has not fulfilled his contract and can therefore be held liable for breach of contract. He will normally have to provide substitute goods in place of those lost or damaged, or make other agreed restitution.

In this respect, the interrelation between the trade term and the other terms of the contract of sale is vital, since the risk falling upon the seller may be eliminated, or at least modified, by various so-called relief clauses or force majeure clauses in the contract of sale.

The basic distinction between C- and D-terms becomes crucial when goods are damaged in transit. With C-terms, the seller has already fulfilled his delivery obligations, while with D-terms the seller may be liable for breach of contract.

It follows that the parties must always observe the fundamental difference between the C-terms and the D-terms and that a seller having sold the goods under D-terms should carefully consider the need to protect himself against breach of contract and non-fulfilment risks by adequate force majeure clauses or other relief clauses in the contract of sale.

The abbreviations: E-, F-, C- and D-terms

The different nature of the trade terms can be evidenced by the grouping of the terms in four categories, using the first letter as an indication of the category to which the term belongs. The first category has only one trade term, namely EXW. But in the other three categories there are three F-terms (FCA, FAS and FOB), four C-terms (CPT, CIP, CFR and CIF) and three D-terms (DAT, DAP and DDP).

It follows from the presentation of the Incoterms® 2010 rules that Group I with terms intended for any mode or modes of transport contains one F-term (FCA), two C- terms (CPT and CIP) and three D-terms (DAT, DAP and DDP), while Group II with terms for sea and inland waterway transport comprise two F- terms (FAS and FOB) and two C-terms (CFR and CIF).

- The letter F signifies that the seller must hand over the goods to a nominated carrier Free of risk and expense to the buyer.

- The letter C signifies that the seller must bear certain Costs even after the critical point for the division of the risk of loss of or damage to the goods has been reached.

- The letter D signifies that the goods must arrive at a stated Destination.

This grouping and identification of the various trade terms should enable merchants to understand the different fundamental meanings of the terms and guide them to the most suitable option.

The Incoterms® 2010 rules

Gategory E		
Departure	**EXW**	Ex Works
Gategory F	**FCA**	Free Carrier
Main carriage	**FAS**	Free Alongside Ship
Unpaid	**FOB**	Free On Board

Gategory C			
Main carriage	**CPT**	Carriage Paid To	
Paid	**CIP**	Carriage and Insurance Paid To	
	CFR	Cost and Freight	
	CIF	Cost, Insurance and Freight	

Gategory D		
	DAT	Delivered at Terminal
	DAP	Delivered at Place
	DDP	Delivered Duty Paid

The term EXW: placing the goods at the disposal of the buyer

EXW represents the seller's minimum obligation, since he only has to place the goods at the disposal of the buyer. Although it may appear from the contract itself or from the surrounding circumstances that the buyer intends to export the goods, it is entirely up to him whether he wishes to do so. According to the trade term, there is no obligation for either party to do anything with respect to export.

Nevertheless, it follows from B2 that the buyer must carry out all tasks of export, import and security clearance, and, as stipulated in A2, the seller merely has to render his assistance in connection with these tasks. The buyer has to reimburse the seller for all costs and charges incurred in rendering this assistance (B6).

Neither of the parties has any obligation to the other with respect to contracts of carriage and insurance. However, if the buyer wishes to have the goods carried from the seller's place he should, for his own benefit, arrange for carriage and cargo insurance.

F-terms and C-terms: the carriage-related terms

F-terms: main carriage not paid by seller

F-terms and pre-carriage

While under the F-terms the seller has to arrange any necessary pre-carriage to reach the agreed point for handing over the goods to the carrier, it is the buyer's function to arrange and pay for the main carriage. Section A3 of the F-terms does not mention anything with respect to pre-carriage, since there is no need to explain how the seller is able to reach the point for the handing over of the goods to the carrier.

FCA and handing over goods for carriage

As noted, FCA is the main F-term which can be used irrespective of the mode of transport and should be used whenever handing over to the carrier is not completed alongside a ship or by placing the goods on board. In the two latter cases, the terms FAS and FOB should be used instead of FCA.

The circumstances defining the handing over of the goods to the carrier differ according to the mode of transport and the nature of the goods. Practices also vary from place to place. Since the buyer has to arrange for the transport, it is vital that he instruct the seller precisely regarding how the goods should be handed over for carriage. He should also ensure that the precise point where this will occur is mentioned in the contract of sale. This is not always possible to do when making the contract, since the exact point may be decided subsequently. In this event, it is important that the seller, when quoting his price, consider the various options available to the buyer for requiring the seller to hand over the goods for carriage. The seller, of course, should know how the goods are to be packed, whether they are to be containerized and whether they should be delivered to a terminal in his vicinity or elsewhere.

Full loads and less-than-full loads

The quantity of the goods will determine whether they are suitable to constitute so-called full loads (railway wagon loads or container loads), or whether they must be delivered to the carrier as break bulk cargo to be stowed by him, usually at his terminal. In the container trade, the important distinction is made between full loads and less-than-full loads (FCL for full container load and LCL for less than full container load).

In practice, the seller often contracts for carriage

Although all of the F-terms clearly place the obligation to contract for carriage on the buyer, in practice the seller frequently performs it when the choice is more or less immaterial to the buyer. This is particularly common when there is only one option available, taking into account the place and the nature of the goods, or when the freight would be the same even though there are several options for carriage.

When there is a "liner service" from the seller's country, the seller frequently contracts for carriage under FOB. This practice is called "FOB additional service". In many cases the practice with respect to road transport is less firm; indeed, it may vary from forwarder to forwarder and from carrier to carrier. Nevertheless, the seller frequently contracts for the road carriage, though it is intended that the buyer should pay for it.

Current commercial practice makes it difficult to set down in a legal text what the parties are obliged to do. But though from a strictly legal point of view the seller is not concerned with the main contract of carriage, his duties according to commercial practice are reflected under the heading A3. If there is such a practice, the seller may contract for carriage on usual terms at the buyer's risk and expense.

When the seller declines or the buyer wants to contract for carriage

The seller may decline to contract for carriage and may notify the buyer accordingly. The buyer may also specifically ask the seller to assist him or tell the seller that he intends to contract for carriage himself.

It is important for the buyer to notify the seller of his intentions if, for instance, he has a special relationship with a carrier making it important for him to exercise his right according to B3 to arrange the contract of carriage.

Buyer's risk if transport is unavailable

Even though the seller under an F-term is requested or intends to perform the contracting for carriage according to commercial practice, the buyer always will bear the risk if, because of unforeseen circumstances, transport facilities fail to be available as contemplated.

Division of loading costs under FOB

When the cargo is delivered containerized or in less-than-full loads to the carrier's terminal, the division of loading costs seldom presents any particular problems. However, the situation is quite different when under FOB the cargo is to be delivered in the traditional manner over the ship's rail.

The custom of the port will decide the extent to which loading costs under FOB should be distributed between seller and buyer. If this is known to both parties, no difficulties should arise. But frequently the buyer may not know the custom of the port in the seller's country and indeed may find out later that the custom works to his disadvantage.

For this reason, it is important that the FOB buyer consider this problem when negotiating the contract of sale and the price for the goods.

C-terms: main carriage paid by seller

Two groups of C-terms

There are two groups of C-terms; one group (CPT and CIP) can be used for any mode of transport, including sea and multimodal transport while the other group can be used only when the goods are intended to be carried by sea (CFR and CIF).

Do not use CFR or CIF for anything other than sea transport

Sometimes the parties fail to observe the important distinction in the previous paragraph, and use CFR and CIF for modes of transport other than carriage by sea. The seller then puts himself in the unfortunate position of being unable to fulfil his fundamental obligation to present a bill of lading, or to present a sea waybill or similar document as required under CFR or CIF A8.

Note, however, that if the buyer intends to sell the goods in transit, he may lose this option if he receives the incorrect transport document. In such a case, he would be able to cancel the contract because of the seller's breach in not providing the correct document. Also, when the market for the goods falls after the contract of sale has been entered into, a buyer could, in certain circumstances, use the seller's breach as a means of avoiding the market loss by cancelling the contract of sale.

Wrongful use of CFR/CIF

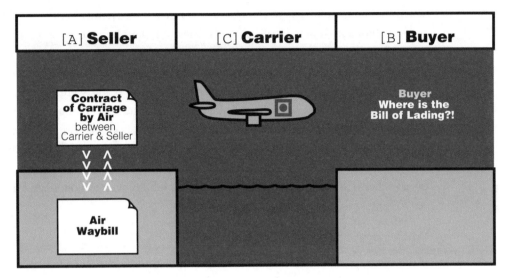

C-terms are not equivalent to D-terms

The C-terms may present some difficulties, since only the point of destination is mentioned after the respective term: for example, in a contract of sale concluded between a buyer in New York and a seller in London, only New York is likely to be mentioned after the C-term, with nothing usually being said about shipment from London. Obviously, this can give rise to the false impression that the goods are to be delivered in New York and that the seller has not fulfilled his obligation until they have in fact been delivered there.

Consequently, it is not uncommon that the contract will indicate, for example, "Delivery New York not later than..." (with a particular date being given). But this notation would demonstrate that the contracting parties failed to understand the fundamental nature of the C-term, since under it the seller fulfils his obligation by shipping the goods from his country.

This confusion arises because the seller undertakes to arrange and pay for the main carriage up to destination. This payment obligation, however, is only in addition to the fundamental obligation to ship the goods from the seller's place.

Two "critical points" under C-terms

Since the C-term must show the extent to which the seller undertakes to arrange and pay for the main contract of carriage – with the addition of insurance under CIF and CIP – indicating the point of destination under C-terms is inevitable. The C-term also establishes that the seller fulfils his delivery obligation by handing over the goods for shipment in his country, and that this has to be accepted as delivery by the buyer (A4 and B4 respectively).

Thus, under the C-terms there will be not only one relevant point as under the F-terms – the point of shipment – but two critical points, one coinciding with the point of shipment under the F-terms, the other indicating the point up to which the seller would have to procure and pay for contract of carriage and insurance. It would be easier for traders to understand the fundamental nature of the C-term if both of these critical points were indicated. However, this is usually not done, since the seller at the time of entering into the contract of sale may prefer to retain a certain liberty with regard to the exact point or port of shipment. A seller in Stockholm, for example, having sold the goods under CFR or CIF to a buyer in New York, may wish to delay deciding whether he wishes to ship the goods directly from Stockholm, or have them carried by road to Gothenburg or perhaps even to Rotterdam for carriage by sea to New York.

Do not stipulate date of arrival under C-terms

If the contract of sale refers to a C-term, but also indicates arrival at destination on a particular date, the contract becomes ambiguous. One would then not know if it was the intention of the contracting parties that the seller will have breached the contract if the goods do not actually arrive at destination on the agreed date, or whether the fundamental nature of the C-term should supersede this interpretation.

In the latter case, the seller's obligation is limited to shipping the goods so that they could arrive at the destination on the agreed date, unless something happens after shipment, which, according to the C-term, would be at the risk of the buyer.

Seller's insurance obligation under CIF and CIP

In the Incoterms rules the C-term exists in two forms: CFR and CPT when there is no insurance obligation for the seller, and CIF and CIP when, according to A3b, the seller must obtain and pay for the insurance. Otherwise, CFR and CPT are identical to CIF and CIP respectively.

Cost of insurance depends on intended transport

Under CFR and CPT, where the seller has no insurance obligation, the buyer should be aware of the relation between the cost of insurance and the intended carriage of the goods. If the goods are deemed to be exposed to greater risks during the transport (for example, during the shipment of goods on deck or in older ships), the insurance premium will become more expensive – if insurance is available at all.

The "minimum cover" principle of CIF and CIP

The obligation of the seller to obtain and pay for cargo insurance under CIF and CIP A3(b) is based on the principle of "minimum cover" as set out in the Institute Cargo Clauses drafted by Lloyd's Market Association (LMA) and International Underwriting Association of London (IUA). But such minimum cover could also follow any other similar set of clauses.

In practice, however, "all risk-insurance" is preferred to less, since the minimum cover is appropriate only when the risk of loss of or damage to the goods in transit is more or less confined to casualties affecting both the means of conveyance and the cargo, such as those resulting from collisions, strandings and fire. In such cases, even the minimum cover would protect the buyer against the risk of having to pay compensation to a shipowner for his expenses in salvaging the ship and cargo, according to the rules relating to general average (the York/Antwerp Rules of 2004).

Unsuitability of minimum cover for manufactured goods

Minimum cover is not suitable for manufactured goods (particularly not for goods of high value) because of the risk of theft, pilferage or improper handling or custody of the goods. Therefore, extended insurance coverage is usually taken out as protection against such risks. A buyer of manufactured goods should stipulate in the contract of sale that the insurance according to CIF or CIP should be extended as indicated. If he does not, the seller can fulfil his insurance obligation by providing only minimum cover (Institute Clauses C).

The buyer may also wish to obtain additional coverage such as insurance against war, riots, other civil commotions, or strikes or other labour disturbances. This would normally be accomplished by specific instructions to the seller. Alternatively, the buyer may himself arrange for appropriate additional insurance. This can be done either case by case or through general arrangements with his insurer.

The question of whether it is correct to follow the principle of minimum insurance coverage has been much debated. However, the traditional "minimum principle" has been retained, primarily due to the difficulty of knowing the insurance requirements of prospective buyers in multiple sales down a chain ("string sales").

Guarding against fraud under CFR and CPT

Statistical evidence indicates that fraud occurs more frequently under the CFR and CPT terms than under other terms, largely because the buyer does not normally have sufficient control over the particular method and the type of transport involved. Therefore, the CFR or CPT buyer is advised to consider specific stipulations in the contract of sale restricting the seller's option to arrange for carriage as he pleases (for example, the buyer can mention a particular shipping line or identify the carrier).

How to prevent delivery until payment has been made

Sellers uncertain about the buyer's ability or willingness to pay the price can take measures to prevent delivery of the goods before payment has been made. There are two ways to do this: (1) instructions to prevent the buyer from obtaining documents required to obtain the goods before payment can be given to a carrier, a freight forwarder or a bank (CAD-Instructions); and (2) instructions to require cash from the buyer on delivery (COD instructions) can be given to the carrier or a freight forwarder, and the bank can be instructed not to release the original(s) of the bill of lading until payment has been made. This would probably best be achieved by means of a documentary collection arranged through the international banking system.

Payment by using the irrevocable documentary credit

Payment can also be arranged by requiring the buyer to open an irrevocable documentary credit (also called a letter of credit, L/C) with the seller as beneficiary. This alternative gives the seller the additional advantage of receiving payment earlier, when the goods are shipped from his own country. He then avoids having to transport the goods to destination before payment, where he could run the risk of the buyer's failing to collect the goods.

As beneficiary under a documentary credit, the seller will be paid provided he presents the stipulated documents to the bank completely complying with the requirements of the L/C and within the period allowed. The bank which is to pay under the documentary credit can also be requested to add its confirmation to the irrevocable undertaking of the bank which opened the credit (the so-called opening or issuing bank). In this case, the seller obtains a promise to receive payment, not only from the issuing bank, but separately from the confirming bank as well.

Documentary credits are often used with C-terms, and in these cases they are fully consistent with the basic nature of the terms. This is because the seller fulfils his shipment obligation with shipment in his own country and only has to provide evidence with the documents stipulated in the documentary credit that will satisfy the paying bank and the buyer that he has fulfilled that obligation.

Nevertheless, buyers should be aware that with documentary credits banks

■ are not concerned with the contract of sale or the contract of carriage;

■ limit their service to the contract of finance as such;

■ do not undertake to check whether the goods in fact correspond to the contract description;

■ only check that the documents "on their face" appear to be in order; and

■ do not assume any responsibility for the solvency or standing of parties having issued the documents.

Thus, the buyer does not receive comprehensive protection merely by using the documentary credit process.

It follows from the previous paragraphs that, with respect to the C-terms

■ **CFR and CIF should never be used when carriage other than carriage by sea is intended;**

■ **the buyer should always consider the need to restrict the seller's options with respect to arranging the carriage and, except in case of "string sales", should require additional insurance coverage from the seller or arrange such insurance himself;**

■ **under no circumstances should a stipulation as to time for delivery be mentioned in connection with arrival at destination: it should be mentioned only in connection with the shipment of the goods; and**

■ **if buyers wish to make sellers responsible for the arrival of the goods at destination at a particular time, D-terms should be used instead of C-terms**

D-terms: delivered terms (DAT, DAP and DDP)

Factors determining use of different D-terms

When choosing among the different D-terms, two factors have to be taken into consideration:

■ the distribution of costs and risks connected with discharging the goods at destination; and

■ the distribution of functions in connection with the clearance of the goods for import.

The trend toward choice of delivered terms

A seller of manufactured goods, whose products have to compete in the country of destination and who has to extend his obligation to the buyer by contract guarantees, often finds it inappropriate to limit his obligation under the contract of sale by fulfilling the contract at some earlier point, for example before the goods are dispatched or before they have reached destination. As one car manufacturer reportedly said: "Although I may be relieved of the risk of damage to my cars sold under an FOB contract, I am not pleased to see how they are being damaged when hopeless efforts are made to squeeze them into a cargo hold of a wholly inappropriate ship."

The seller's need to plan and control cargo movements

Practical problems with respect to arranging the carriage often make terms under which the seller fulfils his obligation by handing over the goods to a carrier inappropriate and less economical. An exporter of goods with a constant flow of cargo in various directions often finds that transport economy (so-called logistics planning) requires him to totally control carriage as well as the delivery at destination. In addition, the seller is often in a better position to obtain competitive freight rates than his buyers.

DES and DEQ for sea transport (now replaced by DAP and DAT)

The terms DES and DEQ are traditional for carriage of goods by sea. The former means that the buyer must take the cargo out of the ship, whereas the latter places the burden on the seller to ensure that the goods are discharged on to the quay. When the goods are to be carried on liner terms, discharging expenses are usually included in the freight, in which case the term DES is out of place. If, on the other hand, the goods are commodities carried in ships to be chartered by the seller, the distinction between DES and DEQ is particularly important. Even though DES and DEQ have disappeared from the Incoterms rules, it is expected that the terms will continue to be used in commodity trading. If so, they will be interpreted either according to the Incoterms 2000 rules or as DAP or DAT under the Incoterms® 2010 rules with the same result.

DES and "Free out" stipulation in charter parties

If the contract of sale is concluded on DES, the seller charters the ship on terms relieving the shipowner from the discharging operation. Thus, the charter party will be concluded between the seller and the shipowner on terms "Free out", when the word "Free" means that discharging operations are not included in the charter party hire. In such cases, the charter party may make clear that the loading operation is also "free" to the shipowner. If so, the loading expenses have to be borne by the seller, since loading and carrying the goods to the agreed destination under delivered terms would fall upon him. The charter party term in such a case would read "Free in and out" (FIO).

FIO stipulations in charter parties and contracts of sale

There are also variants of FIO used when further distinctions are made: for example, "Free in and out stowed and trimmed" (FIOST) and similar expressions in the charter party. These and similar terms can also appear in the contract of sale. But a contract of sale on delivered terms has to deal only with discharging functions and expenses, since it is unnecessary to deal with expenses which inevitably must fall upon the seller before the goods arrive at the agreed destination.

However, the term FIOST is sometimes used in FOB contracts of sale when the seller's obligation is limited to placing the goods on board the ship in the port of shipment. But such a charter party term is out of place in the contract of sale, since the FOB seller is not concerned with discharging operations in the port of destination. Here, if the seller agrees to do more than merely lift the goods over the ship's rail, the correct term in the contract of sale to specify what the seller has to do in connection with the loading of the ship would read "FOB stowed and trimmed".

Buyer needs to know time of arrival

Under the terms DES and DEQ, or DAP and DAT, it is vital that the buyer know the time of the ship's arrival so that the ship is not detained in the port of discharge waiting for the cargo to be removed. It is also important that the goods, when they have been discharged, be removed from the quay as quickly as possible. It is common practice for the seller in the contract of sale to give the buyer notice of the estimated time of the arrival of the ship (ETA), and also for the contract to require the buyer to discharge the ship and remove the cargo from the quay within an agreed time.

Demurrage and dispatch money

If the buyer fails to discharge the ship and remove the cargo from the quay, he may have to reimburse the seller for expenses incurred, "demurrage". Alternatively, the buyer may have to pay port authorities or stevedoring companies for additional storage expenses. To induce the buyer to discharge the cargo, the seller may be prepared to give him an extra bonus for saving time. Corresponding stipulations may also be found in charter parties to the benefit of the seller in his capacity as charterer (so-called dispatch money).

Demurrage can also be charged by the owners or lessors of containers, when the containers have not been unloaded within an agreed period and are unavailable for re-use.

Consistency required between charter party and contract of sale

It is important to make the terms of the charter party and the contract of sale compatible on questions of demurrage and dispatch money. Terms relating to the time the vessel is available for loading and discharge (so-called laytime) and terms relating to demurrage and dispatch are often complicated, since some events – for example, circumstances which could be attributed to the carrier or events beyond the control of either party, such as labour disturbances, government directions or adverse weather conditions – can extend the time available. For these reasons as well, it is necessary that the provisions of the charter party and the contract of sale be consistent.

DAT, DAP and DDP – for all modes of transport

DAT, DAP and DDP can usually be used regardless of the mode of transport. When DAP is used for through rail transport, it signifies that the seller's obligations extend up to the border of the country mentioned after the term. This is usually the border of the buyer's country, but it could also be some third country through which the goods are to be carried in transit.

Avoid "free border" or "franco border"

Terms such as "free border" or "franco border" are even more common in practice than the earlier DAF in the Incoterms 2000 rules now replaced by DAP. Nevertheless, these terms are not to be used, since misunderstandings frequently arise with respect to the extent of the seller's obligations. It is clear that the seller has to bear the costs up to the agreed point, but it is not clear whether that point is a "tariff point" or whether a real "delivery point" is intended. If the latter is the case, the seller is also responsible for what may happen to the goods from the time of dispatch until the agreed point is reached.

As noted in the explanation of C-terms, the mere fact that the seller undertakes to pay costs does not necessarily mean that he also has to assume the risks connected with the carriage. For this reason, terms using only the words "free" or "franco" are to be avoided. The term "delivered" should be used instead, if it is intended that the seller bear the risks as well as the costs for loss of or damage to the cargo or for failure to reach the delivery point. If this is not intended, one of the C-terms, for example CPT or CIP, should be used instead of DAP.

The through railway consignment note

In railway traffic a physical delivery of the goods to the buyer seldom takes place precisely at the border of the buyer's country. The seller often obtains a through consignment note from the railway, covering the whole transit up to the final destination, and also assists the buyer to do whatever is necessary to clear customs and to pass the goods through third countries before they reach the destination. But the seller in these cases can perform these "additional" services at the risk and expense of the buyer in the same way he would under FCA and FOB terms (see the discussion of FCA and FOB above). Then if something goes wrong after the goods have reached the agreed point mentioned after DAP, this would be at the risk and expense of the buyer. Conversely, if something happens which delays the cargo or prevents it from reaching that point, it would be at the seller's risk and expense.

Railway cargo consolidation by freight forwarders

Break bulk cargo is usually handed over to freight forwarders for so-called railway cargo consolidation. In these cases, the freight forwarder unitizes the cargo in full wagon loads and enters into contractual arrangements with the railways on terms which differ from the terms which the seller or buyer could have negotiated with the railway for each individual parcel. Freight forwarders have their own tariffs, and they debit sellers and buyers accordingly.

In railway traffic, the point mentioned after DAP, as discussed earlier, would then serve as the "tariff point", so that the costs relating to the carriage before the point will be debited to the seller and the costs thereafter to the buyer. In most cases, the cargo is not discharged from one railway wagon and re-loaded on another at the point mentioned after DAP. Nevertheless, if something happens to the cargo or if the traffic is interrupted, the point mentioned after DAP would also serve as a point for the division of the risks between seller and buyer.

Presumably, sellers and buyers contracting on the term DAP will not consider more than the division of costs. As noted, the terms CPT and CIP are quite sufficient if only a division of costs between the parties is intended.

DAP and DDP do not include unloading

When cargo is to be collected or delivered at destination, difficulties arise in determining exactly what should be done by the seller and the buyer.

Is it sufficient that the goods arrive on the vehicle provided by the seller? Or do they have to be removed from that vehicle at the risk and expense of the seller? If the latter, can the buyer debit the seller for the work performed by his own personnel in receiving the goods at a ramp in his warehouse? And should the seller load the goods on to a vehicle sent by the buyer to collect the goods from the seller's terminal? Answers to these questions normally follow from commercial practice or from previous dealings between the same contracting parties. Since, in most countries, the seller normally loads the goods on to the buyer's collecting vehicle, while the buyer unloads the goods from the seller's vehicle arriving at his premises or some other place named by the buyer, DAT and DAP, in clause A4, at least reflect the latter practice.

Import clearance under D-terms

It is common practice that the party domiciled in the country arranges export and import and security clearance. Thus the buyer must clear the goods for import and pay duty, VAT and other taxes and charges levied upon import of the goods, unless the parties by choosing DDP have explicitly placed that obligation on the seller.

Seller should avoid DDP if difficulties expected

If any difficulties seem likely to arise in relation to the import of the goods into the buyer's country, the seller should try to avoid using the term DDP.

Even if no difficulties are expected, each party is usually better suited to assess the possible risks in his own country. Therefore, it is normally better that the seller take upon himself the task of clearing the goods for export, while the buyer procures the import formalities and bears any extra costs and risks incurred in that connection.

Also, it may be that the applicable statutory provisions relating to duties, VAT and similar charges require payment from a party domiciled in the country concerned. A party from abroad, having undertaken to pay these charges, cannot then benefit from advantages accorded to parties domiciled in the country of export or import. Moreover, if the costs are paid by a non-resident, difficulties may arise in deducting the expenditure in the VAT forms submitted to the authorities.

Choice of DDP with exclusion of duty and/or other charges

The seller or his freight forwarder may be prepared to clear the goods for import, without paying duty, VAT and other official charges connected with the import clearance. If so, DDP may still be used but with the addition of the phrase "exclusive of duty, VAT and other import charges".

DDP with such an exclusion is not equivalent to the other D-terms since the obligation to clear the goods for import still falls on the DDP seller. It is also possible to use another D-term and then to add that some costs connected with import should be borne by the seller.

DAT or DAP and difficulties of reaching the final destination

Serious difficulties could arise in using the term DAT, DAP when the goods have to pass through customs at an earlier point than the agreed point of destination. If so, the goods may be prevented from reaching the destination point as contemplated if they are held up at the customs station, either because of the failure of the buyer to do whatever is required by the authorities or for other reasons.

Since under DAT and DAP it is the buyer's task to clear the goods for import, all of the above events are at his risk and expense. This may be cold comfort for a seller who has his transport arrangements interrupted at the customs station but who has the remaining obligation to deliver the goods at the agreed final point of destination. Consequently, sellers are advised to be cautious and to avoid agreeing to arrive at a point which may be difficult to reach.

By adding the term "cleared for import", it is possible to use DAT or DAP and still place the obligation to clear the goods for import on the seller. This means that the seller's obligation is limited to the clearance as such and that the duty, as well as other charges levied upon import, will be unpaid and have to be paid by the buyer.

Charges and the DDP seller

It should be underlined that the "charges" to be paid by the DDP-seller concern only such charges as are a necessary consequence of the import as such and thus have to be paid according to the applicable import regulations. This does not include additional charges resulting from warehousing or services obtained from private parties in connection with the import.

SELLER'S AND BUYER'S OBLIGATIONS: AN OVERVIEW

The basic nature of the various trade terms having already been briefly explained, the following section-by-section examination will make it easier for the user of this guide to determine the risks and responsibilities of the parties.

Sections A1, B1: the obligation to exchange goods for money

The essence of any contract of sale is the exchange of goods for money. The Incoterms rules, in sections A1 and B1, simply contain a reminder of this. Needless to say, the contract of sale must specify which goods the seller has to provide and what the buyer must pay for them. In A1 there is also a reminder that the seller should provide the "commercial invoice" and any "evidence of conformity" the contract may stipulate.

Section A9: the seller's packaging obligations

Any particular requirement with respect to checking and marking which the buyer desires solely for his own purposes must be stipulated in the contract of sale. Section A9 makes clear that the costs required solely to place the goods at the buyer's disposal are for the seller's account. In this respect, government agencies in some countries may request that the goods be checked before they are admitted for import or export. Some goods may have to be marked, measured, weighed or counted as a condition for the carrier's acceptance of the goods for carriage. When the contract of sale does not contain detailed provisions on packaging of the goods, or when these cannot be ascertained from previous dealings between the parties, the seller may be uncertain as to what he should do. Under normal circumstances, the seller has to provide some packaging.

However, how the goods should be packed and prepared for the intended voyage may be unclear. A long sea voyage could require strong packaging and special preparations to protect against rusting caused by condensation and humidity. This same degree of protection is unlikely to be required for air carriage of the same cargo.

The seller must pack the goods as required for the mode of transport, but only to the extent that the circumstances of the transport are known to him before the contract of sale is concluded. If these are known, he can take them into consideration when he quotes his price. Therefore, it is important that the buyer duly inform the seller of his intentions, particularly when the contract has been concluded on EXW or under F-terms, when the seller may not otherwise know the buyer's intentions with respect to the carriage.

Section B9: pre-shipment inspection

Pre-shipment inspection (PSI) may be required when the buyer requires a licence or permit from the authorities to ensure that the goods conform with the contract. In these circumstances, the authorities order an inspection and generally engage an independent inspection agency to perform it. Legislation in the country of import will determine whether and to what extent the authorities can require reimbursement of costs paid by them for the inspection; but if reimbursement is required from one of the parties, the buyer will normally bear the cost.

Contractual stipulations relating to inspection usually require the buyer to pay for it. However, there are other variants which require the seller to pay, wholly or partly, for the inspection; in others, the seller has to pay for it to the extent that the inspection shows that the goods were not in condition to satisfy the contract.

PSI should be distinguished from an inspection required by the buyer himself without the involvement of his authorities. Such an inspection may be important for the buyer. if he has any reason to doubt that the seller will hand over goods for shipment in conformity with the contract. Using such an inspection can ascertain whether a commodity – such as oil, ore, foodstuffs, or timber – conforms with the contract of sale.

An inspection can also be arranged when the contract of sale is concluded between parties who are not familiar with one another from previous dealings and who may not intend to establish future commercial relations (as in "one-off" contracts on the spot market).

Finally, an inspection can be a means of avoiding maritime fraud. In some notorious cases it has been possible for a fraudulent seller to obtain payment under a documentary credit by presenting documents relating to a cargo and a ship even though neither the cargo nor the ship existed. Had an inspection been performed in these cases, the outcome could have been quite different. Since the inspection is normally performed in the buyer's interest, section B9 of the Incoterms rules requires the buyer to pay the costs unless otherwise agreed. There is an exception to this principle when the inspection has been mandated by the authorities of the country of export.

Sections A2, B2: the obligation to clear the goods for export and import

A reference to the Incoterms rules may sometimes be made in domestic contracts of sale, although this is not usually necessary or appropriate. The overwhelming usage concerns international contracts of sale when the cargo must be carried from country to country. There it is necessary to decide what the seller and the buyer are required to do to clear the goods for export and import, and in the Incoterms rules this is dealt with under the heading "Licences, authorizations, security clearances and other formalities" (A2, B2).

The division of functions with respect to export and import clearance is important in several ways. First, the parties must know who is responsible for doing what is necessary to obtain any required licences or official authorizations and to submit official forms and requests in the country concerned. Second, the obligation to clear the goods – particularly for import – frequently results in the obligation to pay duty, VAT and other official charges.

Third, the parties must resolve who bears the risk if it is not possible to clear the goods within the agreed time or at all (for example, if there are export or import prohibitions).

Take precautions against the risk of export and import prohibitions

A seller who has undertaken to clear the goods for export – and particularly for import – is well advised to negotiate with his buyer an extension of the time for delivery or the right to terminate the contract in case of unforeseen restrictions or prohibitions relating to export or import. More than this, it is important that the seller not undertake any activity that he or his agent either cannot do or are expressly forbidden to do by the receiving country.

Obtaining assistance to clear customs

A party having undertaken to clear the goods for export or import or to move them through a third country may often need the assistance of the other party to obtain various documents, for example documents showing the origin or ultimate destination of the goods. Therefore, sections A2 or B2 set out the extent to which the seller or the buyer, as the case may be, has to render this assistance to the other party.

Sections A10 and B10 stipulate that the seller and the buyer respectively have to reimburse any costs incurred by the other party for rendering the requested assistance, which is always provided at the risk and expense of the requesting party.

Sections A2, B2 and A10, B10: security measures and the changing role of customs

Security-Measures and the changing role of customs

As a result of the terrorist attacks in the United States on 11 September 2001 (the so called "9/11" attacks), the US Customs service began to collaborate with US Industry under the the Customs Trade Partnership Against Terrorism (C-TPAT). As a result various security measures were initiated in order to prevent the entry into the United States of goods that could be used for terrorist activities. For the purpose of clearance, goods may be subjected to costly and time-consuming procedures involving scanning of containers and inspection and Risk Analysis of global cargo.

Driven by the requirement of Global Supply Chain Security the role of customs authorities changed from the traditional revenue collection to supply chain security and co-operation between customs authorities in countries of export and import intensified. The World Customs Organisation (WCO) subsequently established the WCO SAFE Framework of Standards, which drives various security initiatives including the WCO Data Model that aim to promote a single window efficiency in discovering security threats and avoid delay and costs. This recent WCO instrument seeks to address the simultaneous facilitation and securitization of global trade as well as the authorised economic operator (AEO) concept within the Global Supply Chain. This instrument currently has two Pillars, that of Customs-to-Customs cooperation and Customs-to-Business cooperation. In a sense, the total control approach adopted by customs authorities creates a "new Border", where advance chain-of-custody information on inbound, outbound and transit shipments purports to improve the capability of customs authorities to detect high-risk consignments. In order to alleviate the burden on international trade and to simplify control, the AEO concept offers benefits to reliable traders by simplifying security and safety controls. Mutual recognition of AEOs by customs authorities worldwide would significantly enhance the flow of "innocent cargo" from sellers and buyers due to quicker clearance of such cargo and the additional benefits that can be enjoyed by such traders. Authorised economic operators[1] involved in the international trade supply chain will engage in a self-assessment process measured against predetermined security standards and best practices to ensure that their internal policies and procedures provide adequate safeguards against the compromise of their shipments and containers until they are released from Customs' control at destination. The present status of these efforts is evidenced by the following Resolution:

Resolution of the Customs Co-operation Council on the framework of standards to secure and facilitate global trade

Customs Co-operation Council

Recognizing that the implementation of the principles contained in the WCO Framework of Standards will be an important step in enhancing security of the international trade supply chain and lead to a greater facilitation of legitimate trade;

Noting the increased concern with respect to acts of international terrorism and organized crime and the importance and vulnerability of global trade;

Considering that Customs administrations contribute to the economic and social development of nations through the collection of revenue, and that implementing the Framework of Standards will also be equally important in this regard;

Taking into account the Resolutions of the Customs Co-operation Council on Security and Facilitation of the International Trade Supply Chain (June 2002) and Global Security and Facilitation Measures concerning the International Trade Supply Chain (June2004), and IMO Conference Resolution No. 9 on the enhancement of security in co-operation with the WCO;

Believing in the need for Customs administrations to implement standards regarding integrated Customs procedures and in the need for co-operation between Customs administrations and business;

Noting that Members and Customs or Economic Unions may need to consider modifications to their legal or other provisions to support the implementation of the WCO Framework of Standards.

RESOLVES :

1. To adopt the Framework of Standards to Secure and Facilitate Global Trade.

2. That the Members of the Council and Customs or Economic Unions should :

   2.1. implement as soon as possible in accordance with each administration's capacity and necessary legislative authority the principles, standards and other provisions contained in the WCO Framework of Standards;

---

1. One of the main elements of the security amendment of the Community Customs Code (Regulation (EC) No. 648/2005) is the creation of the AEO concept. On the basis of Article 5a of the security amendments, Member States can grant the AEO status to any economic operator meeting the following common criteria: customs compliance, appropriate record-keeping, financial solvency and, where relevant, security and safety standards.

2.2. encourage any necessary improvements in Customs capability and integrity to provide a comprehensive framework for global trade security;

2.3. identify the required sustainable capacity building measures including the modifications to national legal and administrative rules and procedures, where appropriate, and pursue their realization to enable a comprehensive implementation of the provisions of the Framework of Standards;

2.4. foresee the provision of technical assistance in order to encourage the implementation of the Framework of Standards;

2.5. submit to the WCO an indicative timetable for implementation of the Framework of Standards suitable to their capacities;

2.6. endeavour to secure the full co-operation of business in the implementation of the Frame work of Standards;

2.7. participate in periodic evaluation meetings to assess progress towards implementation;

2.8. provide to the WCO periodic reports on progress towards implementation of the Framework, to be discussed during each evaluation meeting; and

2.9. consider the use of benchmarking methods to evaluate each Member's own implementation process.

3. That Members and Customs or Economic Unions should notify the WCO of their intention to implement the Framework of Standards. The WCO will transmit this information to the Customs administrations of all Members and to those Customs or Economic Unions which have notified the WCO.

4. That those Members and Customs or Economic Unions which have notified the WCO of their intention to implement the Framework of Standards should work with each other to develop mechanisms for mutual recognition of Authorized Economic Operator validations and accreditations and Customs control results, and other mechanisms that may be needed to eliminate or reduce redundant or duplicated validation and accreditation efforts.

It follows from what has been stated that the meaning of "duty paid" and "clearance" of goods for export and import has changed. The traditional checkpoint at the border of the country of importation has developed into a global system of advance control. The responsibilities of border management still remain but the function of governmental agencies has changed. This is demonstrated in particular by the US Customs-Trade Partnerships Against Terrorism (C-TPAT) and other global Customs trade security partnerships such as the EU (AEO), Canada (PIP), Singapore (STP), and Sweden (StairSec) to name but a few.

The impact on the Incoterms rules of the changing role of customs authorities is obvious. While sellers and buyers still have to allocate the duties in clearing the goods for export and import, assistance to provide the required information in advance- such as the Advance Manifest for Customs Border Control and Importer Security Filing (ISF) in United States and other global security Customs Administration areas- has become indispensable. As such assistance is at the cost and risk of the party responsible for the clearance of the goods, the choice of a recognised partner and compliance with the relevant customs administrations' security programmes, in order to enjoy the relevant benefits prescribed in the WCO SAFE Framework of Standards, becomes paramount.

While the main principles of export and import clearance under the Incoterms® 2010 rules remain the same, the duties of the parties to cooperate have become indispensable. Thus, the duty of the seller and the buyer to assist in order to providing the necessary information required for security measures is specifically addressed in clauses A2/B2 and A10/B10 of the various the Incoterms rules.

Sections A3, B3, A4, B4: division of functions, costs and risks between the parties

While it may often be more practical for either the buyer or the seller to be responsible for the whole transport from point of origin to the agreed destination – as is the case under EXW and could be the case under D-terms – the majority of international sales still use terms under which the obligations of carriage are divided between the parties. Under the F-terms pre-carriage is normally arranged by the seller; under the C-terms the seller undertakes only to arrange for the carriage and pay the costs, but the risk is transferred from him to the buyer when the goods are shipped. Presumably, this commercial practice is based to a large extent on the tradition in commodity trading which frequently requires the chartering of ships. In this case, the FAS, FOB and CFR, CIF are still appropriate.

For economy of transport, do not divide functions

A large number of sales transactions now using F- or C-terms involve manufactured goods. In these cases, the optimal transport economy may depend on either the buyer or the seller arranging and paying for the whole of the carriage. This is particularly true when the transport facilities available make it possible for the buyer or the seller to integrate the whole of the transport in one contract of carriage with the operator, even if this involves a contract using more than one mode of transport (so-called multimodal or integrated transport).

In such circumstances, the use of F- and C- terms may well diminish. However, in practice the term FCA can come very close to EXW, particularly if the words "cleared for export" are added after EXW. This is because under both FCA and EXW the buyer may be required to let the carrier pick up the goods at the seller's premises. The buyer is then in the same position under both EXW and FCA, since he is responsible for arranging and paying for the whole transport. But under EXW the seller is obliged only to make the goods available at his premises. The loading on to the carrier's vehicle is at the risk and expense of the buyer unless otherwise agreed.

Additional service to the buyer under F-terms

Although there is a fundamental difference between F-terms (FCA, FAS, FOB) and C-terms (CFR, CIF, CPT and CIP), this distinction is blurred in practice because sellers using F-terms still, as an additional service to the buyer, normally arrange the carriage (but at the buyer's risk and expense).

From a strictly legal viewpoint, parties using the F-terms should not find it necessary to specify how the seller should hand over the goods for carriage, since he simply has to follow (1) what the contract of sale specifically provides, or (2) the buyer's instructions. But the seller – though he has no duty under an F-term to do so – frequently takes care of the interests of the "absent" buyer.

While FCA can be used regardless of the mode of transport, FAS and FOB can be used only when the goods are carried by sea or inland waterway transport.

The distinction between FAS and FOB is well established on the question of handing over the goods for carriage. FAS means that the goods should be placed alongside the ship and FOB that they should be placed on board. Nevertheless, difficulties have always been connected with the use of FOB, since the ship's rail as a point for the division of functions, costs and risks between seller and buyer is seldom practicable.

The reference to the ship's rail may have been appropriate in earlier times when the cargo was lifted parcel by parcel on board the ship by the ship's own crew and equipment. Then "land costs" would fall upon the seller, "ship's costs" upon the buyer.

The custom of the port

Today stevedoring companies usually perform the whole of the loading operation, using either their own cranes or those belonging to the port authorities. Problems then arise as how to divide the bill for their services between the seller and the buyer, since the FOB does not give sufficient guidance. Instead, it is necessary to follow the custom of the port, which unfortunately may vary considerably from one port to another and which can range from

- having the buyer pay for the whole of the loading operation (as if FOB in this respect were equivalent to FAS);

- splitting the costs according to various customs and methods; or

- having the seller pay all costs of the loading.

Caution when using FOB if custom of port not known

A buyer who does not know the custom of the port in the seller's country should be cautious when using FOB and should require a precise stipulation concerning the loading costs. Short expressions are sometimes used for this purpose (for example "FOB stowed" or "FOB stowed and trimmed").

While it may be clear that the seller's obligation to pay the loading costs is extended by these additions, it is not immediately clear to what extent the seller must also bear the risk of loss of or damage to the cargo which could occur subsequent to the passing of the ship's rail. The parties are therefore advised to clarify their intentions in this respect (for example, by adding a phrase such as "FOB stowed, costs and risks in connection with loading on the seller").

Handing over to the carrier under C-terms

When under the C-terms the seller has to arrange and pay for the carriage, handing over of the goods for carriage should not present any particular problem for seller or buyer. This is because the seller has to perform his duties according to the contract of carriage, which he has himself concluded with the carrier.

Dividing the costs of discharge at destination

Difficulties could arise at the other end of the transport, however, when the goods have to be discharged from the ship or from another means of transport.

While delivery from a road, rail or air carrier should normally pose no problem, considerable problems may arise when the goods are carried by sea. Liner shipping companies usually include costs of loading and discharge in their freight rates, but in charter party operations there may be provisions stipulating that the discharging operations should be wholly or partly "free" to the carrier ("free out" stipulations). In these cases the buyer must know the ship's time of arrival and the time available for the discharging operations (the "laytime"). He must also ascertain the extent to which he is exposed to the risk of having to pay compensation (demurrage) to the seller if the laytime is exceeded.

Because of these variations, the rules of interpretation in the Incoterms rules cannot specify how discharging costs should be divided between seller and buyer under the different C-terms. The parties are therefore advised to deal specifically with the relevant points in the contract of sale.

Failing such specific arrangements, guidance must be sought from any custom which the parties have developed between themselves in previous dealings, or from the custom of the port.

Section A8: the seller's duty to provide proof of delivery and the transport document

All terms except EXW require the seller to submit to the buyer formal proof that he has fulfilled his delivery obligation (A8). (The difference in EXW, of course, is that the buyer picks up the goods at the seller's premises or some other indicated point.)

Under the C-terms, when the seller has to arrange and pay for the carriage, the transport document becomes very important, since it must show not only that the goods have been handed over to the carrier by the date agreed, but also that the buyer has an independent right to claim the goods from the carrier at destination.

CFR, CIF and on board documents

A further problem occurs with CFR or CIF, both of which require the seller to provide "the usual transport document for the agreed port of destination". Not surprisingly, container lines prefer to issue the transport document as a receipt for the goods when they are received for carriage, not at some later stage when the container with the cargo is lifted on board the ship.

It is common for the container line, upon the request of the shipper, to convert the "received-for-shipment" bill of lading with an "on board notation". This, however, causes further paperwork and frequently delay for sellers when payment is to be collected under documentary credits requiring an on board bill of lading rather than a received-for-shipment bill of lading to be presented within a prescribed period after the date on which the goods are loaded on board the ship.

Surrender of original bill of lading essential

In some trades, there is a further problem connected with the use of bills of lading. This is caused by the need to present and surrender one original document to the carrier in order to obtain delivery of the goods. Ships frequently arrive at destination before an original bill of lading is available there. In such cases, the goods are often delivered to the buyer against a bill of lading guarantee issued by a bank. This is to protect the carrier if some person other than the person to whom the goods were delivered is the rightful holder of the original bill of lading.

This practice – or rather malpractice – defeats the whole bill of lading system, which depends for its validity on the firm principle that under no circumstances should the goods be delivered except in return for an original bill of lading. If that principle is not strictly followed, one can no longer say that the "bill of lading represents the goods".

Non-negotiable transport documents

In recent years, transport documents other than bills of lading for carriage of goods by sea have been increasingly used. These documents in the "waybill system" are similar to those used for modes of transport other than carriage by sea and when no original document is required to obtain the goods from the carrier at destination. It is sufficient that the consignee be named and that he can properly identify himself, as in the widespread use of air waybills (AWBs) and waybills for international road and rail carriage.

Such documents cannot be used, however, for transferring rights to the goods by the transfer of the document; they are therefore called non-negotiable. They bear various names such as "liner waybills", "ocean waybills", "data freight receipts", "cargo quay receipts" or "sea waybills". Although in such transport documents a buyer or a bank has been named as consignee, the seller and the seller alone enters into a contractual relationship with the carrier when the seller has contracted for carriage. The carrier takes instructions from his contracting party – the seller – and from no one else.

Payment against sea waybills requires caution

If the buyer has paid for the goods in advance, or a bank wishes to use the goods as security for a loan extended to the buyer, it is not sufficient that the buyer or the bank be named as consignee in a non-negotiable document. This is the case because the seller, by new instructions to the carrier, could replace the named consignee with someone else. To protect the buyer or the bank it is therefore necessary that the original instructions from the seller to the carrier to deliver the goods to the named consignee be irrevocable.

It follows that a seller should avoid trade terms such as CFR and CIF obliging him to present a document for transfer of rights to the goods whenever practical difficulties are involved in obtaining and using such documents. It also follows that the buyer should not pay for the goods, and the bank should not rely on security in the goods, merely by accepting transport documents naming the buyer and the bank respectively as consignees, unless such instructions to the carrier are made irrevocable.

The problems of replacing bills of lading by EDI

Apart from the need to agree on a method for using EDI and adopting international message standards, there should be no particular problems when replacing transport documents by electronic messages. However, it is difficult to replace the bill of lading because it is not only proof of the delivery of the goods to the carrier but also a legal symbol often expressed by the principle that "the bill of lading represents the goods".

As noted, the fundamental principle behind the "negotiable" status of the bill of lading stems from the carrier's obligation to deliver the goods to the holder of one original bill of lading and to no one else. Consequently, the possession of the bill of lading has controlled the rightful delivery of the goods to the entitled party at destination.

How can this be replaced by an electronic message? The solution is to obtain the agreement of all parties concerned. First, they must agree to communicate electronically. Second, the agreement must take a particular form with respect to the replacement of bills of lading. The carrier must agree to deliver the goods only as instructed by the party having the right to give him delivery instructions. While, as noted above, this right has traditionally been tied to the possession of the original bill of lading, it can now be vested instead in the person whom the carrier has authorized to give him electronic instructions.

The Incoterms rules CFR and CIF and EDI

The Incoterms 1990 rules, in the trade terms CFR and CIF, section A8, already took the development of EDI into consideration. They did this first by maintaining the traditional principle that, unless otherwise agreed, the transport document must enable the buyer to sell the goods in transit by the transfer of the document to a subsequent buyer. But they also indicated that the transfer could be made by notification to the carrier. In the former case, the negotiable bill of lading is expressly referred to. In the latter, reference is made to a system of notification. In any event, a mere notification to the carrier is not sufficient to replace a bill of lading.

Therefore, parties wishing to replace the bill of lading by electronic messages must necessarily refer to a system, such as BOLERO or similar systems, to enable the buyer to obtain the goods from the carrier at destination and to transfer the rights to the goods to a subsequent buyer while the goods are still being carried.

It follows that the use of EDI requires a particular agreement and a well-developed system following internationally agreed standards, and that the replacement of bills of lading by electronic messages can be implemented only by reference to a notification system such as BOLERO or by electronic procedures as referred to in ART.9-1 of the Rotterdam rules.

The "usual transport document" under CFR and CIF

In the CFR and CIF terms, no reference is made to the on board bill of lading, but under those terms the seller has not fulfilled his delivery obligation until the goods have been placed on board the ship and the document used to show this is still the bill of lading. The bill of lading is critical for the buyer if he intends to sell the goods to another buyer while they are still being carried (sale "afloat"). In these circumstances, transferring the original or the set of originals of the bill of lading can be used to transfer title of the goods to the other party.

Transport document as proof of delivery

Although under the F-terms the buyer must arrange and pay for the carriage – meaning that he enters into a direct contractual relationship with the carrier – the transport document can still be given by the carrier to the seller as proof that the seller has delivered the goods to him. If it is, the transport document will constitute not only evidence of the contract of carriage, but also proof of delivery of the goods to the carrier.

Indeed the seller – in his capacity as a shipper in the contract of carriage – frequently receives the bill of lading from the carrier as proof of delivery of the goods. This often happens, even though from a strictly legal viewpoint it is the buyer who should have received the bill of lading as evidence of the contract made with the carrier, so that the buyer can take delivery of the goods at destination in return for it.

This is further clarified in A8 of the F-terms, which stipulates that the seller must render the buyer, at the buyer's risk and expense, every assistance in obtaining the transport document if the document is not identical with the document proving delivery of the goods to the carrier. Since the possession of the bill of lading is required for the right to give instructions to the carrier and to obtain the cargo from him at destination, it is extremely important that the buyer receive this document from the seller, unless it has been given directly to him by the carrier.

Documents required to obtain delivery under D-terms

Under the D-terms the situation is different from that described in the preceding paragraphs, since the seller has not fulfilled his delivery obligation until the goods have actually arrived in the country of destination. Nevertheless, the buyer may still require a document to enable him to obtain the goods from the carrier at the agreed point of delivery. This may well be the case, for example, if the goods have been sold DAP and the buyer takes delivery from ship. If so, he is normally required to surrender an original bill of lading.

The terms DAT, DAP and DDP may be different in this respect, since the goods under these terms would have been placed on a quay or taken to a terminal at an interior point in the country of destination. But this does not necessarily mean that they have left the custody of the carrier, and a bill of lading, delivery order or warehouse warrant may still be required to obtain them.

Transport documents for carriage by sea

Note the difference between the waybill and the bill of lading:

Waybill

- The goods are delivered to the party named as consignee.
- Other than proof of identity, the consignee does not have to produce documents to claim the goods, and the waybill itself is not a document of title.

Bill of lading

- The goods should be released only in return for an original bill of lading.
- The bill of lading itself represents title to the goods, and is appropriate when the goods may be sold in transit.

The Incoterms rules accept electronic equivalents for transport documents which is generally stated in the A1/B1 clauses.

Delivery orders

Sometimes the goods may have been discharged in bulk, and the buyer has to remove his goods from a larger consignment. One bill of lading could then cover the whole consignment, even though the consignment is intended for several buyers. In these cases, it is customary to split the bill of lading into parts by issuing individual so-called delivery orders; in some cases, there is no physical delivery of the goods to the buyer at the "D point", but the carriage continues without interruption to the final destination.

Sections A4 and B4: the seller's obligation to deliver and the buyer's obligation to take delivery

Delivery at the seller's premises

As noted, contracts requiring the buyer to take delivery of the goods at the seller's premises do not normally cause any particular problems in practice. The facilities at the seller's place will determine whether the cargo will be delivered at a ramp where a driver could place his lorry and where forklift trucks can be used by the seller's personnel to place the goods on the lorry. However, it may not be easy to determine how much stowing of the goods on the lorry should be performed by the driver and how much by the seller's personnel. This necessarily depends on the circumstances and is not resolved by the rule of interpretation in EXW A4, which simply states that the goods should be placed "at the disposal of the buyer at the agreed point, if any, at the named place of delivery, not loaded on any collecting vehicle". This differs from FCA A 4 a) stating that delivery is completed " when the goods have been loaded on the means of transport provided by the buyer".

Delivery at the buyer's premises

The same problem could arise under the D-terms, when it can be very difficult to determine exactly how the seller should arrange to hand over the goods to the buyer. In A4 of all the D-terms, except DAT, it is now clarified that the seller only has to place the goods at the disposal of the buyer on the arriving means of transport ready for unloading.

Delivery at the waterfront under DAP and DAT

Under the terms DAP and DAT (and DES and DEQ in the Incoterms 2000 rules), the cargo will be made available to the buyer in the ship and on the quay respectively. How the cargo should be received at these points (pumping installations, silos, adjoining railway tracks, cargo terminals, etc.) will depend on the circumstances.

The buyer's acceptance of the seller's handing over for carriage

As noted, there are different customs for handing over the cargo to the carrier. Under the C-terms, when the seller arranges and pays for the carriage, he will deliver the cargo to the carrier in the absence of the buyer. Consequently, there will be no physical delivery of the cargo directly to the buyer.

But the buyer must accept that the cargo is handed over to the carrier as stipulated in A4 of the C-terms and be content with the proof of the delivery which the seller must give him according to A8. This is because the C-terms evidence shipment contracts under which, in principle, the seller fulfils his delivery obligation at the place of dispatch or shipment. What happens to the cargo after the seller has fulfilled his delivery obligation is at the risk and expense of the buyer.

The buyer's obligation to receive the goods from the carrier

Nevertheless, it is also important to note that the buyer has an obligation to the seller to receive the goods from the carrier at the named place or port of destination (B4). If a buyer refuses to honour his obligation to pay for the goods in return for a bill of lading, where applicable, and thereby fails to collect the goods from the carrier, the seller may incur expenses due under the contract of carriage he has concluded with the carrier. These costs will then be included in the seller's claim for damages as a result of the buyer's breach of his contractual obligation.

Sections A5 and B5: the transfer from seller to buyer of the risk of loss of or damage to the goods

Whenever "transfer of risks" is referred to in the Incoterms rules A5 and B5, the expression "loss of or damage to the goods" is used. This means physical loss of or damage to the cargo and does not include other risks such as the risk of delay or non-fulfilment of the contract for other reasons.

The "price risk"

If the risk referred to in the Incoterms rules materializes, the buyer has to pay the price even though he does not receive the goods in contractual condition or at all.

This is the so-called "price risk". Nonetheless, damage to the goods may depend upon circumstances attributable to the seller. For example, the seller may have inadequately packaged the goods. If so, the damage will not have resulted from a transportation risk, and the buyer is then entitled not only to avoid paying for the goods but also to hold the seller responsible for breach of contract.

The Incoterms rules do not specifically deal with other consequences if the seller has not fulfilled his delivery obligation. Such questions are left to the applicable law or to the stipulations in the contract of sale. But in the absence of any provisions in the contract, fulfilment of the seller's delivery obligation also means that any further risks or expenses are for the account of the buyer.

Consequently, while under the C-terms the seller has to pay the normal costs of carriage to the carrier, the buyer has to bear any additional costs resulting from circumstances occurring after the seller has fulfilled his delivery obligation. These may include, for example, extra costs for an unexpected transhipment caused by political events or adverse weather conditions which render the previously agreed routing inaccessible.

However, if such events occur before the seller has fulfilled his delivery obligation but after he has entered into the contract of sale, the extent to which he can escape (if at all) his duty to perform the contract will depend on the other terms of the contract or on the applicable law. Thus, the "price risk" should not be confused with the risk of breach of the contract of sale (caused by delay, non-fulfilment, etc.). The remedies available to the affected party for these breaches are not dealt with in the Incoterms rules.

Premature transfer of risk

In some cases, the risk can be transferred from the seller to the buyer even before the seller has fulfilled his delivery obligation. This could happen as a result of (1) the buyer's failure to do what is required of him to enable the seller to deliver the goods to him, or (2) the buyer's failure to take delivery of the goods.

Therefore, the buyer must give such notice to the seller as the latter requires to prepare the delivery (B7), or the buyer must nominate the carrier under F-terms and accept the goods from the carrier as agreed. Moreover, a buyer having undertaken to clear the goods for import must fulfil his obligation to do this within the agreed time so the seller can proceed with the on-carriage of the goods to destination as intended. If the buyer fails to do this, he must bear all additional risks of loss of or damage to the goods resulting from his failure (B5).

Identification of the contract goods

The premature passing of the risk noted in the above paragraphs cannot occur unless it can be ascertained that the goods are intended for the buyer and appropriated to the contract of sale made with him. Or, as expressed in article B5 of the Incoterms rules, the goods must have been set aside or otherwise "clearly identified as the contract goods". This appropriation is normally achieved as soon as the goods have been prepared for carriage, since it would then have been necessary to mark them and/or to name the consignee. But it may be that the goods are to be carried in bulk without such marking or naming of the consignee as would amount to appropriation. Then the risk will not pass until effective appropriation has been made, for example, until the issuance of separate bills of lading or delivery orders for parts of the bulk consignment.

Using force majeure clauses to protect the seller from the "breach of contract risk"

A seller who has undertaken to deliver the goods at a point outside of his control – for example, when the goods are to be delivered under D-terms – should consider the need to protect himself (usually by force majeure or other relief clauses) against the risk of having to provide substitute goods instead of those lost or damaged, or to make other agreed restitution. Otherwise, he could face damages for breach of contract if he fails to do this in time or at all.

Section A3b: the seller's insurance obligation

CIF and CIP are the only the Incoterms rules related directly to insurance coverage. This is because it is important for the buyer to obtain insurance when he has left the responsibility of arranging the contract of carriage and paying the freight to the seller. The seller is then presumed to be in a better position to arrange insurance than the buyer. This could still be the case if the goods are to be carried in chartered ships or if they consist of larger consignments of commodities.

But with manufactured goods, sellers and buyers usually have lasting arrangements with their insurers for exports and imports. Therefore, separate insurance arrangements for each shipment would be unnecessary. This being so, there is no reason to impose an insurance obligation on one party to the benefit of the other, since the better solution is to leave the question of insurance to the parties themselves.

Freedom of insurance restricted

In many countries sellers or buyers may be compelled to take out insurance in their own country – either to minimize expenditure in foreign currencies and/or to support the domestic insurance industry. In these cases, a buyer may be ordered to contract for imports on CFR or CPT terms instead of letting the seller arrange the insurance according to CIF or CIP. Conversely, a seller in these countries may be obliged to sell the goods on CIF or CIP terms for the same reasons.

Sections A7, B7: notices

Conditions for the buyer's giving notice

If there is no specified date or place agreed in the contract and the buyer is entitled to determine

■ the time and/or place when and where he should take delivery under EXW or D-terms;

■ the nomination of the carrier and delivery time under F-terms; or

■ the time for shipping the goods and/or the destination under C-terms,

then the buyer has to give the seller sufficient and timely notice (B7).

Conditions for the seller's giving notice

Conversely, the seller must give the buyer sufficient notice of

■ when and where the goods will be placed at the buyer's disposal under EXW;

■ when and where the goods have been delivered to the carrier under F- and C-terms; and

■ when and where the goods are expected to arrive under D-terms so that the buyer can take appropriate measures in time to receive them (A7).

Information relating to insurance

When under CIF and CIP the seller has to take out insurance for the benefit of the buyer, the seller may require information about particulars of the goods which do not appear in the contract of sale. He may also need to be informed about the buyer's wishes for extended or additional insurance. The buyer must then inform the seller accordingly (B3). When the buyer intends to take out insurance himself, or is obliged to do so under his country's regulations, he may also require additional information from the seller, who must then give such information to the buyer upon request (A3).

Sufficient notice

There are no special requirements in the Incoterms rules that notice be given in a particular form (by letter, telex or telefax). If the parties have agreed to communicate electronically, notice may be given in such form (A1/B1).

Failure to give sufficient notice

Failure to give sufficient notice constitutes a breach of contract which could lead to serious consequences. It could, for example, give the other party the right to cancel the contract. The Incoterms rules deal only with two particular aspects of late or insufficient notice, namely

- the premature passing of the risk (B5); and

- the buyer's liability to pay additional costs (B6).

For the premature passing of the risk as well as for the liability to pay additional costs, the parties must be able to ascertain the goods to which the risk or the additional costs relate. This can only be done if the goods can be identified as the contract of goods, i.e., if they are set aside for the buyer or otherwise clearly identified as being intended for him.

Sections A6, B6, A3, A10 and B10: division of costs between the parties

Division of costs is a most important element in every contract of sale. The parties must know not only who does what but also how costs resulting therefrom should be divided between them. In most cases the fact that a party must do something means that he must also bear the resulting costs, unless otherwise agreed. But there are many exceptions to this principle and uncertainties arise, particularly with respect to services performed by other parties (for example, stevedores engaged for loading and discharge or costs which cannot clearly be attributed to either the buyer's or the seller's functions, such as (a) "semi-official" charges debited on the export or import of the goods, or (b) charges for their storage pending shipment or delivery). Also, difficulties arise with respect to the division of costs whenever additional costs are caused by unexpected events, such as hindrances causing a ship to deviate or to remain in a seaport longer than expected.

Main principle of distribution of costs

The main principle of the division of costs is clear enough: the seller has to pay costs necessary for the goods to reach the agreed point of delivery, and the buyer has to pay any further costs after that point. But as noted, it is not always easy to implement this principle in practice, since the detailed distribution of functions under the various trade terms is not and cannot be fully defined in the Incoterms rules. Instead, failing precise stipulations in the contract of sale, guidance must be sought from other criteria such as commercial practices used earlier by the same parties or the custom of the trade.

The four main categories of costs

The costs referred to in the Incoterms rules can be grouped in four main categories. These include elements relating to

- dispatch, carriage and delivery;

- customs clearance for export and import;

- services or assistance rendered by one party to the other in addition to what the assisting party is required to do under the relevant trade term; and

- insurance.

Costs related to dispatch, carriage and delivery

This category is by far the most important, since it includes costs relating to

- loading at the seller's premises;

- pre-carriage in the country of export;

- making of the contract (booking the cargo for shipment and issuing the relevant transport documents);

- warehousing, storage and handling charges pending dispatch of the cargo from the country of export;

- hire of transportation equipment and appliances in the country of export;

- the main international carriage;

- warehousing, storage and handling charges subsequent to discharge in the country of import;

- hire of transportation equipment and appliances in the country of import;

- on-carriage in the country of import; and

- unloading at the buyer's premises.

Costs for export, import and security clearance

With respect to costs for export and import clearance, a firm distinction should be made between duties, VAT and other official charges and the cost for the clearance itself, which is frequently performed by freight forwarders in their capacity as customs brokers. Clearing of the goods will also include costs to obtain licences, certificates, consular invoices, permits, authorizations, and legalization as well as costs for inspection, customs warehouse charges, customs declarations and freight forwarders' service charges or for providing security-related information or assistance.

Costs for services and assistance

This category relates only to costs which one party may be entitled to claim from the other for services or assistance rendered upon request for the clearing of the goods. These include the seller's assistance for the buyer's export clearance under EXW (A2) and the buyer's assistance for the seller's clearing of the goods under DDP (B2). They may also include costs incurred in obtaining documents which the other party could require for the clearance as well as costs incurred for security-related assistance (A10 and B10 respectively).

Costs of insurance

This category is relevant only when the seller has contracted on CIF or CIP terms requiring that he take out insurance for the benefit of the buyer and also that he pay the premium. Any additional insurance (extended coverage or protection against added risks such as war, riots, or civil commotions, or strikes or other labour disturbances) taken out by the seller at the buyer's request has to be paid for by the buyer, unless otherwise agreed in the contract of sale.

Cost distribution systems

In certain cases – for example, freight forwarding services using a pre-arranged cost distribution system – it may be possible to obtain the more detailed breakdown needed to avoid uncertainty and disputes between the parties over costs. These disputes often concern minor costs, but the time, effort and money spent in resolving the disputes can be out of all proportion.

The parties are therefore advised either to specify the division of such costs not clearly following from the trade term itself, or to agree to apply a pre-arranged cost distribution system. An agreement to use a cost distribution system should be clearly mentioned in conjunction with the trade term by adding the phrase "the Incoterms® 2010 rules with cost distribution according to ...".

GOING THROUGH THE 11 INCOTERMS RULES

GROUP I: ANY MODE OR MODES OF TRANSPORT

EXW FCA CPT CIP DAT DAP DDP: may be chosen for maritime transport and should be chosen for wholly or partly non-maritime transport

EX WORKS
EXW (insert named place of delivery) the Incoterms® 2010 rules

DELIVERY

GUIDANCE NOTE

This rule may be used irrespective of the mode of transport selected and may also be used where more than one mode of transport is employed. It is suitable for domestic trade, while FCA is usually more appropriate for international trade.

"Ex Works" means that the seller delivers when it places the goods at the disposal of the buyer at the seller's premises or at another named place (i.e., works, factory, warehouse, etc.). The seller does not need to load the goods on any collecting vehicle, nor does it need to clear the goods for export, where such clearance is applicable.

The parties are well advised to specify as clearly as possible the point within the named place of delivery, as the costs and risks to that point are for the account of the seller. The buyer bears all costs and risks involved in taking the goods from the agreed point, if any, at the named place of delivery.

EXW represents the minimum obligation for the seller. The rule should be used with care as:

a) The seller has no obligation to the buyer to load the goods, even though in practice the seller may be in a better position to do so. If the seller does load the goods, it does so at the buyer's risk and expense. In cases where the seller is in a better position to load the goods, FCA, which obliges the seller to do so at its own risk and expense, is usually more appropriate.

b) A buyer who buys from a seller on an EXW basis for export needs to be aware that the seller has an obligation to provide only such assistance as the buyer may require to effect that export: the seller is not bound to organize the export clearance. Buyers are therefore well advised not to use EXW if they cannot directly or indirectly obtain export clearance.

c) The buyer has limited obligations to provide to the seller any information regarding the export of the goods. However, the seller may need this information for, e.g., taxation or reporting purposes.

EXW

A THE SELLER'S OBLIGATIONS

A1 General obligations of the seller

The seller must provide the goods and the commercial invoice in conformity with the contract of sale and any other evidence of conformity that may be required by the contract.

Any document referred to in A1-A10 may be an equivalent electronic record or procedure if agreed between the parties or customary.

Comments   The seller must provide the goods in conformity with the contract. It is also usual practice that the seller, in order to be paid, has to invoice the buyer. In addition, the seller must submit any other evidence stipulated in the contract itself that the goods conform with the contract.

This text only serves as a reminder of the seller's main obligation under the contract of sale.

A2 Licences, authorizations, security clearances and other formalities

Where applicable, the seller must provide the buyer, at the buyer's request, risk and expense, assistance in obtaining any export licence, or other official authorization necessary for the export of the goods.

Where applicable, the seller must provide, at the buyer's request, risk and expense, any information in the possession of the seller that is required for the security clearance of the goods.

Comments   Under EXW it is the buyer's obligation to obtain export as well as import licences or other official authorizations. It is therefore the seller under this term who should render the necessary assistance and the buyer who should bear any cost involved. However, the seller must, whenever required, assist the buyer, at his risk and expense, with security clearance.

Since the goods are made available to the buyer at the seller's premises, the seller has no obligation to contract for carriage or insurance. However, he must give the buyer any information he may request for insurance purposes.

A3 Contracts of carriage and insurance

a)   Contract of carriage
The seller has no obligation to the buyer to make a contract of carriage.

b)   Contract of insurance:
The seller has no obligation to the buyer to make a contract of insurance. However, the seller must provide the buyer, at the buyer's request, risk, and expense (if any), with information that the buyer needs for obtaining insurance.

Comments   Since the goods are made available to the buyer at the seller's premises, the seller has no obligation to contract for carriage or insurance. However, he must give the buyer any information he may request for insurance purposes.

EXW

A4   Delivery

The seller must deliver the goods by placing them at the disposal of the buyer at the agreed point, if any, at the named place of delivery, not loaded on any collecting vehicle. If no specific point has been agreed within the named place of delivery, and if there are several points available, the seller may select the point that best suits its purpose. The seller must deliver the goods on the agreed date or within the agreed period.

Comments   Under EXW the seller only has to make the goods available to the buyer at the named place of delivery in the seller's own country, which is usually at the seller's premises. Therefore, this term represents the seller's minimum obligation; delivery at the buyer's premises in the buyer's country would represent the seller's maximum obligation, for example DAT, DAP and DDP. Exactly how delivery should be performed is not specified, but this normally follows what has been done in previous dealings between the same parties or from the custom of the trade.

Frequently, the seller assists the buyer by bringing the goods onto a ramp from which they can be loaded on an arriving vehicle. The seller may also assist the buyer with the loading of the goods on to the vehicle, for example by using a fork-lift truck. If it is intended that the seller should be obliged to assist the buyer as above, this could be made clear by the parties' adding the words "loaded upon departing vehicle" after EXW in the contract of sale.

A5   Transfer of risks

The seller bears all risks of loss of or damage to the goods until they have been delivered in accordance with A4 with the exception of loss or damage in the circumstances described in B5.

Comments   All the Incoterms rules are based on the same principle that the risk of loss of or damage to the goods is transferred from the seller to the buyer when the seller has fulfilled his delivery obligation according to A4.

All the Incoterms rules, in conformity with the general principle of the 1980 CISG (Convention on Contracts for the International Sale of Goods), connect the transfer of the risk with the delivery of the goods and not with other circumstances, such as the passing of ownership or the time of the conclusion of the contract. Neither the Incoterms rules nor CISG deal with transfer of title to the goods or other property rights with respect to the goods.

The passing of risk of loss of or damage to the goods concerns the risk of fortuitous events (accidents) and does not include loss or damage caused by the seller or the buyer, for example through inadequate packing or marking of the goods. Therefore, even if damage occurs subsequent to the transfer of the risk, the seller may still be responsible if the damage could be attributed to the fact that the goods were not delivered in conformity with the contract (see A1 and the comments to A9).

A5 of all the Incoterms rules contain the phrase "with the exception of loss or damage in circumstances described in B5". This means that there are exceptions to the main rule in the circumstances described in B5 which may result in a premature passing of the risk because of the buyer's failure properly to fulfil his obligations (see the comments to B5).

EXW

A6   Allocation of costs

The seller must pay all costs relating to the goods until they have been delivered in accordance with A4, other than those payable by the buyer as envisaged in B6.

Comments   As is the case with the transfer of the risk of loss of or damage to the goods, all the Incoterms rules follow the same rule, that the division of costs occurs at the delivery point. All costs occurring before the seller has fulfilled his obligation to deliver according to A4 are for his account, while further costs are for the account of the buyer (see the comments to B6). This rule is made subject to the provisions of B6, which indicates that the buyer may have to bear additional costs incurred by his failure to take delivery or to give appropriate notice to the seller.

Since under EXW the seller's obligation is limited to placing the goods at the disposal of the buyer, all further costs have to be borne by the buyer once the goods have been placed at his disposal. The seller has no duty to bear any costs incurred for export or security clearance, since under B2 this is the buyer's obligation.

A7   Notice to the buyer

The seller must give the buyer any notice needed to enable the buyer to take delivery of the goods.

Comments   The seller must give the buyer sufficient notice as to when the goods will be available at the agreed or chosen delivery point, so that the buyer can make preparations in time to take delivery according to B4. There is no stipulation in the Incoterms rules spelling out the consequences of the seller's failure to give such notice. But it follows from the Incoterms rules that the seller's failure constitutes a breach of contract. This means that the seller could be held responsible for such a breach, according to the law applicable to the contract of sale.

A8   Delivery document

The seller has no obligation to the buyer.

Comments   Since the seller makes the goods available at his premises, or a named place of delivery in his own country, no delivery document is required.

A9   Checking – packaging – marking

The seller must pay the costs of those checking operations (such as checking quality, measuring, weighing, counting) that are necessary for the purpose of delivering the goods in accordance with A4.

The seller must, at its own expense, package the goods, unless it is usual for the particular trade to transport the type of goods sold unpackaged. The seller may package the goods in the manner appropriate for their transport, unless the buyer has notified the seller of specific packaging requirements before the contract of sale is concluded. Packaging is to be marked appropriately.

EXW

Comments   It is necessary for the buyer to ensure that the seller has duly fulfilled his obligation with respect to the condition of the goods. This is particularly important if the buyer is called upon to pay for the goods before he has received and checked them. However, the seller has no duty to arrange and pay for inspection of the goods before shipment, unless this has been specifically agreed in the contract of sale.

The goods must also be adequately packed. But the seller may not know the buyer's intentions concerning the mode of transport and the ultimate destination. There is a considerable difference between a short journey to an adjoining country and an intercontinental carriage by sea, which may expose the goods to the risk of breakage or corrosion from humidity and condensation.

The seller is obliged to pack the goods for a long and difficult carriage only if he knows that this will actually occur. Therefore, it is advisable for the buyer to inform the seller accordingly, or, better still, to specify the required packaging in the contract of sale.

A10   Assistance with information and related costs

The seller must, where applicable, in a timely manner, provide to or render assistance in obtaining for the buyer, at the buyer's request, risk and expense, any documents and information, including security-related information, that the buyer needs for the export and/or import of the goods and/or for their transport to the final destination.

Comments   Since it is for the buyer to do whatever is necessary with respect to export, transit and import and security clearance, he may well need the seller's assistance to obtain documents (for example, a certificate of origin, health certificate, clean report of finding, import licence, security-related information) or equivalent electronic data interchange (EDI) messages issued or transmitted in the country of delivery or import. But any cost incurred by the seller in rendering this assistance must be reimbursed to him by the buyer, according to B10.

EXW

B THE BUYER'S OBLIGATIONS

B1 General obligations of the buyer

The buyer must pay the price of the goods as provided in the contract of sale.

Any document referred to in B1-B10 may be an equivalent electronic record or procedure if agreed between the parties or customary.

Comments The buyer must pay the price agreed in the contract of sale. B1 constitutes a reminder of this main obligation, which corresponds with the seller's obligation to provide the goods in conformity with the contract of sale, as stipulated in A1.

B2 Licences, authorizations, security clearances and other formalities

Where applicable, it is up to the buyer to obtain, at its own risk and expense, any export and import licence.or other official authorization and carry out all customs formalities for the export of the goods.

Comments Since the seller only makes the goods available to the buyer in the country of export, it is for the buyer to do whatever is necessary with respect to the clearance of the goods for export, transit, import and security. A prohibition of export or import will not relieve the buyer from his obligation under the contract of sale. However, contracts of sale frequently contain "relief clauses" to the benefit of both parties in such cases. These clauses may stipulate that the affected party will be given the benefit of an extension of time to fulfil his obligation, or, under the worst circumstances, the right to avoid the contract. It may also be possible to obtain such relief under the law applicable to the contract of sale.

Before accepting the obligation to clear the goods for export, the buyer should ascertain that the regulations of the seller's country do not prevent him as a non-resident from applying for an export licence or from performing whatever tasks are necessary to clear the goods for export and security. Normally, no such difficulties will be encountered, since measures in this regard can be taken by freight forwarders (customs brokers) on the buyer's behalf. If the buyer wishes to avoid the obligation to clear the goods for export, the words "cleared for export" could be added after EXW.

B3 Contracts of carriage and insurance

a) Contract of carriage
The buyer has no obligation to the seller to make a contract of carriage.

b) Contract of insurance
The buyer has no obligation to the seller to make a contract of insurance.

Comments The buyer has no obligation to the seller under the contract of sale to contract for carriage, except as required in order to take delivery according to B4. He would, of course, nevertheless arrange for carriage in his own interest.

EXW

B4 Taking delivery

The buyer must take delivery of the goods when A4 and A7 have been complied with.

Comments The buyer must take delivery of the goods when they have been placed at his disposal at the agreed time and place as stipulated in A4. His failure to do so will not relieve him from his obligation to pay the price and could result in a premature passing of the risk of loss of or damage to the goods or make him liable to pay additional costs according to B5 and B6.

B5 Transfer of risks

The buyer bears all risks of loss of or damage to the goods from the time they have been delivered as envisaged in A4.

If the buyer fails to give notice in accordance with B7, then the buyer bears all risks of loss of or damage to the goods from the agreed date or the expiry date of the agreed period for delivery, provided that the goods have been clearly identified as the contract goods.

Comments According to the main rule, while the seller under A5 bears the risk of loss of or damage to the goods until the delivery point, the buyer has to bear the risk thereafter. The delivery point is different under the different terms. In EXW and all D-terms, the goods are simply placed "at the disposal of the buyer" at the relevant point, while under the F- and C-terms the delivery point is related to the handing over of the goods to the carrier in the country of dispatch or shipment (see the comments to A4 of these terms). In the terms used for goods intended to be carried by sea, reference is made to delivery alongside the named vessel (FAS A4) or delivery onboard the vessel (FOB, CFR, CIF).

Consequences of buyer's failure to give notice

While the seller under EXW and all D-terms can transfer the risk by his own act of placing the goods at the buyer's disposal, he may be prevented from doing so by the buyer's failure to give notice according to B7. This can occur when it is the buyer's responsibility to determine (1) the time within a stipulated period when the goods are to be made available or (2) the place of delivery (see the comments to B7). The failure to perform these tasks results in a premature passing of the risk: it is not acceptable that the buyer should be able to delay the delivery and the passing of the risk longer than contemplated when the contract of sale was made. Therefore, his failure to notify according to B7 will cause the risk to pass "from the agreed date or the expiry date of any period fixed for taking delivery".

Identification of the contract goods and the passing of risk

The risk, however, cannot pass until the goods have been duly identified as the contract goods. If the goods are unascertained, i.e., goods of a certain kind which the seller will deliver to his various buyers, passing of risk occurs only when the goods are "clearly identified as the contract goods".

EXW

B6   Allocation of costs

The buyer must:

a)   pay all costs relating to the goods from the time they have been delivered as envisaged in A4;

b)   pay any additional costs incurred by failing either to take delivery of the goods when they have been placed at its disposal or to give appropriate notice in accordance with B7, provided that the goods have been clearly identified as the contract goods;

c)   pay, where applicable, all duties, taxes and other charges, as well as the costs of carrying out customs formalities payable upon export; and

d)   reimburse all costs and charges incurred by the seller in providing assistance as envisaged in A2.

Comments   Although the seller's obligation is limited to placing the goods at the disposal of the buyer at the seller's own premises, EXW A4 does not indicate exactly how this should be done. In practice, the seller will often assist the buyer by bringing the goods onto a ramp from which they can be loaded on to a vehicle for carriage from the seller's place. Or the seller may assist the buyer with the loading of the goods on to this vehicle, for example by placing them on to the vehicle by the use of a fork-lift truck. In these cases, sellers will not usually debit their buyers with costs for work performed by the seller's own personnel and/or for the use of the seller's own equipment. However, if the goods are to be taken from an independent warehouse and the seller stands to incur external costs, he would, according to the main principle of B6, be entitled to debit such costs to the buyer.

Normally, the extent to which the seller will assist the buyer free of charge in removing the goods from the seller's premises will be determined from previous dealings between the same parties or from the custom of the trade. If, however, the parties agree that the seller should be obliged to perform the loading of the goods, the words "loaded upon departing vehicle" may be added after EXW in the contract of sale.

Notice and identification of goods

Whenever the buyer is entitled to determine the time or place of taking delivery, his failure to notify the seller according to B7 will not only cause the risk of loss of or damage to the goods to pass prematurely but also make him liable to pay any additional costs caused thereby, for example extra costs for storage and insurance. However, this liability occurs only if the goods have been identified as the contract goods (see the comments concerning "identification" under B5).

Buyer clears goods for export

Under EXW the buyer has to clear the goods for export. Consequently, he will have to pay "where applicable, all duties, taxes and other charges as well as the costs of carrying out customs formalities payable upon export" and reimburse the seller for any assistance the seller provides in performing these tasks.

EXW

B7   Notices to the seller

The buyer must, whenever it is entitled to determine the time within an agreed period and/or the point of taking delivery within the named place, give the seller sufficient notice thereof.

Comments   As discussed in the comments to B5 and B6, the failure of the buyer to notify the seller of the time for shipping the goods or the destination – when the buyer in the contract of sale has been given the option to determine these matters – may cause the risk of the loss of or damage to the goods to pass before the goods have been delivered according to A4. In addition, it can make the buyer liable to pay any additional costs incurred by the seller as a result of the buyer's failure.

B8   Proof of delivery

The buyer must provide the seller with appropriate evidence of having taken delivery.

Comments   The buyer should provide the seller with a customary receipt for the goods. This receipt could be indicated on a packing list or provided by some other document which could constitute "appropriate evidence".

B9   Inspection of goods

The buyer must pay the costs of any mandatory pre-shipment inspection, including inspection mandated by the authorities of the country of export.

Comments   As noted in the comments to A9, the buyer has to pay for any costs of checking the goods, unless the contract determines that these costs should be wholly or partly borne by the seller. In some cases, the contract may provide that the costs should be borne by the seller if the inspection reveals that the goods do not conform with the contract.

Pre-shipment inspection

In some countries, where import licences or permission to obtain foreign currency for the payment of the price may be required, the authorities may demand an inspection of the goods before shipment, to ensure that the goods conform with the contract. (This is usually called pre-shipment inspection, PSI.) If this is the case, the inspection is normally arranged by instructions from the authorities to an inspection company, which they appoint. The costs following from this inspection have to be paid by the authorities. Any reimbursement to the authorities for the inspection costs, however, must be made by the buyer, unless otherwise specifically agreed between the buyer and the seller.

EXW

B10   Assistance with information and related costs

The buyer must, in a timely manner, advise the seller of any security information requirements so that the seller may comply with A10.

The buyer must reimburse the seller for all costs and charges incurred by the seller in providing or rendering assistance in obtaining documents and information as envisaged in A10.

Comments   As discussed in the comments to A10, the seller has to render the buyer assistance in obtaining the documents or electronic messages and information which may be required for the transit, import and security-clearance of the goods. However, this assistance is rendered at the buyer's risk and expense. Therefore, B10 stipulates that the buyer must pay all costs and charges incurred in obtaining these documents or electronic messages. He will also have to reimburse the seller for the seller's costs in rendering his assistance in these matters.

FREE CARRIER

FCA (insert named place of delivery) the Incoterms® 2010 rules

DELIVERY

GUIDANCE NOTE

This rule may be used irrespective of the mode of transport selected and may also be used where more than one mode of transport is employed.

"Free Carrier" means that the seller delivers the goods to the carrier or another person nominated by the buyer at the seller's premises or another named place. The parties are well advised to specify as clearly as possible the point within the named place of delivery, as the risk passes to the buyer at that point.

If the parties intend to deliver the goods at the seller's premises, they should identify the address of those premises as the named place of delivery. If, on the other hand, the parties intend the goods to be delivered at another place, they must identify a different specific place of delivery.

FCA requires the seller to clear the goods for export, where applicable. However, the seller has no obligation to clear the goods for import, pay any import duty or carry out any import customs formalities.

FCA

A THE SELLER'S OBLIGATIONS

A1 General obligations of the seller

The seller must provide the goods and the commercial invoice in conformity with the contract of sale and any other evidence of conformity that may be required by the contract.

Any document referred to in A1-A10 may be an equivalent electronic record or procedure if agreed between the parties or customary.

Comments   The seller must provide the goods in conformity with the contract. It is also usual practice that the seller, in order to be paid, has to invoice the buyer. In addition, the seller must submit any other evidence stipulated in the contract itself that the goods conform with the contract.

This text only serves as a reminder of the seller's main obligation under the contract of sale.

A2 Licences, authorizations, security clearances and other formalities

Where applicable, the seller must obtain, at its own risk and expense, any export licence or other official authorization and carry out all customs formalities necessary for the export of the goods.

Comments   The seller has to clear the goods for export and assume any risk or expense which this involves. Consequently, if there is an export prohibition or if there are particular taxes on the export of the goods – and if there are other government-imposed requirements which may render the export of the goods more expensive than contemplated – all of these risks and costs must be borne by the seller. However, contracts of sale usually contain particular provisions which the seller may invoke to protect himself in the event of these contingencies. Under CISG and corresponding provisions in various national Sale of Goods Acts, unforeseen or reasonably unforeseeable export prohibitions may relieve the seller from his obligations under the contract of sale.

A3 Contracts of carriage and insurance

a)   Contract of carriage
The seller has no obligation to the buyer to make a contract of carriage. However, if requested by the buyer or if it is commercial practice and the buyer does not give an instruction to the contrary in due time, the seller may contract for carriage on usual terms at the buyer's risk and expense. In either case, the seller may decline to make the contract of carriage and, if it does, shall promptly notify the buyer.

b)   Contract of insurance
The seller has no obligation to the buyer to make a contract of insurance. However, the seller must provide the buyer, at the buyer's request, risk, and expense (if any), with information that the buyer needs for obtaining insurance.

FCA

Comments   The F-terms all mean that the seller's obligation is limited to handing over the goods to the carrier nominated by the buyer. Consequently, the seller has no obligation to contract for carriage. Nevertheless, if arranging for the carriage is not difficult and if the freight rate would be more or less the same regardless of whether the seller or the buyer contracts with the carrier, it is often more practical for the seller to contract for carriage at the buyer's risk and expense. This explains why, in many cases, a commercial practice has developed to this effect.

It should be stressed, however, that the seller has no obligation to contract for carriage as noted above and that the buyer does not have to let him do so. If there is a commercial practice between the parties, then under F-terms the seller may contract for carriage as an additional service to the buyer, unless the buyer in due time has instructed the seller not to do so.

Therefore, if it is possible for the buyer to obtain a better freight rate than the seller, or if there are other reasons for him to exercise his right to contract for carriage (for example, government directions), he must inform the seller accordingly, preferably when the contract of sale is made. Otherwise, problems and additional expenses may follow if both parties contract for carriage assuming that the other party did not.

Conversely, the seller must promptly inform the buyer if for some reason he does not wish to follow the buyer's request to contract for carriage or to adhere to commercial practice. Otherwise, additional expenses and risks may occur as a result of the failure to arrange for carriage in due time. In any event, the seller does not incur any risk in complying with the buyer's request or with commercial practice, since whatever he does or intends to do is at the buyer's risk and expense.

If transport becomes temporarily unavailable or more expensive, the buyer under all F-terms has to bear these risks.

The seller, even under F-terms, has to contract for any carriage required to reach the place where the parties have agreed that the goods should be handed over for carriage, as, for example, when the goods are to be carried from an inland point to an ocean carrier to be named by the buyer. Such pre-carriage would then be for the seller's account.

A4   Delivery

The seller must deliver the goods to the carrier or another person nominated by the buyer at the agreed point, if any, at the named place on the agreed date or within the agreed period. Delivery is completed:

a)   if the named place is the seller's premises, when the goods have been loaded on the means of transport provided by the buyer.

b)   In any other case, when the goods are placed at the disposal of the carrier or another person nominated by the buyer on the seller's means of transport ready for unloading.

FCA

If no specific point has been notified by the buyer under B7 d) within the named place of delivery, and if there are several points available, the seller may select the point that best suits its purpose.

Unless the buyer notifies the seller otherwise, the seller may deliver the goods for carriage in such a manner as the quantity and/or nature of the goods may require.

Comments   FCA, as first presented in the Incoterms1980 rules (where it was referred to as FRC), was originally intended to solve the particular problems arising from changed cargo handling techniques, such as containerization or other means of assembling parcel cargo in transportation units before the vehicle of transport arrived. In such cases, FCA should be used instead of FOB, the latter of which is intended to be used in cases where the seller tenders the goods to the ship. By using FCA instead of FOB, the point of delivery is moved to the prior point where the goods are delivered to the carrier, either at his cargo terminal or to a vehicle sent to pick up the goods after they have been containerized or otherwise assembled in transportation units at the seller's premises.

Stipulations on handing over and delivery advisable in contract of sale

It is vital for the seller to know at the time he makes his offer what he may be required to do according to the contract of sale, since this may well affect his costs and should therefore be reflected in the price. Ideally, in the contract of sale the parties should agree on a precise point for the delivery of the goods to the carrier and make clear how the goods should be handed over to him, for example by naming the carrier's cargo terminal and specifying if the goods should be delivered containerized or not.

Also, it is necessary to clarify who should be responsible for loading the goods on to the buyer's collecting vehicle and unloading them from the seller's vehicle used to bring the goods to the place where they should be handed over to the carrier.

In the Incoterms® 2010 rules it is the seller who has the duty to load the goods on to the buyer's collecting vehicle, and the seller only has to bring the goods for on-carriage on the seller's means of transport ready for unloading by the buyer.

If at the time the contract of sale is concluded, the buyer wishes later to have the option to decide (1) the point where the goods should be handed over for carriage or (2) the mode of transport, it is important to determine the extent of the buyer's options concerning these matters and the time within which he must exercise them. If the buyer is not given options but the contract mentions a place where the carrier has several receiving points, the seller "may select the point that best suits his purpose".

Normally, it would follow from the mode of transport and the carrier's receiving point exactly how the goods should be handed over for carriage. But, as noted in the preceding paragraph, there may be different alternatives for the handing over, and failing precise stipulations or instructions in the contract of sale, the goods may be handed over to the carrier "in such a manner as the quantity and/or nature of the goods may require".

FCA

The quantity and nature of the goods will determine whether the goods should be containerized by the seller as homogeneous cargo in one full load in a so-called FCL-container, or by the carrier at his cargo terminal as parcel cargo together with cargo from other shippers in a so-called LCL-container.

Who is a carrier ?

Since the carrier under FCA is named by the buyer, it is normally not necessary to decide whether the entity named can be regarded as a "carrier" according to the law applicable to the contract of sale and the contract of carriage. The seller merely has to accept the buyer's nomination. Therefore, the buyer is not compelled to name someone who has the status of a carrier in a legal sense; he could also name "another person" (for example, a freight forwarder).

However, the problem of deciding whether the person engaged for the carriage is a "carrier" in the legal sense may arise whenever the seller chooses this person in accordance with A3. The seller must then "contract for carriage on usual terms at the buyer's risk and expense", and unless otherwise agreed, arrange a contract of carriage and not merely a contract of forwarding agency.

A contract of carriage may be entered into with operators which do not physically perform the carriage as long as they assume liability as carriers for the carriage.

A5   Transfer of risks

The seller bears all risks of loss of or damage to the goods until they have been delivered in accordance with A4, with the exception of loss or damage in the circumstances described in B5.

Comments   All the Incoterms rules are based on the same principle, that the risk of loss of or damage to the goods is transferred from the seller to the buyer when the seller has fulfilled his delivery obligation according to A4.

All the Incoterms rules, in conformity with the general principle of CISG, connect the transfer of the risk with the delivery of the goods and not with other circumstances, such as the passing of ownership or the time of the conclusion of the contract. Neither the Incoterms rules nor CISG deals with transfer of title to the goods or other property rights with respect to the goods.

The passing of risk for loss of or damage to the goods concerns the risk of fortuitous events (accidents) and does not include loss or damage caused by the seller or the buyer, for example through inadequate packing or marking of the goods. Therefore, even if damage occurs subsequent to the transfer of the risk, the seller may still be responsible if the damage could be attributed to the fact that the goods were not delivered in conformity with the contract (see A1 and the comments to A9).

FCA

A5 of all the Incoterms rules contain the phrase "with the exception of loss or damage in circumstances described in B5". This means that there are exceptions to the main rule in the circumstances described in B5 which may result in a premature passing of the risk because of the buyer's failure properly to fulfil his obligations (see the comments to B5).

A6   Allocation of costs

The seller must pay

a)   all costs relating to the goods until they have been delivered in accordance with A4, other than those payable by the buyer as envisaged in B6; and

b)   where applicable, the costs of customs formalities necessary for export, as well as all duties, taxes, and other charges payable upon export.

Comments   As is the case with the transfer of the risk of loss of or damage to the goods, all the Incoterms rules follow the same rule, that the division of costs occurs at the delivery point. All costs occurring before the seller has fulfilled his obligation to deliver according to A4 are for his account, while further costs are for the account of the buyer (see the comments to B6). This rule is made subject to the provisions of B6, which indicates that the buyer may have to bear additional costs incurred by his failure to nominate a carrier that takes the goods into his charge or to give appropriate notice to the seller.

Since the seller's obligation is limited to handing over the goods to the carrier named by the buyer, all further costs have to be borne by the buyer once the goods have been delivered in this way. The seller must, however, pay the costs of customs formalities as well as all duties, taxes and other official charges payable upon export.

A7   Notices to the buyer

The seller must, at the buyer's risk and expense, give the buyer sufficient notice either that the goods have been delivered in accordance with A4 or that the carrier or another person nominated by the buyer has failed to take the goods within the time agreed.

Comments   The seller must give the buyer sufficient notice as to when the goods will be available at the agreed or chosen delivery point, so that the buyer can make preparations in time to take delivery according to B4. There is no stipulation in the Incoterms rules spelling out the consequences of the seller's failure to give such notice. But it follows from the Incoterms rules that the seller's failure constitutes a breach of contract. This means that the seller could be held responsible for such a breach, according to the law applicable to the contract of sale.

The seller must also inform the buyer if the carrier nominated by the buyer fails to take the goods into his charge at the time agreed. There is no similar stipulation in the other Incoterms rules, since under all C- and D- terms, the consequences of any failure of the carrier to take the goods into his charge have to be borne by the seller.

FCA

A8 Delivery document

The seller must provide the buyer, at the seller's expense, with the usual proof that the goods have been delivered in accordance with A4.

The seller must provide assistance to the buyer, at the buyer's request, risk and expense, in obtaining a transport document.

Comments Since the seller has to hand over the goods for carriage, the carrier normally gives him a receipt which is usually identical to the transport document such as a received for shipment bill of lading or multimodal transport document. If so, that document serves as evidence not only of the contract of carriage – which under F-terms is made by or on behalf of the buyer – but also of the delivery of the goods to the carrier.

If, however, the seller receives a document other than the transport document – for example, a so-called mate's receipt when the goods have been loaded onboard a ship chartered by the buyer – he should, upon the buyer's request, assist the buyer to obtain the transport document. This assistance is rendered at the buyer's risk and expense.

A9 Checking – packaging – marking

The seller must pay the costs of those checking operations (such as checking quality, measuring, weighing, counting) that are necessary for the purpose of delivering the goods in accordance with A4, as well any pre-shipment inspection mandated by the authority of the country of export.

The seller must, at its own expense, package the goods, unless it is usual for the particular trade to transport the type of goods sold unpackaged. The seller may package the goods in the manner appropriate for their transport, unless the buyer has notified the seller of specific packaging requirements before the contract of sale is concluded. Packaging is to be marked appropriately.

Comments It is necessary for the buyer to ensure that the seller has duly fulfilled his obligation with respect to the condition of the goods. This is particularly important if the buyer is called upon to pay for the goods before he has received and checked them. However, the seller has no duty to arrange and pay for inspection of the goods before shipment, unless this has been mandated by the authorities in the country of export or specifically agreed in the contract of sale.

The goods must also be adequately packed. But the seller may not know the buyer's intentions concerning the mode of transport and the ultimate destination. There is a considerable difference between a short journey to an adjoining country and an intercontinental carriage by sea, which may expose the goods to the risk of breakage or corrosion from humidity and condensation.

The seller is obliged only to pack the goods for a long and difficult carriage if he knows that this will actually occur. Therefore, it is advisable for the buyer to inform the seller accordingly, or, better still, to specify the required packaging in the contract of sale.

FCA

A10   Assistance with information and related costs

The seller must, where applicable, in a timely manner, provide to or render assistance in obtaining for the buyer, at the buyer's request, risk and expense, any documents and information, including security-related information, that the buyer needs for the import of the goods and/or for their transport to the final destination.

The seller must reimburse the buyer for all costs and charges incurred by the buyer in providing or rendering assistance in obtaining documents and information as envisaged in B10.

Comments   Since it is for the buyer to do whatever is necessary with respect to transit, import and security clearance, he may well need the seller's assistance to obtain documents (for example, a certificate of origin, health certificate, clean report of finding, import licence) issued or transmitted in the country of delivery and/or origin. But any cost incurred by the seller in rendering this assistance must be reimbursed to him by the buyer, according to B10. Similarly, the seller must reimburse the buyer for any assistance provided by him according to B10.

Also, the seller may be requested to provide the buyer with information relating to the goods which the buyer may require for security-related clearance of the goods.

FCA

B THE BUYER'S OBLIGATIONS

B1   General obligations of the buyer

The buyer must pay the price of the goods as provided in the contract of sale.

Any document referred to in B1-B10 may be an equivalent electronic record or procedure if agreed between the parties or customary.

Comments   The buyer must pay the price agreed in the contract of sale. B1 constitutes a reminder of this main obligation, which corresponds with the seller's obligation to provide the goods in conformity with the contract of sale, as stipulated in A1.

B2   Licences, authorizations, security clearances and other formalities

Where applicable, it is up to the buyer to obtain, at its own risk and expense, any import licence or other official authorization and carry out all customs formalities for the import of the goods and for their transport through any country.

Comments   Since the seller fulfils his obligations by handing over the goods for carriage and clearing the goods for export, the buyer has to take care of any necessary transit formalities and clear the goods for import. These obligations of the buyer are specifically mentioned in B2.

B3   Contracts of carriage and insurance

a)   Contract of carriage
The buyer must contract at its own expense for the carriage of the goods from the named place of delivery, except when the contract of carriage is made by the seller as provided for in A3 a).

b)   Contract of insurance
The buyer has no obligation to the seller to make a contract of insurance.

Comments   Under all F-terms the buyer has the obligation to contract for carriage, though the seller may, as an additional service, arrange for carriage at the buyer's risk and expense. However, the contract for carriage starts "from the named place", and any prior carriage (pre-carriage) would have to be arranged by the seller (see A3).

B4   Taking delivery

The buyer must take delivery of the goods when they have been delivered as envisaged in A4.

Comments   The buyer must take delivery of the goods when they have been placed at his disposal at the agreed time and place as stipulated in A4. His failure to do so will not relieve him of his obligation to pay the price and could result in a premature passing of the risk of loss of or damage to the goods, or make him liable to pay additional costs according to B5 and B6.

FCA

B5   Transfer of risks

The buyer bears all risks of loss of or damage to the goods from the time they have been delivered as envisaged in A4.

If
a)   the buyer fails in accordance with B7 to notify the nomination of a carrier or another person as envisaged in A4 or to give notice; or

b)   the carrier or person nominated by the buyer as envisaged in A4 fails to take the goods into its charge,

then, the buyer bears all risks of loss of or damage to the goods:
(i)   from the agreed date, or in the absence of an agreed date,
(ii)   from the date notified by the seller under A7 within the agreed period; or, if no such date has been notified,
(iii)   from the expiry date of any agreed period for delivery,

provided that the goods have been clearly identified as the contract goods.

Comments   According to the main rule, while the seller under A5 bears the risk of loss of or damage to the goods until the delivery point, the buyer has to bear the risk thereafter. The delivery point is different under the different terms. In EXW and all D-terms the goods are simply placed "at the disposal of the buyer" at the relevant point, while under the F- and C-terms the delivery point is related to the handing over of the goods to the carrier in the country of dispatch or shipment (see the comments to A4 of these terms). In the terms used for goods intended to be carried by sea, reference is made to delivery alongside the named vessel (FAS) or delivery onboard the vessel (FOB, CFR, CIF).

The seller cannot – as under EXW and the D-terms – cause the goods to be delivered and the risk to pass unless he receives instructions or contracts for carriage under the C-terms or on behalf of the buyer (see the comments to FCA A3a). When the buyer is responsible for making the contract of carriage and nominating the carrier and that carrier fails to take the goods into his charge, the buyer incurs the same liability as he would had he failed properly to nominate the carrier or to notify the seller of matters required for handing over the goods for carriage.

Identification of the contract goods and premature passing of risk

For risk to pass prematurely, it is required that the goods be identified as the contract goods. When the goods have been prepared for dispatch they have also normally been identified as the contract goods. But a failure of the buyer to give sufficient notice of the date or period of shipment according to B7 causes the seller to defer his preparations. If so, it may not be possible to identify some goods stored at the seller's premises or in an independent cargo terminal as the contract goods on the "agreed date or the expiry date of any period stipulated for delivery". The risk would then not pass until the identification has been made.

FCA

B6 Allocation of costs

The buyer must pay

a) all costs relating to the goods from the time they have been delivered as envisaged in A4, except, where applicable, the costs of customs formalities necessary for export, as well as all duties, taxes, and other charges payable upon export as referred to in A6 b);

b) any additional costs incurred, either because:
   (i) the buyer fails to nominate a carrier or another person as envisaged in A4, or
   (ii) the carrier or person nominated by the buyer as envisaged in A4 fails to take the goods into its charge, or
   (iii) the buyer has failed to give appropriate notice in accordance with B7,

provided that the goods have been clearly identified as the contract goods; and

c) where applicable, all duties, taxes and other charges as well as the costs of carrying out customs formalities payable upon import of the goods and the costs for their transport through any country.

Comments Under FCA the seller fulfils his delivery obligation according to A4 by handing over the goods to the carrier. The buyer must pay the freight and other costs occurring subsequent to the delivery of the goods to the carrier.

Since the buyer has to contract for carriage, he would also have to pay any additional costs incurred because the carrier or person named by him fails to take the goods into his charge.

Whenever the buyer is entitled to determine the time or place of taking delivery, his failure to notify the seller according to B7 will not only cause the risk of loss of or damage to the goods to pass prematurely but also make him liable to pay any additional costs caused thereby, for example, extra costs for storage and insurance.

The liability to pay additional costs as noted above occurs only if the goods have been identified as the contract goods (see the comments on "identification" in B5).

B7 Notices to the seller

The buyer must notify the seller of

a) the name of the carrier or another person nominated as envisaged in A4 within sufficient time as to enable the seller to deliver the goods in accordance with that article;

b) where necessary, the selected time within the period agreed for delivery when the carrier or person nominated will take the goods;

c) the mode of transport to be used by the person nominated; and

d) the point of taking delivery within the named place.

Comments As discussed in the comments to B5 and B6, the failure of the buyer to notify the seller of the time for shipping the goods or the destination – when the buyer in the contract of sale has been given the option to determine these matters – may cause the risk of the loss of or damage to the goods to pass before the goods have been delivered according to A4. In addition, it can make the buyer liable to pay any additional costs incurred by the seller as a result of the buyer's failure.

FCA

The buyer's notice should inform the seller of the name of the carrier as well as of any further particulars relating to the delivery of the goods for carriage (such as the mode of transport and the exact point and time for the delivery) unless, of course, the carrier has been chosen by the seller according to A3.

B8   Proof of delivery

The buyer must accept the proof of delivery provided as envisaged in A8.

Comments   The seller has to provide proof of delivery, and the buyer must accept that proof if it conforms with the contract and with the requirements of A8 (see comments to A8). If the buyer rejects a conforming document giving proof (for example, by instructions to a bank not to pay the seller under a documentary credit), he commits a breach of contract which would give the seller remedies available for the breach under the contract of sale (for example, a right to cancel the contract or to claim damages for breach). However, the buyer is not obliged to accept a document which does not provide adequate proof of delivery, for example, if there are notations on the document showing that the goods are defective or if the document indicates that the goods have been provided in less than the agreed quantity. The document is then considered to be "unclean".

B9   Inspection of goods

The buyer must pay the costs of any mandatory pre-shipment inspection, except when such inspection is mandated by the authorities of the country of export.

Comments   As noted in the comments to A9, the buyer has to pay for any costs of checking the goods, unless the contract determines that these costs should be wholly or partly borne by the seller. In some cases, the contract may provide that the costs should be borne by the seller if the inspection reveals that the goods do not conform with the contract.

In some countries, where import licences or permission to obtain foreign currency for the payment of the price may be required, the authorities may demand an inspection of the goods before shipment, to ensure that the goods are in conformity with the contract. (This is usually called pre-shipment inspection, PSI.) If this is the case, the inspection is normally arranged by instructions from the authorities to an inspection company, which they appoint. The costs following from this inspection have to be paid by the authorities. Any reimbursement to the authorities for the inspection costs, however, must be made by the buyer, unless mandated by the authorities of the country of export or otherwise specifically agreed between the buyer and the seller.

FCA

B10 Assistance with information and related costs

The buyer must, in a timely manner, advise the seller of any security information requirements so that the seller may comply with A10.

The buyer must reimburse the seller for all costs and charges incurred by the seller in providing or rendering assistance in obtaining documents and information as envisaged in A10.

The buyer must, where applicable, in a timely manner, provide to or render assistance in obtaining for the seller, at the seller's request, risk and expense, any documents and information, including security-related information, that the seller needs for the transport and export of the goods and for their transport through any country.

Comments   As discussed in the comments to A10, the seller has to assist the buyer in obtaining the documents or electronic messages and information which may be required for the transit, import and security-related clearance of the goods. However, this assistance is rendered at the buyer's risk and expense. Therefore, B10 stipulates that the buyer must pay all costs and charges incurred in obtaining these documents or electronic messages. He will also have to reimburse the seller for the seller's costs in rendering his assistance in connection with these matters or in contracting for carriage in accordance with A3.

CARRIAGE PAID TO

CPT (insert named place of destination) the Incoterms® 2010 rules

DELIVERY

GUIDANCE NOTE

This rule may be used irrespective of the mode of transport selected and may also be used where more than one mode of transport is employed.

"Carriage Paid To" means that the seller delivers the goods to the carrier or another person nominated by the seller at an agreed place (if any such place is agreed between the parties) and that the seller must contract for and pay the costs of carriage necessary to bring the goods to the named place of destination.

When CPT, CIP, CFR or CIF are used, the seller fulfils its obligation to deliver when it hands the goods over to the carrier and not when the goods reach the place of destination.

This rule has two critical points, because risk passes and costs are transferred at different places. The parties are well advised to identify as precisely as possible in the contract both the place of delivery, where the risk passes to the buyer, and the named place of destination to which the seller must contract for the carriage. If several carriers are used for the carriage to the agreed destination and the parties do not agree on a specific point of delivery, the default position is that risk passes when the goods have been delivered to the first carrier at a point entirely of the seller's choosing and over which the buyer has no control. Should the parties wish the risk to pass at a later stage (e.g., at an ocean port or airport), they need to specify this in their contract of sale.

The parties are also well advised to identify as precisely as possible the point within the agreed place of destination, as the costs to that point are for the account of the seller. The seller is advised to procure contracts of carriage that match this choice precisely. If the seller incurs costs under its contract of carriage related to unloading at the named place of destination, the seller is not entitled to recover such costs from the buyer unless otherwise agreed between the parties.

CPT requires the seller to clear the goods for export, where applicable. However, the seller has no obligation to clear the goods for import, pay any import duty or carry out any import customs formalities.

CPT

A THE SELLER'S OBLIGATIONS

A1 General obligations of the seller

The seller must provide the goods and the commercial invoice in conformity with the contract of sale and any other evidence of conformity that may be required by the contract.

Any document referred to in A1-A10 may be an equivalent electronic record or procedure if agreed between the parties or customary.

Comments The seller must provide the goods in conformity with the contract. It is also usual practice that the seller, in order to be paid, has to invoice the buyer. In addition, the seller must submit any other evidence stipulated in the contract itself that the goods conform with that contract.

This text only serves as a reminder of the seller's main obligation under the contract of sale.

A2 Licences, authorizations, security clearances and other formalities

Where applicable, the seller must obtain, at its own risk and expense, any export licence or other official authorization and carry out all customs formalities necessary for the export of the goods, and for their transport through any country prior to delivery.

Comments The seller has to clear the goods for export and assume any risk or expense which this involves. Consequently, if there is an export prohibition or if there are particular taxes on the export of the goods – and if there are other government-imposed requirements which may render the export of the goods more expensive than contemplated – all of these risks and costs must be borne by the seller. However, contracts of sale usually contain particular provisions which the seller may invoke to protect himself in the event of these contingencies. Under CISG and corresponding provisions in various national Sale of Goods Acts, unforeseen or reasonably unforeseeable export prohibitions may relieve the seller from his obligations under the contract of sale.

A3 Contracts of carriage and insurance

a) Contract of carriage
The seller must contract or procure a contract for the carriage of the goods from the agreed point of delivery, if any, at the place of delivery to the named place of destination or, if agreed, any point at that place. The contract of carriage must be made on usual terms at the seller's expense and provide for carriage by the usual route and in a customary manner. If a specific point is not agreed or is not determined by practice, the seller may select the point of delivery and the point at the named place of destination that best suit its purpose.

b) Contract of insurance
The seller has no obligation to the buyer to make a contract of insurance. However, the seller must provide the buyer, at the buyer's request, risk, and expense (if any), with information that the buyer needs for obtaining insurance.

CPT

Comments   The seller's obligation to contract for carriage is basically the same under all C-terms, in that the seller fulfils his delivery obligation upon handing over the goods for carriage in the country of shipment, but with the additional obligation to arrange and pay for the carriage up to the agreed point in the country of destination. Since CFR and CIF can only be used when the goods are intended for carriage by sea or inland waterway transport, CPT and CIP respectively must be used as alternatives to CFR and CIF when the goods are intended to be carried by other modes of transport (air, road, rail, unnamed or multimodal transport). But they should also be used whenever the goods are not handed over for sea transport to the ship, for example, transport of containerized cargo or in roll on-roll off traffic when the goods are carried in railway wagons, trailers or semi-trailers on ferries.

In all C-terms, the seller must, unless otherwise agreed, contract for carriage "on usual terms" and "by the usual route". In CFR and CIF reference is made to a vessel of the type normally used for the transport of goods of the type sold. Since CPT and CIP are not confined to sea carriage but may be used for all modes of transport, reference is not made to the vehicle of transport but instead to the "customary manner" of transportation.

The seller has no obligation to provide insurance for the benefit of the buyer (compare CIP where the seller has to provide insurance).

However, he must give the buyer any information he may request for insurance purposes.

A4   Delivery

The seller must deliver the goods by handing them over to the carrier contracted in accordance with A3 on the agreed date or within the agreed period.

Comments   While delivery under CFR and CIF must be made on board the vessel at the port of shipment, the goods under CPT and CIP must be handed over "to the carrier". Therefore, the delivery obligation is no longer related to the means of conveyance – the vessel – but to the carrier as such.

CPT and CIP should be the preferred terms, when in practice delivery is not intended to be made directly to a vessel. When the parties intend to use several carriers – for example, a pre-carriage by road or rail from the seller's premises at an inland point for further carriage by sea to the agreed destination – the seller has fulfilled his delivery obligation under CPT and CIP when the goods have been handed over for carriage to the first carrier. In this respect, there is an important difference between CPT and CIP on the one hand and CFR and CIF on the other.

In the latter two terms, delivery is not completed until the goods have reached a vessel at the port of shipment. Therefore, the principle that the delivery is completed when the goods have been handed over to the first carrier cannot apply under CFR and CIF unless the pre-carriage is performed by sea, for example, by a so-called feeder ship to an ocean-going vessel for further carriage.

CPT

A5 Transfer of risks

The seller bears all risks of loss of or damage to the goods until they have been delivered in accordance with A4, with the exception of loss or damage in the circumstances described in B5.

Comments All of the Incoterms rules are based on the same principle that the risk of loss of or damage to the goods is transferred from the seller to the buyer when the seller has fulfilled his delivery obligation according to A4.

All of the Incoterms rules, in conformity with the general principle of CISG, connect the transfer of the risk with the delivery of the goods and not with other circumstances, such as the passing of ownership or the time of the conclusion of the contract. Neither the Incoterms rules nor CISG deals with transfer of title to the goods or other property rights with respect to the goods.

The passing of risk of loss of or damage to the goods concerns the risk of fortuitous events (accidents) and does not include loss or damage caused by the seller or the buyer, for example, inadequate packing or marking of the goods. Therefore, even if damage occurs subsequent to the transfer of the risk, the seller may still be responsible if the damage could be attributed to the fact that the goods were not delivered in conformity with the contract (see A1 and the comments to A9).

A5 of all the Incoterms rules contain the phrase "with the exception of loss or damage in the circumstances described in B5". This means that there are exceptions to the main rule concerning the passing of risk under the circumstances mentioned in B5, which may result in a premature passing of the risk because of the buyer's failure to fulfil his obligations properly (see the comments to B5)

A6 Allocation of costs

The seller must pay

a) all costs relating to the goods until they have been delivered in accordance with A4, other than those payable by the buyer as envisaged in B6;

b) the freight and all other costs resulting from A3 a), including the costs of loading the goods and any charges for unloading at the place of destination that were for the seller's account under the contract of carriage; and

c) where applicable, the costs of customs formalities necessary for export, as well as all duties, taxes and other charges payable upon export, and the costs for their transport through any country that were for the seller's account under the contract of carriage.

Comments As is the case with the transfer of the risk for loss of or damage to the goods, all of the Incoterms rules follow the same rule, that the division of costs occurs at the delivery point.

All costs occurring before the seller has fulfilled his obligation to deliver according to A4 are for his account, while further costs are for the account of the buyer (see the comments to B6). This rule is made subject to the provisions of B6, which indicates that the buyer may have to bear additional costs incurred by his failure to give appropriate notice to the seller.

CPT

A7   Notices to the buyer

The seller must notify the buyer that the goods have been delivered in accordance with A4. The seller must give the buyer any notice needed in order to allow the buyer to take measures that are normally necessary to enable the buyer to take the goods.

Comments   The seller must give the buyer sufficient notice that the goods have been dispatched, as well as other relevant information, so that the buyer can make preparations in time to take delivery according to B4. There is no stipulation in the Incoterms rules spelling out the consequences of the seller's failure to give such notice. But it follows from the Incoterms rules that the seller's failure constitutes a breach of contract. This means that the seller could be held responsible for the breach according to the law applicable to the contract of sale.

A8   Delivery document

If customary or at the buyer's request, the seller must provide the buyer, at the seller's expense, with the usual transport document[s] for the transport contracted in accordance with A3.

This transport document must cover the contract goods and be dated within the period agreed for shipment. If agreed or customary, the document must also enable the buyer to claim the goods from the carrier at the named place of destination and enable the buyer to sell the goods in transit by the transfer of the document to a subsequent buyer or by notification to the carrier. When such a transport document is issued in negotiable form and in several originals, a full set of originals must be presented to the buyer.

Comments   In all shipment contracts – and particularly contracts under the so-called C-terms, which require the seller to arrange and pay for the contract of carriage – it is vital for the buyer to know that the seller has fulfilled his obligation to perform these tasks and to deliver the goods to the carrier. The transport document constitutes proof of such delivery.

Non-negotiable transport documents

Generally, it suffices for the parties to refer to the "usual transport document" obtained from the carrier when the goods are handed over to him. But in maritime carriage, different documents can be used. While traditionally, negotiable bills of lading were used for carriage of goods by sea, other documents have appeared in recent years, for example, transport documents which are non-negotiable and similar to those used for other modes of transport. These alternative documents have different names – "liner waybills", "ocean waybills", "cargo quay receipts", "data freight receipts" or "sea waybills". The term "sea waybill" is frequently used to include all of the various non-negotiable transport documents used for carriage of goods by sea.

Unfortunately, international conventions and national laws do not yet provide specific regulations for these non-negotiable transport documents. (The exception is in the United States, where a non-negotiable bill of lading is recognized; this is the "straight bill of lading".) For this reason, the Comité Maritime International (CMI) in June 1990 adopted Uniform Rules for Sea Waybills. The parties should refer to these Rules in the contract of carriage to avoid any legal uncertainties stemming from the use of non-negotiable documents (see Annex 1).

CPT

When sale of goods in transit is intended ,the parties should choose one of the terms in Group II for transport by sea and inland waterways (FAS, FOB, CFR, CIF).

A9   Checking – packaging – marking

The seller must pay the costs of those checking operations (such as checking quality, measuring, weighing, counting) that are necessary for the purpose of delivering the goods in accordance with A4, as well as the costs of any pre-shipment inspection mandated by the authority of the country of export.

The seller must, at its own expense, package the goods, unless it is usual for the particular trade to transport the type of goods sold unpackaged. The seller may package the goods in the manner appropriate for their transport, unless the buyer has notified the seller of specific packaging requirements before the contract of sale is concluded. Packaging is to be marked appropriately.

Comments   It is necessary for the buyer to ensure that the seller has duly fulfilled his obligation with respect to the condition of the goods. This is particularly important if the buyer is called upon to pay for the goods before he has received and checked them. However, the seller has no duty to arrange and pay for inspection of the goods before shipment, unless this is mandated by authorities in the country of export or has been specifically agreed in the contract of sale.

The goods must also be adequately packed. Since the seller arranges the carriage, he is in a good position to decide the packing required for the transport of the goods. However, if he knows the ultimate destination and circumstances relating to the carriage he may be required to pack the goods accordingly. The goods should also be marked in accordance with applicable standards and regulations.

A10   Assistance with information and related costs

The seller must, where applicable, in a timely manner, provide to or render assistance in obtaining for the buyer, at the buyer's request, risk and expense, any documents and information, including security-related information, that the buyer needs for the import of the goods and/or for their transport to the final destination.

The seller must reimburse the buyer for all costs and charges incurred by the buyer in providing or rendering assistance in obtaining documents and information as envisaged in B10.

Comments   The seller has the obligation to clear the goods for export, but he has no obligation after shipment to bear any costs or risks connected either with the transit through another country or with import clearance of the goods at destination. However, he has the duty to render assistance to the buyer in obtaining any documents or equivalent electronic messages which may be required for these purposes. The buyer, however, must reimburse the seller for any expenses which the seller might have incurred in connection with this assistance. Moreover, if something goes wrong, the buyer will have to assume the risk. Similarly, the seller must reimburse the buyer for any assistance provided by him according to B10.

The seller may also be requested to provide the buyer with information related to the goods which the buyer requires for security-related clearance of the goods.

CPT

CPT

B THE BUYER'S OBLIGATIONS

B1   General obligations of the buyer

The buyer must pay the price of the goods as provided in the contract of sale.

Any document referred to in B1-B10 may be an equivalent electronic record or procedure if agreed between the parties or customary.

Comments   The buyer must pay the price agreed in the contract of sale. B1 constitutes a reminder of this main obligation, which corresponds with the seller's obligation to provide the goods in conformity with the contract of sale, as stipulated in A1.

B2   Licences, authorizations, security clearances and other formalities

Where applicable, it is up to the buyer to obtain, at its own risk and expense, any import licence or other official authorization and carry out all customs formalities for the import of the goods and for their transport through any country.

Comments   The buyer must take care of the import and security clearance and bear any costs and risks in connection with it. Therefore, an import prohibition will not relieve the buyer of his obligation to pay for the goods, unless there is a particular "relief clause" in the contract of sale which he invokes to obtain this relief. Such clauses may provide for the extension of time or the right to avoid the contract under the applicable law (see the comments to A2).

The buyer must also do whatever may be needed to pass the goods through a third country after they have been shipped (dispatched) from the seller's country, unless this obligation is for the seller's account under the contract of carriage.

B3   Contracts of carriage and insurance

a) Contract of carriage
The buyer has no obligation to the seller to make a contract of carriage.

b) Contract of insurance
The buyer has no obligation to the seller to make a contract of insurance. However, the buyer must provide the seller, upon request, with the necessary information for obtaining insurance.

Comments   Although B3(a) merely stipulates "No obligation" for the buyer, on-carriage from the port of destination is necessary in most cases, and it is the buyer's responsibility to do whatever is required for this purpose. But the seller is not concerned with the further carriage of the goods, and the buyer has no obligation to the seller in this respect. Whatever the buyer does is in his own interest and is not covered by the contract of sale.

CPT

B4   Taking delivery

The buyer must take delivery of the goods when they have been delivered as envisaged in A4 and receive them from the carrier at the named place of destination.

Comments   Here, the two critical points under the C-term appear again. Since the seller fulfils his obligation by handing over the goods to the carrier at the place of dispatch (A4), it is for the buyer to accept such delivery under B4. But the buyer also has a further obligation to receive the goods from the carrier at the named port of destination. This is not something he does only in his own interest (as in B3) but is an obligation to the seller, who has concluded the contract of carriage with the carrier.

The fact that the buyer must take delivery of the goods when as they have been delivered in accordance with A4 does not, of course, preclude him from raising claims against the seller if the goods do not conform with the contract.

B5   Transfer of risks

The buyer bears all risks of loss of or damage to the goods from the time they have been delivered as envisaged in A4.

If the buyer fails to give notice in accordance with B7, it must bear all risks of loss of or damage to the goods from the agreed date or the expiry date of the agreed period for delivery, provided that the goods have been clearly identified as the contract goods.

Comments   According to the main rule, while the seller under A5 bears the risk of loss of or damage to the goods until the delivery point, the buyer has to bear the risk thereafter. The delivery point is different under the different terms. In EXW and all D-terms the goods are simply placed "at the disposal of the buyer" at the relevant point, while under the F- and C-terms the delivery point is related to the handing over of the goods to the carrier in the country of dispatch or shipment (see the comments to A4 of these terms). In the terms used for goods intended to be carried by sea, reference is made to delivery alongside the named vessel (FAS) or delivery on board the vessel (FOB, CFR, CIF).

The buyer's failure to give notice according to B7, which relates to the "time for dispatching the goods and/or the named place of destination or the point of receiving the goods within that place" (see the comments to B7) may result in a premature passing of the risk: it is unacceptable to allow the buyer to delay the delivery and passing of the risk longer than contemplated when the contract of sale was made. Therefore, his failure to notify according to B7 will cause the risk to pass "from the agreed date or the expiry date of the period agreed for delivery".

The risk, however, cannot pass until the goods have been appropriated to the contract. If the goods are unascertained – i.e. goods of a certain kind which the seller will deliver to various buyers – appropriation occurs only when the goods are "clearly identified as the contract goods".

CPT

B6   Allocation of costs

The buyer must, subject to the provisions of A3 a), pay

a)   all costs relating to the goods from the time they have been delivered as envisaged in A4, except, where applicable, the costs of customs formalities necessary for export, as well as all duties, taxes, and other charges payable upon export as referred to in A6 c);

b)   all costs and charges relating to the goods while in transit until their arrival at the agreed place of destination, unless such costs and charges were for the seller's account under the contract of carriage;

c)   unloading costs, unless such costs were for the seller's account under the contract of carriage;

d)   any additional costs incurred if the buyer fails to give notice in accordance with B7, from the agreed date or the expiry date of the agreed period for dispatch, provided that the goods have been clearly identified as the contract goods; and

e)   where applicable, all duties, taxes and other charges, as well as the costs of carrying out customs formalities payable upon import of the goods and the costs for their transport through any country, unless included within the cost of the contract of carriage.

Comments   While the seller has to pay all costs required to bring the goods to the place of dispatch and to deliver the goods to the carrier (as well as unloading charges at the place of destination, provided they have been included in the freight), the buyer has to pay any further costs which may arise after the seller has fulfilled these obligations. In this sense, the transfer of the risk also determines the division of costs; if something occurs as a result of contingencies after shipment – such as strandings, collisions, strikes, government directions, hindrances because of ice or other weather conditions – any additional costs charged by the carrier as a result of these contingencies, or otherwise occurring, will be for the account of the buyer.

Failure to give notice and premature passing of risk

The failure to give appropriate notice in accordance with B7 not only results in a premature transfer of the risks (see comments to B5) but also imposes on the buyer the responsibility to pay any additional costs as a consequence. In this case, the obligation to pay these additional costs occurs only if the goods have been identified as the contract goods (as discussed in the comments to B5).

Buyer's duties in clearing goods for import

As noted in the comments to B2, the buyer has the duty to clear the goods for import; it is then established in B6 that he has to pay the costs arising from the clearance ("duties, taxes and other charges as well as the costs of carrying out customs formalities"). The buyer also has to pay any duties, taxes and other charges arising in connection with the transit of the goods through another country after they have been delivered by the seller in accordance with A4 unless these costs were for the seller's account under the contract of carriage.

CPT

B7   Notices to the seller

The buyer must, whenever it is entitled to determine the time for dispatching the goods and/or the named place of destination or the point of receiving the goods within that place, give the seller sufficient notice thereof.

Comments   As discussed in the comments to B5 and B6, the failure of the buyer to notify the seller of the time for dispatching the goods and/or the named place of destination or the point of receiving the goods within that place – when the buyer in the contract of sale has been given the option to determine these matters – may cause the risk of the loss of or damage to the goods to pass before the goods have been delivered according to A4. In addition, it can make the buyer liable to pay any additional costs incurred by the seller as a result of the buyer's failure.

B8   Proof of delivery

The buyer must accept the transport document provided as envisaged in A8 if it is in conformity with the contract.

Comments   The buyer has to accept the transport document if it conforms with the contract and with the requirements of A8 (see the comments to A8). If the buyer rejects a conforming transport document (for example, by instructions to a bank not to pay the seller under a documentary credit), he commits a breach of contract, which would give the seller remedies available for such a breach under the contract of sale.

These remedies could include, for example, a right to cancel the contract or to claim damages for breach. However, the buyer is not obliged to accept a document which does not provide adequate proof of delivery, for example, one which has notations on it showing that the goods are defective or that they have been provided in less than the agreed quantity. In these cases, the document is termed "unclean".

B9   Inspection of goods

The buyer must pay the costs of any mandatory pre-shipment inspection, except when such inspection is mandated by the authorities of the country of export.

Comments   As discussed in the comments to A9, the buyer has to pay for any costs of checking the goods unless the contract states that these costs should be borne wholly or partly by the seller. In some cases, the contract may provide that the costs should be borne by the seller if the inspection reveals that the goods do not conform with the contract.

In some countries, where import licences or permission to obtain foreign currency for the payment of the price may be required, the authorities may demand an inspection of the goods before shipment, to ensure that the goods are in conformity with the contract. (This is usually called pre-shipment inspection, PSI.) If this is the case, the inspection is normally arranged by instructions from the authorities to an inspection company, which they

CPT

appoint. The costs following from this inspection have to be paid by the authorities. Any reimbursement to the authorities for the inspection costs, however, must be made by the buyer, unless mandated by the authorities of the country of export or specifically agreed between the buyer and the seller.

B10   Assistance with information and related costs

The buyer must, in a timely manner, advise the seller of any security information requirements so that the seller may comply with A10.

The buyer must reimburse the seller for all costs and charges incurred by the seller in providing or rendering assistance in obtaining documents and information as envisaged in A10.

The buyer must, where applicable, in a timely manner, provide to or render assistance in obtaining for the seller, at the seller's request, risk and expense, any documents and information, including security-related information, that the seller needs for the transport and export of the goods and for their transport through any country.

Comments   As discussed in the comments to A10, the seller has to render the buyer assistance in obtaining the documents or electronic messages and information which may be required for the transit and import and security-clearance of the goods. However, this assistance is rendered at the buyer's risk and expense. Therefore, B10 stipulates that the buyer must pay all costs and charges incurred in obtaining these documents or electronic messages. He will also have to reimburse the seller for the seller's costs in rendering his assistance in these matters.

CARRIAGE AND INSURANCE PAID TO
CIP (insert named place of destination) the Incoterms® 2010 rules

DELIVERY

GUIDANCE NOTE

This rule may be used irrespective of the mode of transport selected and may also be used where more than one mode of transport is employed.

"Carriage and Insurance Paid to" means that the seller delivers the goods to the carrier or another person nominated by the seller at an agreed place (if any such place is agreed between the parties) and that the seller must contract for and pay the costs of carriage necessary to bring the goods to the named place of destination.

The seller also contracts for insurance cover against the buyer's risk of loss of or damage to the goods during the carriage. The buyer should note that under CIP the seller is required to obtain insurance only on minimum cover. Should the buyer wish to have more insurance protection, it will need either to agree as much expressly with the seller or to make its own extra insurance arrangements.

When CPT, CIP, CFR or CIF are used, the seller fulfils its obligation to deliver when it hands the goods over to the carrier and not when the goods reach the place of destination.

This rule has two critical points, because risk passes and costs are transferred at different places. The parties are well advised to identify as precisely as possible in the contract both the place of delivery, where the risk passes to the buyer, and the named place of destination to which the seller must contract for carriage. If several carriers are used for the carriage to the agreed destination and the parties do not agree on a specific point of delivery, the default position is that risk passes when the goods have been delivered to the first carrier at a point entirely of the seller's choosing and over which the buyer has no control. Should the parties wish the risk to pass at a later stage (e.g., at an ocean port or an airport), they need to specify this in their contract of sale.

The parties are also well advised to identify as precisely as possible the point within the agreed place of destination, as the costs to that point are for the account of the seller. The seller is advised to procure contracts of carriage that match this choice precisely. If the seller incurs costs under its contract of carriage related to unloading at the named place of destination, the seller is not entitled to recover such costs from the buyer unless otherwise agreed between the parties.

CIP

A   THE SELLER'S OBLIGATIONS

A1, A2, A3(a) A4 to A10
See the comments to CPT A1, A2,A3 (a) A4 to A10.

A3(b)   Contract of insurance
The seller must obtain at its own expense cargo insurance complying at least with the minimum cover as provided by Clauses (C) of the Institute Cargo Clauses (LMA/IUA) or any similar clauses. The insurance shall be contracted with underwriters or an insurance company of good repute and entitle the buyer, or any other person having an insurable interest in the goods, to claim directly from the insurer.

When required by the buyer, the seller shall, subject to the buyer providing any necessary information requested by the seller, provide at the buyer's expense any additional cover, if procurable, such as cover as provided by Clauses (A) or (B) of the Institute Cargo Clauses (LMA/IUA) or any similar clauses, and/or cover complying with the Institute War Clauses and/or Institute Strikes Clauses (LMA/IUA) or any similar clauses.

The insurance shall cover, at a minimum, the price provided in the contract plus 10% (i.e., 110%) and shall be in the currency of the contract.

The insurance shall cover the goods from the point of delivery set out in A4 and A5 to at least the named place of destination.

The seller must provide the buyer with the insurance policy or other evidence of insurance cover.

Moreover, the seller must provide the buyer, at the buyer's request, risk, and expense (if any), with information that the buyer needs to procure any additional insurance.

Comments   The only difference between the CPT and the CIP term is that the latter requires the seller to also obtain and pay for cargo insurance. This is particularly important for the buyer, since under CIP the risk of loss of or damage to the goods will pass from the seller to the buyer when the goods have been delivered to the carrier at the place of dispatch (see CPT A5).

In addition, it is vital for the buyer to be given the right to claim against the insurer independently of the seller. For this purpose it may be necessary to provide the buyer with the insurance policy under which the insurer makes his undertaking directly to the buyer.

Seller need only provide "minimum cover"
It is important to note that the seller only has to provide for so-called "minimum cover". Such limited cover is suitable only for bulk cargoes, which normally do not suffer loss or damage in transit unless something happens to the means of conveyance as well as to the cargo (strandings, collisions, fire, etc.). The buyer and seller are therefore advised to agree that the seller should provide a more suitable insurance cover. The buyer should then specify the extended cover he prefers.
Under Clauses C of the Institute Cargo Clauses (LMA/IUA) cover is available in categories A, B and C. The C category provides the minimum cover, and the cover is extended

CIP

progressively in categories B and A. However, even the most extended cover does not provide for what is misleadingly called "all-risk insurance". Furthermore, there are other important exceptions which insurance does not cover, for example, cases when the loss of the goods has been caused by insolvency or fraud, or when financial loss has been incurred by delay in delivery.

Duration of insurance cover

The duration of the insurance cover must coincide with the carriage and must protect the buyer from the moment he has to bear the risk of loss of or damage to the goods (i.e. from the moment the goods have been delivered to the carrier at the place of dispatch). It must extend until the goods arrive at the agreed place of destination or an agreed pont within that place.

Some risks require additional cover

Some particular risks require additional insurance, and if the buyer requests it, the seller must arrange this additional cover at the buyer's expense – for example, insurance against the risks of war, strikes, riots and civil commotion – if this cover can possibly be arranged.

Amount of the insurance cover

The amount of the insurance should correspond to the price provided in the contract, plus 10 per cent. The additional 10 per cent is intended to cover the average profit which buyers of goods expect from the sale. The insurance should be provided in the same currency as stipulated in the contract for the price of the goods. Consequently, if the price of the goods is to be paid in convertible currency, the seller may not provide insurance in other than convertible currency.

CIP

B   THE BUYER'S OBLIGATIONS

B1 to B2, B3(a), and B4 to B10

See the comments to CPT B1 B2, B3(a), and B4 to B10

B3(b)   Contract of insurance

The buyer has no obligation to the seller to make a contract of insurance. However, the buyer must provide the seller, upon request, with any information necessary for the seller to procure any additional insurance requested by the buyer as envisaged in A3 b).

Comments   It is vital for the buyer to understand that the seller only has to take out minimum insurance cover. This cover in most cases is insufficient when manufactured goods are involved. In the contract of sale, therefore, the buyer should require the seller to take out additional cover. If, however, the contract does not deal with this matter at all, the seller's obligation is limited as stipulated in A3, and the buyer has to arrange and pay for any additional insurance cover required.

In most cases the seller will know how to arrange the insurance from the contract of sale (from the invoice value of the goods, their destination, etc). However, the buyer has to provide the seller upon request with any information necessary for the seller to procure additional insurance requested by the buyer.

DELIVERED AT TERMINAL

DAT (insert named terminal at port or place of destination) the Incoterms® 2010 rules

DELIVERY

GUIDANCE NOTE

This rule may be used irrespective of the mode of transport selected and may also be used where more than one mode of transport is employed.

"Delivered at Terminal" means that the seller delivers when the goods, once unloaded from the arriving means of transport, are placed at the disposal of the buyer at a named terminal at the named port or place of destination. "Terminal" includes any place, whether covered or not, such as a quay, warehouse, container yard or road, rail or air cargo terminal. The seller bears all risks involved in bringing the goods to and unloading them at the terminal at the named port or place of destination.

The parties are well advised to specify as clearly as possible the terminal and, if possible, a specific point within the terminal at the agreed port or place of destination, as the risks to that point are for the account of the seller. The seller is advised to procure a contract of carriage that matches this choice precisely.

Moreover, if the parties intend the seller to bear the risks and costs involved in transporting and handling the goods from the terminal to another place, then the DAP or DDP rules should be used.

DAT requires the seller to clear the goods for export, where applicable. However, the seller has no obligation to clear the goods for import, pay any import duty or carry out any import customs formalities.

DAT

A THE SELLER'S OBLIGATIONS

A1 General obligations of the seller

The seller must provide the goods and the commercial invoice in conformity with the contract of sale and any other evidence of conformity that may be required by the contract.

Any document referred to in A1-A10 may be an equivalent electronic record or procedure if agreed between the parties or customary.

Comments The seller must provide the goods in conformity with the contract. It is also usual practice that the seller, in order to be paid, has to invoice the buyer. In addition, the seller must submit any other evidence stipulated in the contract itself that the goods conform with that contract.

This text only serves as a reminder of the seller's main obligation under the contract of sale.

A2 Licences, authorizations, security clearances and other formalities

Where applicable, the seller must obtain, at its own risk and expense, any export licence and other official authorization and carry out all customs formalities necessary for the export of the goods and for their transport through any country prior to delivery.

Comments Since the term DAT is evidence of an arrival contract, the seller has to do whatever may be necessary for the goods to reach the agreed place for delivery. This means the seller is responsible for export clearance of the goods as well as any transit formalities involved in the transport of the goods through another country before arrival at the agreed destination.

Unforeseen or reasonably unforeseeable prohibitions

The seller's obligations under DAT may become more expensive than contemplated as a result of reasonably unforeseeable circumstances. However, contracts of sale usually contain provisions which the seller may invoke to protect himself in the event of these contingencies. Under CISG and corresponding provisions in various national Sale of Goods Acts, unforeseen or reasonably unforeseeable prohibitions may relieve the seller from his obligations under the contract of sale.

A3 Contracts of carriage and insurance

a) Contract of carriage
The seller must contract at its own expense for the carriage of the goods to the named terminal at the agreed port or place of destination. If a specific terminal is not agreed or is not determined by practice, the seller may select the terminal at the agreed port or place of destination that best suits its purpose.

b) Contract of insurance
The seller has no obligation to the buyer to make a contract of insurance. However, the seller must provide the buyer, at the buyer's request, risk, and expense (if any), with information that the buyer needs for obtaining insurance.

DAT

Comment   Under all D-terms, the seller must ensure that the goods actually arrive at destination. It follows from this that the seller must arrange and pay for any carriage of the goods.

Under the D-terms, the seller's choice of transport is only of importance to the buyer insofar as it affects the buyer's obligation to receive the goods from the carrier. If the seller chooses an unusual mode of transport which makes it more difficult or expensive for the buyer to receive the goods from the carrier, any additional costs or risks caused by the seller's choice of transport will be for the seller's account.

Normally, the point mentioned after the D-term will indicate where the goods should be delivered at destination. But if there are several alternatives available, and the contract of sale or commercial practice does not indicate which alternative the seller must choose, he may select the point at the named place of destination which best suits its purpose.

A4   Delivery

The seller must unload the goods from the arriving means of transport and must then deliver them by placing them at the disposal of the buyer at the named terminal referred to in A3 a) at the port or place of destination on the agreed date or within the agreed period.

Comments   Under all D-terms, the seller must place the goods at the disposal of the buyer at destination. The precise point for the delivery of the goods depends upon the D-term chosen. According to DAT A4, the goods should be placed at the disposal of the buyer UNLOADED from the arriving means of transport (note the difference under DAP!).

A5   Transfer of risks

The seller bears all risks of loss of or damage to the goods until they have been delivered in accordance with A4 with the exception of loss or damage in the circumstances described in B5.

Comments   All of the Incoterms rules are based on the same principle that the risk of loss of or damage to the goods is transferred from the seller to the buyer when the seller has fulfilled his delivery obligation according to A4.

All of the Incoterms rules, in conformity with the general principle of CISG, connect the transfer of the risk with the delivery of the goods and not with other circumstances, such as the passing of ownership or the time of the conclusion of the contract. Neither the Incoterms rules nor CISG deals with transfer of title to the goods or other property rights with respect to the goods.

The passing of risk of loss of or damage to the goods concerns the risk of fortuitous events (accidents) and does not include loss or damage caused by the seller or the buyer, for example, inadequate packing or marking of the goods. Therefore, even if damage occurs subsequent to the transfer of the risk, the seller may still be responsible if the damage could be attributed to the fact that the goods were not delivered in conformity with the contract (see A1 and the comments to A9).

DAT

A5 of all the Incoterms rules contain the phrase "with the exception of loss or damage in the circumstances described in B5". This means that there are exceptions to the main rule concerning the passing of risk under the circumstances mentioned in B5, which may result in a premature passing of the risk because of the buyer's failure properly to fulfil his obligations (see the comments to B5).

A6   Allocation of costs

The seller must pay
a)   in addition to costs resulting from A3 a), all costs relating to the goods until they have been delivered in accordance with A4, other than those payable by the buyer as envisaged in B6; and

b)   where applicable, the costs of customs formalities necessary for export as well as all duties, taxes and other charges payable upon export and the costs for their transport through any country, prior to delivery in accordance with A4.

Comments   As is the case with the transfer of the risk of loss of or damage to the goods, all of the Incoterms rules follow the same rule, that the division of costs occurs at the delivery point. All costs occurring before the seller has fulfilled his obligation to deliver according to A4 are for his account, while further costs are for the account of the buyer (see the comments to B6). This rule is made subject to the provisions of B6, which indicates that the buyer may have to bear additional costs incurred by his failure to give appropriate notice to the seller.

Since under D-terms, the seller does not fulfil his obligation until the goods have actually arrived at destination and been placed at the disposal of the buyer, the seller has to do everything required to achieve this. Nevertheless, A3 in all D-terms still stipulates that the seller must contract for carriage; and A6 of all D-terms stipulates that he must pay the costs resulting from A3 for the carriage of the goods and pay the costs of customs formalities as well as all duties, taxes and other charges payable upon export (and in the case of DDP also import) of the goods, prior to delivery. Needless to say, any transit costs incurred subsequent to delivery will have to be paid by the buyer.

A7   Notices to the buyer

The seller must give the buyer any notice needed in order to allow the buyer to take measures that are normally necessary to enable the buyer to take delivery of the goods.

Comments   The seller must give the buyer sufficient notice as to the estimated time of arrival (ETA) of the vessel, if used for the transport, and other essential notices, so that the buyer can make preparations in time to take delivery according to B4. There is no stipulation in the Incoterms rules spelling out the consequences of the seller's failure to give such notice. But it follows from the Incoterms rules that the seller's failure constitutes a breach of contract. This means that the seller could be held responsible for the breach according to the law applicable to the contract of sale.

DAT

A8   Delivery document

The seller must provide the buyer, at the seller's expense, with a document enabling the buyer to take delivery of the goods as envisaged in A4/B4.

Comments   Whenever a document is required in order to enable the buyer to take delivery, the seller has to provide him with such a document. If the goods are delivered directly to the buyer he must give a receipt indicating , in his own interest, any non-conformity.

A9   Checking – packaging – marking

The seller must pay the costs of those checking operations (such as checking quality, measuring, weighing, counting) that are necessary for the purpose of delivering the goods in accordance with A4, as well as the costs of any pre-shipment inspection mandated by the authority of the country of export.

The seller must, at its own expense, package the goods, unless it is usual for the particular trade to transport the type of goods sold unpackaged. The seller may package the goods in the manner appropriate for their transport, unless the buyer has notified the seller of specific packaging requirements before the contract of sale is concluded. Packaging is to be marked appropriately.

Comments   It is important that the buyer ensure that the seller has duly fulfilled his obligation with respect to the condition of the goods, particularly if the buyer is called upon to pay for the goods before he has received and checked them. However, the seller has no duty to arrange and pay for the inspection of the goods unless this is mandated by the authorities of the country of export or specifically agreed in the contract of sale.

A10   Assistance with information and related costs

The seller must, where applicable, in a timely manner, provide to or render assistance in obtaining for the buyer, at the buyer's request, risk and expense, any documents and information, including security-related information, that the buyer needs for the import of the goods and/or for their transport to the final destination.

The seller must reimburse the buyer for all costs and charges incurred by the buyer in providing or rendering assistance in obtaining documents and information as envisaged in B10.

Comments   DAT requires the buyer to clear the goods for import. The buyer has to reimburse the seller for any costs it may incur in rendering any assistance (see B10).

DAT

B THE BUYER'S OBLIGATIONS

B1 General obligations of the buyer

The buyer must pay the price of the goods as provided in the contract of sale.

Any document referred to in B1-B10 may be an equivalent electronic record or procedure if agreed between the parties or customary.

Comments The buyer must pay the price agreed in the contract of sale. B1 constitutes a reminder of this main obligation, which corresponds with the seller's obligation to provide the goods in conformity with the contract of sale, as stipulated in A1.

B2 Licences, authorizations, security clearances and other formalities

Where applicable, the buyer must obtain, at its own risk and expense, any import licence or other official authorization and carry out all customs formalities for the import of the goods.

Comments Although the seller has to make the goods available to the buyer in the country of destination and clear the goods for export and transit, it is for the buyer to do whatever is necessary with respect to the clearance of the goods for import (see the comments to A2).

B3 Contracts of carriage and insurance

a) Contract of carriage
The buyer has no obligation to the seller to make a contract of carriage.

b) Contract of insurance
The buyer has no obligation to the seller to make a contract of insurance. However, the buyer must provide the seller, upon request, with the necessary information for obtaining insurance.

Comments Although B3 merely stipulates "No obligation" for the buyer, on-carriage from the port of destination is necessary in most cases, and it is the buyer's responsibility to do whatever is required for this purpose. But the seller is not concerned with the further carriage of the goods, and the buyer has no obligation to the seller in this respect. The words "No obligation" mean that whatever the buyer does is in his own interest and is not covered by the contract of sale.

B4 Taking delivery

The buyer must take delivery of the goods when they have been delivered as envisaged in A4.

Comments As in all D-terms, B4 has wording stating that the buyer shall take delivery as soon as the goods have been placed at his disposal in accordance with A4. The seller, according to A4 in the D-terms, shall place the goods at the buyer's disposal "on the agreed date or within the agreed period".

DAT

If the goods are placed at the buyer's disposal earlier than agreed, the buyer is not obliged to take delivery before the agreed time, though it may normally be in his own interest to do so. If the goods are placed at the buyer's disposal too late, the buyer may hold the seller responsible for breach of contract according to the applicable law. He may also recover damages from the seller or, in the event of a fundamental breach, cancel the contract.

B5   Transfer of risks

The buyer bears all risks of loss of or damage to the goods from the time they have been delivered as envisaged in A4.

If
a)   the buyer fails to fulfil its obligations in accordance with B2, then it bears all resulting risks of loss of or damage to the goods; or

b)   the buyer fails to give notice in accordance with B7, then it bears all risks of loss of or damage to the goods from the agreed date or the expiry date of the agreed period for delivery,

provided that the goods have been clearly identified as the contract goods.

Comments   According to the main rule, while the seller under A5 bears the risk of loss of or damage to the goods until the delivery point, the buyer has to bear the risk thereafter. The delivery point is different under the different terms. In EXW and all D-terms the goods are simply placed "at the disposal of the buyer" at the relevant point, while under the F- and C-terms the delivery point is related to the handing over of the goods to the carrier in the country of dispatch or shipment (see the comments to A4 of these terms). In the terms used for goods intended to be carried by sea, reference is made to delivery alongside the named vessel (FAS) or delivery onboard the vessel (FOB, CFR, CIF).

Consequences of buyer's failure to comply with B2, or to give notice
Whenever the seller undertakes to deliver the goods at an interior point in the country of destination it is important that the buyer complies with his obligation to clear the goods for import (B 2). If he fails to do so, the risk of loss of or damage to the goods would pass to him before the goods have arrived at the delivery point. While the seller under EXW and all D-terms can transfer the risk by his own act of placing the goods at the buyer's disposal, he may be prevented from doing so by the buyer's failure to fulfill his obligation to clear the goods for import or give notice according to B7. This can occur when it is the buyer's responsibility to determine (1) the time within a stipulated period when the goods are to be made available or (2) the place of delivery (see the comments to B7). The failure to perform these tasks results in a premature passing of the risk: it is not acceptable that the buyer should be able to delay the delivery and passing of the risk longer than contemplated when the contract of sale was made. Therefore, his failure to notify according to B7 will cause the risk to pass from the agreed date or the expiry date of any period stipulated for delivery.

DAT

Identification of the contract goods and premature passing of risk

The risk, however, cannot pass until the goods have been "identitifed as the contract goods". If the goods are unascertained – i.e., goods of a certain kind which the seller will deliver to various buyers – identification only occurs when the goods are clearly set aside or otherwise identified as the contract goods.

This appropriation will normally be made when the seller has handed over the goods for carriage and the consignment has been marked as intended for the buyer – unless the cargo is carried in bulk and intended to be appropriated between different buyers only upon the arrival of the goods at destination.If so, identification may be made so that each buyer is allotted its proportion of the bulk. The Incoterms 2000 rules used the word "appropriation" to clarify this. No change is intended by deleting this word in the Incoterms® 2010 rules.

B6   Allocation of costs

The buyer must pay

a)   all costs relating to the goods from the time they have been delivered as envisaged in A4;

b)   any additional costs incurred by the seller if the buyer fails to fulfil its obligations in accordance with B2, or to give notice in accordance with B7, provided that the goods have been clearly identified as the contract goods; and

c)   where applicable, the costs of customs formalities as well as all duties, taxes and other charges payable upon import of the goods.

Comments   Since according to A4 the goods are made available to the buyer unloaded from the arriving means of transport (compare DEQ of the earlier versions of the Incoterms rules), the buyer is relieved of the obligation to pay for the costs of unloading. However, once the goods have been placed at his disposal in accordance with A4, the buyer must pay any costs for the storage and further carriage of the goods to their final destination.Also, he must pay any additional costs caused by his failure to fulfil his obligation to clear the goods for import according to B2.

If the buyer fails to take delivery or to take such measures as are needed for on-carriage, he will have to bear any additional costs incurred thereby. At this stage, the seller will normally have identified the goods as the contract goods (through the process of appropriation). But if he has not done so – for example, if the goods arrive at destination in bulk for later appropriation by delivery orders or otherwise – the buyer does not have to bear any additional costs relating to the goods until they have been duly appropriated. Subject to the goods having been appropriated as noted above, the buyer also has to pay any additional costs incurred as a result of his failure to notify the seller according to B7 of the time or place of taking delivery, for example additional storage and insurance costs.

DAT

B7 Notice to the seller

The buyer must, whenever it is entitled to determine the time within an agreed period and/or the point of taking delivery at the named terminal, give the seller sufficient notice thereof.

Comments   As discussed in the comments to B5 and B6, the failure of the buyer to notify the seller of the time and place of taking delivery – when the buyer in the contract of sale has been given the option to determine these matters – may cause the risk of the loss of or damage to the goods to pass before the goods have been delivered according to A4. In addition, it can make the buyer liable to pay any additional costs incurred by the seller as a result of the buyer's failure.

B8 Proof of delivery

TThe buyer must accept the delivery document provided as envisaged in A8.

Comments   The buyer has to accept the delivery document if it conforms with the contract and with the requirements of A8 (see the comments to A8). If the buyer rejects the document (for example, by instructions to a bank not to pay the seller under a documentary credit), he commits a breach of contract, which would give the seller remedies available for such a breach under the contract of sale.

These remedies could include, for example, a right to cancel the contract or to claim damages for breach. However, the buyer is not obliged to accept a document which does not provide adequate proof of delivery, for example, one which has notations on it showing that the goods are defective or that they have been provided in less than the agreed quantity. In these cases, the document is termed "unclean".

B9 Inspection of goods

The buyer must pay the costs of any mandatory pre-shipment inspection, except when such inspection is mandated by the authorities of the country of export.

Comments   As noted in the comments to A9, the buyer has to pay for any costs of checking the goods, unless the contract determines that these costs should be wholly or partly borne by the seller. In some cases, the contract may provide that the costs should be borne by the seller if the inspection reveals that the goods do not conform with the contract.

In some countries, where import licences or permission to obtain foreign currency for the payment of the price may be required, the authorities may demand an inspection of the goods before shipment, to ensure that the goods are in conformity with the contract. (This is usually called pre-shipment inspection, PSI.) If this is the case, the inspection is normally arranged by instructions from the authorities to an inspection company, which they appoint. The costs following from this inspection have to be paid by the authorities. Any reimbursement to the authorities for the inspection costs, however, must be made by the buyer unless the inspection is mandated by the authorities of the country of export or the buyer and the seller specifically agree otherwise.

DAT

B10   Assistance with information and related costs

The buyer must, in a timely manner, advise the seller of any security information requirements so that the seller may comply with A10.

The buyer must reimburse the seller for all costs and charges incurred by the seller in providing or rendering assistance in obtaining documents and information as envisaged in A10.

The buyer must, where applicable, in a timely manner, provide to or render assistance in obtaining for the seller, at the seller's request, risk and expense, any documents and information, including security-related information, that the seller needs for the transport and export of the goods and for their transport through any country.

Comments   Since the buyer has the obligation to clear the goods for import, he may require the seller's assistance to obtain the necessary documents and information. The seller must render this assistance when requested by the buyer to do so, but the seller does this at the buyer's risk and expense.

DELIVERED AT PLACE
DAP (insert named place of destination) the Incoterms® 2010 rules

DELIVERY

GUIDANCE NOTE

This rule may be used irrespective of the mode of transport selected and may also be used where more than one mode of transport is employed.

"Delivered at Place" means that the seller delivers when the goods are placed at the disposal of the buyer on the arriving means of transport ready for unloading at the named place of destination. The seller bears all risks involved in bringing the goods to the named place.

The parties are well advised to specify as clearly as possible the point within the agreed place of destination, as the risks to that point are for the account of the seller. The seller is advised to procure contracts of carriage that match this choice precisely. If the seller incurs costs under its contract of carriage related to unloading at the place of destination, the seller is not entitled to recover such costs from the buyer unless otherwise agreed between the parties.

DAP requires the seller to clear the goods for export, where applicable. However, the seller has no obligation to clear the goods for import, pay any import duty or carry out any import customs formalities. If the parties wish the seller to clear the goods for import, pay any import duty and carry out any import customs formalities, the DDP term should be used.

DAP

A THE SELLER'S OBLIGATIONS

A1 General obligations of the seller

The seller must provide the goods and the commercial invoice in conformity with the contract of sale and any other evidence of conformity that may be required by the contract.

Any document referred to in A1-A10 may be an equivalent electronic record or procedure if agreed between the parties or customary.

Comments   The seller must provide the goods in conformity with the contract. It is also usual practice that the seller, in order to be paid, has to invoice the buyer. In addition, the seller must submit any other evidence stipulated in the contract itself that the goods conform with that contract.

This text only serves as a reminder of the seller's main obligation under the contract of sale.

A2 Licences, authorizations, security clearances and other formalities

Where applicable, the seller must obtain, at its own risk and expense, any export licence and other official authorization and carry out all customs formalities necessary for the export of the goods and for their transport through any country prior to delivery.

Comments   The seller has to clear the goods for export and assume any risk or expense which this involves. Consequently, if there is an export prohibition or if there are particular taxes on the export of the goods – and if there are other government-imposed requirements which may render the export of the goods more expensive than contemplated – all of these risks and costs must be borne by the seller. However, contracts of sale usually contain particular provisions which the seller may invoke to protect himself in the event of these contingencies. Under CISG and corresponding provisions in various national Sale of Goods Acts, unforeseen or reasonably unforeseeable export prohibitions may relieve the seller from his obligations under the contract of sale.

A2 stipulates that the seller has to do whatever may be necessary with respect to prior transit formalities. This is the case even when the goods are to be carried through several countries before they reach the point named after DAP in the contract of sale.

A3 Contracts of carriage and insurance

a)   Contract of carriage
The seller must contract at its own expense for the carriage of the goods to the named place of destination or to the agreed point, if any, at the named place of destination. If a specific point is not agreed or is not determined by practice, the seller may select the point at the named place of destination that best suits its purpose.

DAP

b) Contract of insurance
The seller has no obligation to the buyer to make a contract of insurance. However, the seller must provide the buyer, at the buyer's request, risk, and expense (if any), with information that the buyer needs for obtaining insurance.

Comments   Under all D-terms, the seller must ensure that the goods actually arrive at destination. It follows from this that the seller must arrange and pay for any carriage of the goods. Under the D-terms, the seller's choice of transport is only of importance to the buyer insofar as it affects the buyer's obligation to receive the goods from the carrier. If the seller chooses an unusual mode of transport which makes it more difficult or expensive for the buyer to receive the goods from the carrier, any additional costs or risks caused by the seller's choice of transport will be for the seller's account.

Normally, the point mentioned after the D-term will indicate where the goods should be delivered at destination. But if there are several alternatives available, and the contract of sale or commercial practice does not indicate which alternative the seller must choose, he "may select the point at the named place of destination that best suits its purpose".

A4   Delivery

The seller must deliver the goods by placing them at the disposal of the buyer on the arriving means of transport ready for unloading at the agreed point, if any, at the named place of destination on the agreed date or within the agreed period.

Comments   Under all D-terms the seller must place the goods "at the disposal of the buyer" at destination. The Incoterms® 2010 rules specify that under DAP the goods are placed at the disposal of the buyer "on the arriving means of transport ready for unloading" (see also DDP A4).

If in the contract of sale only the frontier of the country concerned is named and not the point at that frontier where the delivery should take place (the contract may say, for example, "DAP Italian border"), the seller can then select the point at the border which best suits his purpose.

DAP may be used irrespective of the intended mode of transport. Rail carriage usually continues past the border without any discharge of the goods from the railway wagon and re-loading on to another one. Consequently, there will be no real "placing of the goods at the disposal of the buyer". Instead, the seller, on the buyer's request, may provide the buyer with a through railway consignment note to the place of final destination in the country of import (see the comments to DAP A8).

DAP

A5   Transfer of risks

The seller bears all risks of loss of or damage to the goods until they have been delivered in accordance with A4, with the exception of loss or damage in the circumstances described in B5.

Comments   All of the Incoterms rules are based on the same principle that the risk of loss of or damage to the goods is transferred from the seller to the buyer when the seller has fulfilled his delivery obligation according to A4.

All of the Incoterms rules, in conformity with the general principle of CISG, connect the transfer of the risk with the delivery of the goods and not with other circumstances, such as the passing of ownership or the time of the conclusion of the contract. Neither the Incoterms rules nor CISG deals with transfer of title to the goods or other property rights with respect to the goods.

The passing of risk of loss of or damage to the goods concerns the risk of fortuitous events (accidents) and does not include loss or damage caused by the seller or the buyer, for example, inadequate packing or marking of the goods. Therefore, even if damage occurs subsequent to the transfer of the risk, the seller may still be responsible if the damage could be attributed to the fact that the goods were not delivered in conformity with the contract (see A1 and the comments to A9).

A5 of all of the Incoterms rules contains the phrase "with the exception of loss or damage in the circumstances described in B5". This means that there are exceptions to the main rule concerning the passing of risk under the circumstances mentioned in B5, which may result in a premature passing of the risk because of the buyer's failure to fulfil his obligations properly (see the comments to B5).

A6   Allocation of costs

The seller must pay

a)   in addition to costs resulting from A3 a), all costs relating to the goods until they have been delivered in accordance with A4, other than those payable by the buyer as envisaged in B6;

b)   any charges for unloading at the place of destination that were for the seller's account under the contract of carriage; and

c)   where applicable, the costs of customs formalities necessary for export as well as all duties, taxes and other charges payable upon export and the costs for their transport through any country, prior to delivery in accordance with A4.

Comments   As is the case with the transfer of the risk of loss of or damage to the goods, all of the Incoterms rules follow the same rule, that the division of costs occurs at the delivery point. All costs occurring before the seller has fulfilled his obligation to deliver according to A4 are for his account, while further costs are for the account of the buyer (see the comments to B6). This rule is made subject to the provisions of B6, which indicates that the buyer may have to bear additional costs incurred by his failure to give appropriate notice to the seller.

Since under D-terms the seller does not fulfil his obligation until the goods have actually arrived at destination and been placed at the disposal of the buyer, the seller has to do everything required to achieve this. A3 in all D-terms still stipulates that the seller must contract for carriage; and A6 of all D-terms stipulates that he must pay the costs resulting from A3 for the carriage of the goods and, where applicable, the costs relating to customs formalities, duties, taxes and other charges prior to delivery in accordance with A4. Needless to say, any transit costs incurred subsequent to delivery will have to be paid by the buyer.

A7 Notices to the buyer

The seller must give the buyer any notice needed in order to allow the buyer to take measures that are normally necessary to enable the buyer to take delivery of the goods.

Comments The seller must give the buyer sufficient notice as to when the goods are available at the agreed or chosen delivery point, so that the buyer can make preparations in time to take delivery according to B4. There is no stipulation in the Incoterms rules spelling out the consequences of the seller's failure to give such notice. But it follows from the Incoterms rules that the seller's failure constitutes a breach of contract. This means that the seller could be held responsible for the breach according to the law applicable to the contract of sale.

A8 Delivery document

The seller must provide the buyer, at the seller's expense, with a document enabling the buyer to take delivery of the goods as envisaged in A4/B4.

Comments Whenever a document is required in order to enable the buyer to take delivery, the seller has to provide him with such a document. If the goods are delivered directly to the buyer he must give a receipt indicating, in his own interest, any non-conformity. However, as noted in the comments to DAP A4, goods carried by rail will frequently remain on the railway wagon and continue to the final destination. The seller must then provide the buyer with the usual through document of transport if the seller has agreed to contract for on-carriage, at the buyer's risk and expense.

A9 Checking – packaging – marking

The seller must pay the costs of those checking operations (such as checking quality, measuring, weighing, counting) that are necessary for the purpose of delivering the goods in accordance with A4, as well as the costs of any pre-shipment inspection mandated by the authority of the country of export.

DAP

The seller must, at its own expense, package the goods, unless it is usual for the particular trade to transport the type of goods sold unpackaged. The seller may package the goods in the manner appropriate for their transport, unless the buyer has notified the seller of specific packaging requirements before the contract of sale is concluded. Packaging is to be marked appropriately.

Comments   It is important that the buyer ensure that the seller has duly fulfilled his obligation with respect to the condition of the goods, particularly if the buyer is called upon to pay for the goods before he has received and checked them. However, the seller has no duty to arrange and pay for the inspection of the goods before shipment, unless this is mandated by the authorities in the country of export or specifically agreed in the contract of sale.

A10   Assistance with information and related costs

The seller must, where applicable, in a timely manner, provide to or render assistance in obtaining for the buyer, at the buyer's request, risk and expense, any documents and information, including security-related information, that the buyer needs for the import of the goods and/or for their transport to the final destination.

The seller must reimburse the buyer for all costs and charges incurred by the buyer in providing or rendering assistance in obtaining documents and information as envisaged in B10.

Comments   The seller has the obligation to carry out all customs and security-related formalities for the export of the goods and for their prior transit. But he has no obligation after the goods have reached the agreed point place to bear any costs and risks for their transit through another country or for import or security-related clearance. However, he has the duty to render the buyer assistance in obtaining the documents (for example, a certificate of origin, a health certificate, a clean report of findings, an import licence or security-related information) which may be required for import clearance of the goods.

The buyer, in turn, must reimburse the seller for any expenses which the seller might have incurred in connection with this assistance. Moreover, if something goes wrong, the buyer will have to assume the risk.

DAP

B THE BUYER'S OBLIGATIONS

B1 General obligations of the buyer

The buyer must pay the price of the goods as provided in the contract of sale.

Any document referred to in B1-B10 may be an equivalent electronic record or procedure if agreed between the parties or customary.

Comments The buyer must pay the price agreed in the contract of sale. B1 constitutes a reminder of this main obligation, which corresponds with the seller's obligation to provide the goods in conformity with the contract of sale, as stipulated in A1.

B2 Licences, authorizations, security clearances and other formalities

Where applicable, the buyer must obtain, at its own risk and expense, any import licence or other official authorization and carry out all customs formalities for the import of the goods.

Comments The buyer must take care of the import and security clearance and bear any costs and risks in connection with it. Therefore, an import prohibition will not relieve the buyer of his obligation to pay for the goods, unless there is a particular "relief clause" in the contract of sale which he invokes to obtain this relief. Such clauses may provide for the extension of time or the right to avoid the contract under the applicable law (see the comments to A2).

B3 Contracts of carriage and insurance

a) Contract of carriage
The buyer has no obligation to the seller to make a contract of carriage.

b) Contract of insurance
The buyer has no obligation to the seller to make a contract of insurance. However, the buyer must provide the seller, upon request, with the necessary information for obtaining insurance.

Comments Although B3 merely stipulates "No obligation" for the buyer, on-carriage from the place of delivery is sometimes necessary, particularly in railway traffic, where the seller may agree to assist the buyer. (see DAP A4 and A8). Otherwise, the seller is not concerned with the further carriage of the goods and the buyer has no obligation to the seller in this respect. The words "No obligation" mean that whatever the buyer does is in his own interest and is not covered by the contract of sale.

DAP

B4 Taking delivery

The buyer must take delivery of the goods when they have been delivered as envisaged in A4.

Comments   As in all D-terms, B4 has wording stating that the buyer shall take delivery as soon as the goods have been placed at his disposal in accordance with A4. The seller, according to A4 in the D-terms, shall place the goods at the buyer's disposal "at the agreed point, if any, at the named place of destination on the agreed date or within the agreed period".

If the goods are placed at the buyer's disposal earlier than agreed, the buyer is not obliged to take delivery before the agreed time, though it may normally be in his own interest to do so. If the goods are placed at the buyer's disposal too late, the buyer may hold the seller responsible for breach of contract according to the applicable law. He may also recover damages from the seller or, in the event of a fundamental breach, cancel the contract.

B5 Transfer of risks

The buyer bears all risks of loss of or damage to the goods from the time they have been delivered as envisaged in A4.

If
a) the buyer fails to fulfil its obligations in accordance with B2, then it bears all resulting risks of loss of or damage to the goods; or

b) the buyer fails to give notice in accordance with B7, then it bears all risks of loss of or damage to the goods from the agreed date or the expiry date of the agreed period for delivery,

provided that the goods have been clearly identified as the contract goods.

Comments   According to the main rule, while the seller under A5 bears the risk of loss of or damage to the goods until the delivery point, the buyer has to bear the risk thereafter. The delivery point is different under the different terms. In EXW and all D-terms the goods are simply placed "at the disposal of the buyer" at the relevant point, while under the F- and C-terms the delivery point is related to the handing over of the goods to the carrier in the country of dispatch or shipment (see the comments to A4 of these terms). In the terms used for goods intended to be carried by sea, reference is made to delivery alongside the named vessel (FAS) or delivery onboard the vessel (FOB, CFR, CIF).

Consequences of buyer's failure to comply with B2 or to give notice

Whenever the seller undertakes to deliver the goods at an interior point in the country of destination it is important that the buyer complies with his obligation to clear the goods for import (B2). If he fails to do so, the risk of loss of or damage to the goods would pass to him before the goods have arrived at the delivery point. While the seller under EXW and all D-terms can transfer the risk by his own act of placing the goods at the buyer's disposal, he may be prevented from doing so by the buyer's failure to give notice according to B7. This can occur when it is the buyer's responsibility to determine (1) the time within a stipulated period when the goods are to be made available or (2) the point or place of delivery (see the comments to B7). The failure to perform these tasks results

DAP

in a premature passing of the risk: it is not acceptable that the buyer should be able to delay the delivery and passing of the risk longer than contemplated when the contract of sale was made. Therefore, his failure to notify according to B7 will cause the risk to pass from the agreed date or the expiry date of the agreed period for delivery.

Identification of the contract goods and premature passing of risk

The risk, however, cannot pass until the goods "have been clearly identified as the contract goods". If the goods are unascertained – i.e., goods of a certain kind which the seller will deliver to various buyers – appropriation occurs only when the goods are " identified as the contract goods".

This identification will normally be made when the seller has handed over the goods for carriage and the consignment has been marked as intended for the buyer – unless the cargo is carried in bulk and intended to be appropriated between different buyers only upon the arrival of the goods at destination.If so, identification may be made so that each buyer is allotted its proportion of the bulk. The Incoterms 2000 rules used the word "appropriation" to clarify this. No change is intended by deleting this word in the Incoterms® 2010 rules.

B6   Allocation of costs

The buyer must pay

a)   all costs relating to the goods from the time they have been delivered as envisaged in A4;

b)   all costs of unloading necessary to take delivery of the goods from the arriving means of transport at the named place of destination, unless such costs were for the seller's account under the contract of carriage;

c)   any additional costs incurred by the seller if the buyer fails to fulfil its obligations in accordance with B2 or to give notice in accordance with B7, provided that the goods have been clearly identified as the contract goods; and

d)   where applicable, the costs of customs formalities, as well as all duties, taxes and other charges payable upon import of the goods.

Comments   If, as stipulated in A4, the goods are placed at the disposal of the buyer at the named place or point of destination ready for unloading by the buyer (compare DES of the earlier versions of the Incoterms rules), the buyer, under DAP B6 would have to pay all costs from the time the goods have been made available to him in this manner.

When DAP is used for railway traffic, the goods will usually remain on the same railway wagon, and the point mentioned in the contract will then primarily serve as a point for dividing the railway freight between the parties (i.e., as a tariff point). The seller has to bear all costs and risks until that point has been reached.

DAP

Under all D-terms, the buyer has to take delivery of the goods at the agreed point and time. The same principle governs even if there is no delivery in the physical sense, for example, if the goods remain on the same vehicle when it passes the agreed delivery point. If the buyer fails to take delivery or to take the required measures for on-carriage, he will have to bear any additional costs incurred thereby.

Appropriation required if goods arrive in bulk

At the delivery stage, the seller will normally have identified the goods as the contract goods. But if he has not done so – for example, if the goods arrive at destination in bulk for later appropriation by delivery orders or otherwise – the buyer does not have to bear any additional costs relating to the goods until they have been duly appropriated.

Subject to the goods having been appropriated, the buyer then has to pay any additional costs incurred as a result of his failure to notify the seller of the time or place of taking delivery according to B7, for example, additional storage and insurance costs.

Buyer's duties in clearing goods for import

As noted in the comments to B2, the buyer has the duty to clear the goods for import; B6 declares that he also has to pay the costs arising in that connection ("the costs of customs formalities as well as all duties, taxes and other charges"). The buyer also has to pay any duties, taxes and other charges arising with regard to the transit of the goods through another country, after they have been delivered by the seller in accordance with A4.

B7   Notices to the seller

The buyer must, whenever it is entitled to determine the time within an agreed period and/or the point of taking delivery within the named place of destination, give the seller sufficient notice thereof.

Comments   As discussed in the comments to B5 and B6, the failure of the buyer to notify the seller of the time and place of taking delivery – when the buyer in the contract of sale has been given the option to determine these matters – may cause the risk of the loss of or damage to the goods to pass before the goods have been delivered according to A4. In addition, it can make the buyer liable to pay any additional costs incurred by the seller as a result of the buyer's failure.

B8   Proof of delivery

The buyer must accept the delivery document provided as envisaged in A8.

Comments   The buyer has to accept the delivery document if it conforms with the contract and with the requirements of A8 (see the comments to A8). If the buyer rejects the document (for example, by instructions to a bank not to pay the seller under a documentary credit), he commits a breach of contract, which would give the seller remedies available for such a breach under the contract of sale.

These remedies could include, for example, a right to cancel the contract or to claim damages for breach. However, the buyer is not obliged to accept a document which does not provide adequate proof of delivery, for example, one which has notations on it showing that the goods are defective or that they have been provided in less than the agreed quantity. In these cases, the document is termed "unclean".

B9   Inspection of goods

The buyer must pay the costs of any mandatory pre-shipment inspection, except when such inspection is mandated by the authorities of the country of export.

Comments   As noted in the comments to A9, the buyer has to pay for any costs of checking the goods, unless the contract determines that these costs should be wholly or partly borne by the seller. In some cases, the contract may provide that the costs should be borne by the seller if the inspection reveals that the goods do not conform with the contract.

In some countries, where import licences or permission to obtain foreign currency for the payment of the price may be required, the authorities may demand an inspection of the goods before shipment, to ensure that the goods are in conformity with the contract. (This is usually called pre-shipment inspection, PSI.) If this is the case, the inspection is normally arranged by instructions from the authorities to an inspection company, which they appoint. The costs following from this inspection have to be paid by the authorities. Any reimbursement to the authorities for the inspection costs, however, must be made by the buyer, unless the inspection is mandated by the authorities of the country of export or the buyer and the seller specifically agreed otherwise.

B10   Assistance with information and related costs

The buyer must, in a timely manner, advise the seller of any security information requirements so that the seller may comply with A10.

The buyer must reimburse the seller for all costs and charges incurred by the seller in providing or rendering assistance in obtaining documents and information as envisaged in A10.

The buyer must, where applicable, in a timely manner, provide to or render assistance in obtaining for the seller, at the seller's request, risk and expense, any documents and information, including security-related information, that the seller needs for the transport and export of the goods and for their transport through any country.

Comments   As discussed in the comments to A10, the seller has to render the buyer assistance in obtaining the documents or electronic messages and information which may be required for the transit, import and security-clearance of the goods. However, this assistance is rendered at the buyer's risk and expense. Therefore, B10 stipulates that the buyer must pay all costs and charges incurred in obtaining these documents or electronic messages. He will also have to reimburse the seller for the seller's costs in rendering his assistance in these matters.

DAP

According to A8, the seller may have to provide the buyer with a through document of transport. This may also involve other measures, such as obtaining exchange control authorization, permits, other documents or certified copies thereof. The buyer must, at his risk and expense, provide the seller with these documents, when the seller requests that he do so.

DELIVERED DUTY PAID
DDP (insert named place of destination) the Incoterms® 2010 rules

DELIVERY

↓

GUIDANCE NOTE

This rule may be used irrespective of the mode of transport selected and may also be used where more than one mode of transport is employed.

"Delivered Duty Paid" means that the seller delivers the goods when the goods are placed at the disposal of the buyer, cleared for import on the arriving means of transport ready for unloading at the named place of destination. The seller bears all the costs and risks involved in bringing the goods to the place of destination and has an obligation to clear the goods not only for export but also for import, to pay any duty for both export and import and to carry out all customs formalities.

DDP represents the maximum obligation for the seller. The parties are well advised to specify as clearly as possible the point within the agreed place of destination, as the costs and risks to that point are for the account of the seller. The seller is advised to procure contracts of carriage that match this choice precisely. If the seller incurs costs under its contract of carriage related to unloading at the place of destination, the seller is not entitled to recover such costs from the buyer unless otherwise agreed between the parties.

The parties are well advised not to use DDP if the seller is unable directly or indirectly to obtain import clearance.

If the parties wish the buyer to bear all risks and costs of import clearance, the DAP rule should be used.

Any VAT or other taxes payable upon import are for the seller's account unless expressly agreed otherwise in the sale contract.

DDP

A THE SELLER'S OBLIGATIONS

A1 General obligations of the seller

The seller must provide the goods and the commercial invoice in conformity with the contract of sale and any other evidence of conformity that may be required by the contract.

Any document referred to in A1-A10 may be an equivalent electronic record or procedure if agreed between the parties or customary.

Comments   The seller must provide the goods in conformity with the contract. It is also usual practice that the seller, in order to be paid, has to invoice the buyer. In addition, the seller must submit any other evidence stipulated in the contract itself that the goods conform with that contract.

This text only serves as a reminder of the seller's main obligation under the contract of sale.

A2 Licences, authorizations, security clearances and other formalities

Where applicable, the seller must obtain, at its own risk and expense, any export and import licence and other official authorization and carry out all customs formalities necessary for the export of the goods, for their transport through any country and for their import.

Comments   Since the term DDP is evidence of an arrival contract, the seller has to do whatever may be necessary for the goods to reach the agreed place/point for delivery. This means the seller is responsible for export and import clearance of the goods, as well as any transit of the goods through third countries.

Before agreeing to sell the goods under DDP, the seller should be sure that the regulations of the buyer's country do not prevent him as a non-resident from applying for any necessary import licence. Normally no such difficulties will be encountered, since the application for licences can be made by freight forwarders (customs brokers) on the seller's behalf.

Advisable to exclude payment of some charges

It may be advisable for the parties to exclude the payment of any charges relating to the "internal" fiscal system in the country of import (such as VAT levied upon import) from the seller's obligation to pay. If this is not done, any right to deduct these expenses or to benefit from particular tax advantages available only to residents could be lost. The charges intended to be excluded should then be identified in conjunction with the DDP term in the contract of sale, for example, by using a phrase such as "DDP VAT unpaid".

Unforeseen or reasonably unforeseeable prohibitions

The seller's obligations under DDP may become more expensive than contemplated as a result of reasonably unforeseeable circumstances.

DDP

However, contracts of sale usually contain provisions which the seller may invoke to protect himself in the event of these contingencies. Under CISG and corresponding provisions in various national Sale of Goods Acts, unforeseen or reasonably unforeseeable export prohibitions may relieve the seller from his obligations under the contract of sale.

If the seller wishes to avoid the obligation of clearing the goods for import, he should add the phrase "not cleared for import" after DDP.

A3   Contracts of carriage and insurance

a)   Contract of carriage
The seller must contract at its own expense for the carriage of the goods to the named place of destination or to the agreed point, if any, at the named place of destination. If a specific point is not agreed or is not determined by practice, the seller may select the point at the named place of destination that best suits its purpose.

b)   Contract of insurance
The seller has no obligation to the buyer to make a contract of insurance. However, the seller must provide the buyer, at the buyer's request, risk, and expense (if any), with information that the buyer needs for obtaining insurance.

Comments   Under DDP the seller must ensure that the goods actually arrive at destination. It follows from this that the seller must arrange and pay for any carriage of the goods.
Under the D-terms, the seller's choice of transport is only of importance to the buyer insofar as it affects the buyer's obligation to receive the goods from the carrier. If the seller chooses an unusual transport which makes it more difficult or expensive for the buyer to receive the goods from the carrier, any additional costs or risks caused by the seller's choice of transport will be for the seller's account.

Normally, the point mentioned after the D-term will indicate where the goods should be delivered at destination. But if there are several alternatives available, and the contract of sale or commercial practice does not indicate which alternative the seller must choose, he "may select the point at the named place of destination that best suits its purpose".

A4   Delivery

The seller must deliver the goods by placing them at the disposal of the buyer on the arriving means of transport ready for unloading at the agreed point, if any, at the named place of destination on the agreed date or within the agreed period.

Comments   Under DDP the seller must place the goods at the disposal of the buyer on the arriving means of transport ready for unloading by the buyer (same as DAP). It is important to note the difference between DDP and DAT in this respect.

DDP

A5 Transfer of risks

The seller bears all risks of loss of or damage to the goods until they have been delivered in accordance with A4, with the exception of loss or damage in the circumstances described in B5.

Comments   All of the Incoterms rules are based on the same principle that the risk of loss of or damage to the goods is transferred from the seller to the buyer when the seller has fulfilled his delivery obligation according to A4.

All of the Incoterms rules, in conformity with the general principle of CISG, connect the transfer of the risk with the delivery of the goods and not with other circumstances, such as the passing of ownership or the time of the conclusion of the contract. Neither the Incoterms rules nor CISG deals with transfer of title to the goods or other property rights with respect to the goods.

The passing of risk of loss of or damage to the goods concerns the risk of fortuitous events (accidents) and does not include loss or damage caused by the seller or the buyer, for example, inadequate packing or marking of the goods. Therefore, even if damage occurs subsequent to the transfer of the risk, the seller may still be responsible if the damage could be attributed to the fact that the goods were not delivered in conformity with the contract (see A1 and the comments to A9).

A5 of all of the Incoterms rules contains the phrase "with the exception of loss or damage in circumstances described in B5". This means that there are exceptions to the main rule concerning the passing of risk under the circumstances mentioned in B5, which may result in a premature passing of the risk because of the buyer's failure properly to fulfil his obligations (see the comments to B5).

A6 Allocation of costs

The seller must pay

a) in addition to costs resulting from A3 a), all costs relating to the goods until they have been delivered in accordance with A4, other than those payable by the buyer as envisaged in B6;

b) any charges for unloading at the place of destination that were for the seller's account under the contract of carriage; and

c) where applicable, the costs of customs formalities necessary for export and import as well as all duties, taxes and other charges payable upon export and import of the goods, and the costs for their transport through any country prior to delivery in accordance with A4.

Comments   As is the case with the transfer of the risk of loss of or damage to the goods, all of the Incoterms rules follow the same rule, that the division of costs occurs at the delivery point. All costs occurring before the seller has fulfilled his obligation to deliver according to A4

DDP

are for his account, while further costs are for the account of the buyer (see the comments to B6). This rule is made subject to the provisions of B6, which indicates that the buyer may have to bear additional costs incurred by his failure to give appropriate notice to the seller.

Since under D-terms, the seller does not fulfil his obligation until the goods have actually arrived at destination and been placed at the disposal of the buyer, the seller has to do everything required to achieve this. Nevertheless, A3 in all D-terms still stipulates that the seller must contract for carriage; and A6 of all D-terms stipulates that he must pay the costs resulting from A3 for the carriage of the goods, and, where applicable, the costs of customs formalities necessary for export and import as well as all duties, taxes and other charges prior to delivery in accordance with A4. Needless to say, any transit costs incurred subsequent to delivery will have to be paid by the buyer.

A7   Notices to the buyer

The seller must give the buyer any notice needed in order to allow the buyer to take measures that are normally necessary to enable the buyer to take delivery of the goods.

Comments The seller must give the buyer any notice required for the buyer for taking delivery according to B4, so that he can make preparations in time to take delivery according to B4. There is no stipulation in the Incoterms rules spelling out the consequences of the seller's failure to give such notice. But it follows from the Incoterms rules that the seller's failure constitutes a breach of contract. This means that the seller could be held responsible for the breach according to the law applicable to the contract of sale.

A8   Delivery document

The seller must provide the buyer, at the seller's expense, with a document enabling the buyer to take delivery of the goods as envisaged in A4/B4.

Comments Whenever a document is required in order to enable the buyer to take delivery, the seller has to provide him with such a document. If the goods are delivered directly to the buyer he must give a receipt indicating , in his own interest, any non-conformity.

Documents can be replaced by EDI messages when the parties have agreed to communicate   electronically.

A9   Checking-packaging-marking

The seller must pay the costs of those checking operations (such as checking quality, measuring, weighing, counting) that are necessary for the purpose of delivering the goods in accordance with A4, as well as the costs of any pre-shipment inspection mandated by the authority of the country of export or of import.

DDP

The seller must, at its own expense, package the goods, unless it is usual for the particular trade to transport the type of goods sold unpackaged. The seller may package the goods in the manner appropriate for their transport, unless the buyer has notified the seller of specific packaging requirements before the contract of sale is concluded. Packaging is to be marked appropriately.

Comments It is important that the buyer ensure that the seller has duly fulfilled his obligation with respect to the condition of the goods, particularly if the buyer is called upon to pay for the goods before he has received and checked them. However, the seller has no duty to arrange and pay for the inspection of the goods before dispatch unless mandated by authorities or specifically agreed in the contract of sale.

A10   Assistance with information and related costs

The seller must, where applicable, in a timely manner, provide to or render assistance in obtaining for the buyer, at the buyer's request, risk and expense, any documents and information, including security-related information, that the buyer needs for the transport of the goods to the final destination, where applicable, from the named place of destination.

The seller must reimburse the buyer for all costs and charges incurred by the buyer in providing or rendering assistance in obtaining documents and information as envisaged in B10.

Comments DDP requires the seller to clear the goods for import, but if the seller so requests the buyer must assist in obtaining any documents (for example, a certificate of origin, a health certificate, a clean report of findings, an import licence) or information for security-related clearance which the seller may require for these purposes. The seller, however, has to reimburse the buyer for any costs the buyer may incur in rendering this assistance. Also, the seller may have to render a similar assistance to the buyer required for further transport of the goods and the buyer has to reimburse the seller for such assistance (B10).

B THE BUYER'S OBLIGATIONS

B1 General obligations of the buyer

The buyer must pay the price of the goods as provided in the contract of sale.

Any document referred to in B1-B10 may be an equivalent electronic record or procedure if agreed between the parties or customary.

Comments   The buyer must pay the price agreed in the contract of sale. B1 constitutes a reminder of this main obligation, which corresponds with the seller's obligation to provide the goods in conformity with the contract of sale, as stipulated in A1.

B2 Licences, authorizations, security clearances and other formalities

Where applicable, the buyer must provide assistance to the seller, at the seller's request, risk and expense, in obtaining any import licence or other official authorization for the import of the goods.

Comments   Since the seller has to make the goods available to the buyer in the country of destination, it is for the seller to do whatever is necessary with respect to the clearance (including security-related clearance) of the goods for export, transit and import.

B3 Contracts of carriage and insurance

a)   Contract of carriage
The buyer has no obligation to the seller to make a contract of carriage.

b)   Contract of insurance
The buyer has no obligation to the seller to make a contract of insurance. However, the buyer must provide the seller, upon request, with the necessary information for obtaining insurance.

Comments   Although B3 merely stipulates "No obligation" for the buyer, on-carriage from the place of destination may be necessary in some cases, and it is the buyer's responsibility to do whatever is required for this purpose. But the seller is not concerned with the further carriage of the goods, except assisting the buyer at his risk and expense as set forth in A10. The words "No obligation" mean that whatever the buyer does is in his own interest and is not covered by the contract of sale.

B4 Taking delivery

The buyer must take delivery of the goods when they have been delivered as envisaged in A4.

Comments   As in all D-terms, B4 has wording stating that the buyer shall take delivery as soon as the goods have been placed at his disposal in accordance with A4. The seller, according to A4

DDP

in the D-terms, shall place the goods at the buyer's disposal "on the agreed date or within the agreed period".

If the goods are placed at the buyer's disposal earlier than agreed, the buyer is not obliged to take delivery before the agreed time, though it may normally be in his own interest to do so. If the goods are placed at the buyer's disposal too late, the buyer may hold the seller responsible for breach of contract according to the applicable law. He may also recover damages from the seller or, in the event of a fundamental breach, cancel the contract.

B5   Transfer of risks

The buyer bears all risks of loss of or damage to the goods from the time they have been delivered as envisaged in A4.

If
a)   the buyer fails to fulfil its obligations in accordance with B2, then it bears all resulting risks of loss of or damage to the goods; or

b)   the buyer fails to give notice in accordance with B7, then it bears all risks of loss of or damage to the goods from the agreed date or the expiry date of the agreed period for delivery,

provided that the goods have been clearly identified as the contract goods.

Comments   According to the main rule, while the seller under A5 bears the risk of loss of or damage to the goods until the delivery point, the buyer has to bear the risk thereafter. The delivery point is different under the different terms. In EXW and all D-terms the goods are simply placed "at the disposal of the buyer" at the relevant point, while under the F- and C-terms the delivery point is related to the handing over of the goods to the carrier in the country of dispatch or shipment (see the comments to A4 of these terms). In the terms used for goods intended to be carried by sea, reference is made to delivery alongside the named vessel (FAS) or delivery onboard the vessel (FOB, CFR, CIF).

Consequences of buyer's failure to give notice

While the seller under EXW and all D-terms can transfer the risk by his own act of placing the goods at the buyer's disposal, he may be prevented from doing so by the buyer's failure to give notice according to B7. This can occur when it is the buyer's responsibility to determine (1) the time within a stipulated period when the goods are to be made available or (2) the place or point of delivery (see the comments to B7). The failure to perform these tasks results in a premature passing of the risk: it is not acceptable that the buyer should be able to delay the delivery and the passing of the risk longer than contemplated when the contract of sale was made. Therefore, his failure to notify according to B7 will cause the risk to pass "from the agreed date or the expiry date of the agreed period for delivery".

Identification of the contract goods and premature passing of risk

The risk, however, cannot pass until the goods have been identified as the contract goods. If the goods are unascertained – i.e. goods of a certain kind which the seller will deliver to various buyers – appropriation only occurs when the goods are clearly set aside as the contract goods.

This appropriation will normally be made when the seller has handed over the goods for carriage and the consignment has been marked as intended for the buyer – unless the cargo is carried in bulk and intended to be appropriated between different buyers only upon the arrival of the goods at destination.

B6   Allocation of costs

The buyer must pay

a)   all costs relating to the goods from the time they have been delivered as envisaged in A4;

b)   all costs of unloading necessary to take delivery of the goods from the arriving means of transport at the named place of destination, unless such costs were for the seller's account under the contract of carriage; and

c)   any additional costs incurred if it fails to fulfil its obligations in accordance with B2 or to give notice in accordance with B7, provided that the goods have been clearly identified as the contract goods.

Comments   Under DDP the parties have to specify the place of delivery as the buyer must pay any further costs subsequent to the delivery of the goods to that place.

The buyer must pay any additional costs which may arise if he fails to take delivery as agreed or if he fails to notify the seller of the time and place of delivery according to B7. The buyer's obligation to pay additional costs in these cases is subject to the identification of the goods as the contract goods (appropriation).

Since under DDP the seller has to clear the goods for import, the buyer does not have to pay any costs in that regard.

B7   Notices to the seller

The buyer must, whenever it is entitled to determine the time within an agreed period and/or the point of taking delivery within the named place of destination, give the seller sufficient notice thereof.

Comments   As discussed in the comments to B5 and B6, the failure of the buyer to notify the seller of the time and place of taking delivery – when the buyer in the contract of sale has been given the option to determine these matters – may cause the risk of the loss of or damage to the goods to pass before the goods have been delivered according to A4. In addition, it can make the buyer liable to pay any additional costs incurred by the seller as a result of the buyer's failure.

DDP

B8   Proof of delivery

The buyer must accept the proof of delivery provided as envisaged in A8.

Comments   The buyer has to accept the document if it conforms with the contract and with the requirements of A8 (see the comments to A8). If the buyer rejects the document (for example, by instructions to a bank not to pay the seller under a documentary credit), he commits a breach of contract, which would give the seller remedies available for such a breach under the contract of sale.

B9   Inspection of goods

The buyer has no obligation to the seller to pay the costs of any mandatory pre-shipment inspection mandated by the authority of the country of export or of import.

Comments   As noted in the comments to A9, the buyer has to pay for any costs of checking the goods, unless the contract determines that these costs should be wholly or partly borne by the seller. In some cases, the contract may provide that the costs should be borne by the seller if the inspection reveals that the goods do not conform with the contract.

In some countries, where import licences or permission to obtain foreign currency for the payment of the price may be required, the authorities may demand an inspection of the goods before shipment, to ensure that the goods are in conformity with the contract. (This is usually called pre-shipment inspection, PSI.) If this is the case, the inspection is normally arranged by instructions from the authorities to an inspection company, which they appoint. The costs following from this inspection have to be paid by the authorities. Any reimbursement to the authorities for the inspection costs, however, must be made by the seller, unless otherwise specifically agreed between the buyer and the seller.

B10   Assistance with information and related costs

The buyer must, in a timely manner, advise the seller of any security information requirements so that the seller may comply with A10.

The buyer must reimburse the seller for all costs and charges incurred by the seller in providing or rendering assistance in obtaining documents and information as envisaged in A10.

The buyer must, where applicable, in a timely manner, provide to or render assistance in obtaining for the seller, at the seller's request, risk and expense, any documents and information, including security-related information, that the seller needs for the transport, export and import of the goods and for their transport through any country.

Comments   Since the seller has the obligation to clear the goods for import, he may require the buyer's assistance to obtain the necessary documents or EDI messages. The buyer must render this assistance when requested by the seller to do so, but this is done at the seller's risk and expense.

GROUP II: SEA AND INLAND WATERWAY TRANSPORT
FAS FOB CFR CIF:
should only be chosen for maritime transport

FREE ALONGSIDE SHIP

FAS (insert named port of shipment) the Incoterms® 2010 rules

GUIDANCE NOTE

This rule is to be used only for sea or inland waterway transport.

"Free Alongside Ship" means that the seller delivers when the goods are placed alongside the vessel (e.g., on a quay or a barge) nominated by the buyer at the named port of shipment. The risk of loss of or damage to the goods passes when the goods are alongside the ship, and the buyer bears all costs from that moment onwards.

The parties are well advised to specify as clearly as possible the loading point at the named port of shipment, as the costs and risks to that point are for the account of the seller and these costs and associated handling charges may vary according to the practice of the port.

The seller is required either to deliver the goods alongside the ship or to procure goods already so delivered for shipment. The reference to "procure" here caters for multiple sales down a chain ('string sales'), particularly common in the commodity trades.

Where the goods are in containers, it is typical for the seller to hand the goods over to the carrier at a terminal and not alongside the vessel. In such situations, the FAS rule would be inappropriate, and the FCA rule should be used.

FAS requires the seller to clear the goods for export, where applicable. However, the seller has no obligation to clear the goods for import, pay any import duty or carry out any import customs formalities.

FAS

A THE SELLER'S OBLIGATIONS

A1 General obligations of the seller

The seller must provide the goods and the commercial invoice in conformity with the contract of sale and any other evidence of conformity that may be required by the contract.

Any document referred to in A1-A10 may be an equivalent electronic record or procedure if agreed between the parties or customary.

Comments The seller must provide the goods in conformity with the contract. It is also usual practice that the seller, in order to be paid, has to invoice the buyer. In addition, the seller must submit any other evidence stipulated in the contract itself that the goods conform with the contract.

This text only serves as a reminder of the seller's main obligation under the contract of sale.

A2 Licences, authorizations, security clearances and other formalities

Where applicable, the seller must obtain, at its own risk and expense, any export licence or other official authorization and carry out all customs formalities necessary for the export of the goods.

Comments Under FAS it is the seller's obligation to clear the goods for export and to obtain any export licence or other official authorization. This is a change compared with FAS as interpreted in the versions of the Incoterms rules before 2000. The seller's obligation to clear the goods for export is now the same as under FOB (see the comments to FOB A2).

A3 Contracts of carriage and insurance

a) Contract of carriage
The seller has no obligation to the buyer to make a contract of carriage. However, if requested by the buyer or if it is commercial practice and the buyer does not give an instruction to the contrary in due time, the seller may contract for carriage on usual terms at the buyer's risk and expense. In either case, the seller may decline to make the contract of carriage and, if it does, shall promptly notify the buyer.

b) Contract of insurance
The seller has no obligation to the buyer to make a contract of insurance. However, the seller must provide the buyer, at the buyer's request, risk, and expense (if any), with information that the buyer needs for obtaining insurance.

Comments Since in A4 the goods should only be placed alongside the vessel named by the buyer, the seller has no obligation to contract for carriage or insurance. However, he must give the buyer any information he may request for insurance purposes.

FAS

A4   Delivery

The seller must deliver the goods either by placing them alongside the ship nominated by the buyer at the loading point, if any, indicated by the buyer at the named port of shipment or by procuring the goods so delivered. In either case, the seller must deliver the goods on the agreed date or within the agreed period and in the manner customary at the port.

If no specific loading point has been indicated by the buyer, the seller may select the point within the named port of shipment that best suits its purpose. If the parties have agreed that delivery should take place within a period, the buyer has the option to choose the date within that period.

Comments   The seller fulfils his obligation to deliver the goods by placing them alongside the named vessel in the port of shipment, either on the quay or in lighters. Once this has been done, any further risks and costs in loading the goods onboard are for the account of the buyer. When the goods are sold in transit, further sellers would not physically deliver the goods alongside but would sell them procured delivered alongside by the first seller.

A5   Transfer of risks

The seller bears all risks of loss of or damage to the goods until they have been delivered in accordance with A4 with the exception of loss or damage in the circumstances described in B5.

Comments   All of the Incoterms rules are based on the same principle, that the risk of loss of or damage to the goods is transferred from the seller to the buyer when the seller has fulfilled his delivery obligation according to A4.

All of the Incoterms rules, in conformity with the general principle of CISG, connect the transfer of the risk with the delivery of the goods and not with other circumstances, such as the passing of ownership or the time of the conclusion of the contract. Neither the Incoterms rules nor CISG deals with transfer of title to the goods or other property rights with respect to the goods.

The passing of risk for loss of or damage to the goods concerns the risk of fortuitous events (accidents) and does not include loss or damage caused by the seller or the buyer, for example through inadequate packing or marking of the goods. Therefore, even if damage occurs subsequent to the transfer of the risk, the seller may still be responsible if the damage could be attributed to the fact that the goods were not delivered in conformity with the contract (see A1 and the comments to A9).

A5 of all of the Incoterms rules contain the phrase "with the exception of loss or damage in the circumstances described in B5". This means that there are exceptions to the main rule in the circumstances described in B5 which may result in a premature passing of the risk because of the buyer's failure properly to fulfil his obligations (see the comments to B5).

FAS

A6   Allocation of costs

The seller must pay

a)   all costs relating to the goods until they have been delivered in accordance with A4, other than those payable by the buyer as envisaged in B6; and

b)   where applicable, the costs of customs formalities necessary for export as well as all duties, taxes and other charges payable upon export.

Comments   As is the case with the transfer of the risk for loss of or damage to the goods, all of the Incoterms rules follow the same rule, that the division of costs occurs at the delivery point. All costs occurring before the seller has fulfilled his obligation to deliver according to A4 are for his account, while further costs are for the account of the buyer (see the comments to B6). This rule is made subject to the provisions of B6, which indicates that the buyer may have to bear additional costs incurred by his failure to nominate a carrier that takes the goods into his charge or to give appropriate notice to the seller.

Since under FAS the seller's obligation is limited to delivering the goods alongside the vessel named by the buyer, all further costs have to be borne by the buyer once the goods have been made available in this manner.

A7   Notices to the buyer

The seller must, at the buyer's risk and expense, give the buyer sufficient notice either that the goods have been delivered in accordance with A4 or that the vessel has failed to take the goods within the time agreed.

Comments   The seller must give the buyer sufficient notice concerning when the goods have been placed alongside the named vessel or that the vessel has failed to take the goods within the time agreed. There is no stipulation in the Incoterms rules spelling out the consequences of the seller's failure to give this notice. But it follows from the Incoterms rules that the seller's failure constitutes a breach of contract. This means that the seller could be held responsible for the breach according to the law applicable to the contract of sale.

A8   Delivery document

The seller must provide the buyer, at the seller's expense, with the usual proof that the goods have been delivered in accordance with A4.

Unless such proof is a transport document, the seller must provide assistance to the buyer, at the buyer's request, risk and expense, in obtaining a transport document.

Comments   Since the seller's obligation is limited to placing the goods alongside the named vessel, he may not always receive a receipt or a transport document from the carrier. The seller must then provide some other document to prove that the goods have been delivered. When requested by the buyer, the seller must assist the buyer to obtain the transport document. This assistance is at the buyer's risk and expense.

FAS

A9   Checking – packaging – marking

The seller must pay the costs of those checking operations (such as checking quality, measuring, weighing, counting) that are necessary for the purpose of delivering the goods in accordance with A4, as well as the costs of any pre-shipment inspection mandated by the authority of the country of export.

The seller must, at its own expense, package the goods, unless it is usual for the particular trade to transport the type of goods sold unpackaged. The seller may package the goods in the manner appropriate for their transport, unless the buyer has notified the seller of specific packaging requirements before the contract of sale is concluded. Packaging is to be marked appropriately.

Comments   It is necessary for the buyer to ensure that the seller has duly fulfilled his obligation with respect to the condition of the goods. This is particularly important if the buyer is called upon to pay for the goods before he has received and checked them. However, the seller has no duty to arrange and pay for inspection of the goods before shipment, unless this has been mandated by the authorities in the country of export or specifically agreed in the contract of sale.

The goods must also be adequately packed. But the seller may not know the buyer's intentions with respect to the ultimate destination. There is a considerable difference between a short journey to an adjoining country and an intercontinental carriage by sea, which may expose the goods to the risk of breakage or corrosion from humidity and condensation.

A10   Assistance with information and related costs

The seller must, where applicable, in a timely manner, provide to or render assistance in obtaining for the buyer, at the buyer's request, risk and expense, any documents and information, including security-related information, that the buyer needs for the import of the goods and/or for their transport to the final destination.

The seller must reimburse the buyer for all costs and charges incurred by the buyer in providing or rendering assistance in obtaining documents and information as envisaged in B10.

Comments   Since it is for the buyer to do whatever is necessary with respect to transit and import clearance, he may well need the seller's assistance to obtain documents (for example, a certificate of origin, a health certificate, a clean report of finding, import licence) issued or transmitted in the country of delivery or import. But any cost incurred by the seller in rendering this assistance must be reimbursed to him by the buyer, according to B10. Similarly, the seller must reimburse the buyer for any assistance provided by him according to B10.

Also, the seller may be requested to provide the buyer with information relating to the goods which the buyer may require for security-related clearance of the goods.

FAS

B THE BUYER'S OBLIGATIONS

B1 General obligations of the buyer

The buyer must pay the price of the goods as provided in the contract of sale.

Any document referred to in B1-B10 may be an equivalent electronic record or procedure if agreed between the parties or customary.

Comments The buyer must pay the price agreed in the contrcat of sale. B1 constitutes a reminder of this main obligation, which correspond with the seller's obligation to provide the goods in conformity with the contract of sale, as stipulated in A1.

B2 Licences, authorizations, security clearances and other formalities

Where applicable, it is up to the buyer to obtain, at its own risk and expense, any import licence or other official authorization and carry out all customs formalities for the import of the goods and for their transport through any country.

Comments The seller, according to A2, makes the goods available to the buyer in the country of shipment cleared for export, but it is for the buyer to do whatever is necessary with respect to the clearance of the goods for transit and import. A prohibition of import, governmental or otherwise, will not relieve the buyer from his obligation under the contract of sale. However, contracts of sale frequently contain "relief clauses" to the benefit of both parties in such cases. These clauses may stipulate that the affected party will be given the benefit of an extension of time to fulfil his obligation or, under the worst circumstances, the right to avoid the contract. It may also be possible to obtain such relief under the law applicable to the contract of sale.

B3 Contracts of carriage and insurance

a)   Contract of carriage
The buyer must contract, at its own expense for the carriage of the goods from the named port of shipment, except where the contract of carriage is made by the seller as provided for in A3 a).

b)   Contract of insurance
The buyer has no obligation to the seller to make a contract of insurance.

Comments In a strictly legal sense, the buyer under FAS has no obligation to the seller to contract for carriage except as required for the buyer to take delivery according to B4. This, however, still obliges the buyer to name and arrange for a vessel, so that the seller can deliver the goods alongside. Indeed, in practice the buyer normally arranges for carriage in his own interest and does not let the ship remain in the port of loading. In this regard, FAS stipulates that the buyer must "contract at its own expense for the carriage of the goods from the named port of shipment".

FAS

B4   Taking delivery

The buyer must take delivery of the goods when they have been delivered as envisaged in A4.

Comments   The buyer must take delivery of the goods when they have been placed alongside the vessel as stipulated in A4. His failure to do so would not relieve him from his obligation to pay the price and could further result in a premature passing of the risk of loss of or damage to the goods or make him liable to pay additional costs according to B5 and B6.

B5   Transfer of risks

The buyer bears all risks of loss of or damage to the goods from the time they have been delivered as envisaged in A4.

If
a)   the buyer fails to give notice in accordance with B7; or

b)   the vessel nominated by the buyer fails to arrive on time, or fails to take the goods or closes for cargo earlier than the time notified in accordance with B7;

then the buyer bears all risks of loss of or damage to the goods from the agreed date or the expiry date of the agreed period for delivery, provided that the goods have been clearly identified as the contract goods.

Comments   According to the main rule, while the seller under A5 bears the risk of loss of or damage to the goods until the delivery point, the buyer has to bear the risk thereafter. The delivery point is different under the different terms. In EXW and all D-terms the goods are simply placed "at the disposal of the buyer" at the relevant point, while under the F- and C-terms the delivery point is related to the handing over of the goods to the carrier in the country of dispatch or shipment (see the comments to A4 of these terms). In the terms used for goods intended to be carried by sea, reference is made to delivery alongside the named vessel (FAS) or delivery onboard the vessel (FOB, CFR, CIF).

Premature passing of risk

The buyer's failure to notify the seller of the vessel name, loading place and required delivery time may result in a premature passing of the risk, as it cannot be accepted that the buyer should be able to delay the delivery and passing of the risk longer than contemplated when the contract of sale was made. Thus, his failure to notify according to B7 will cause the risk to pass "from the agreed date or the expiry date of the agreed period for delivery".

A further problem can arise if the vessel fails to arrive in time, since in these cases the goods cannot be placed alongside as contemplated. Consequently, a premature passing of the risk could occur in these circumstances. The same result could also occur if the vessel is unable to take the goods, or closes for cargo earlier than the time notified. In this latter case, the goods will be at the buyer's risk.

FAS

For the risk to pass prematurely, it is required that the goods be identified as the contract goods. When the goods have been prepared for dispatch they have also normally been appropriated to the contract goods. But a failure of the buyer to give sufficient notice of the date or period of shipment according to B7 causes the seller to defer his preparations. If so, it may not be possible to identify some goods stored at the seller's premises or in an independent cargo terminal as the contract goods on the agreed date or the expiry date of any agreed period for delivery. The risk would then not pass until the identification has been made.

B6 Allocation of costs

The buyer must pay

a) all costs relating to the goods from the time they have been delivered as envisaged in A4, except, where applicable, the costs of customs formalities necessary for export as well as all duties, taxes, and other charges payable upon export as referred to in A6 b);

b) any additional costs incurred, either because:
   (i) the buyer has failed to give appropriate notice in accordance with B7, or
   (ii) the vessel nominated by the buyer fails to arrive on time, is unable to take the goods, or closes for cargo earlier than the time notified in accordance with B7,

   provided that the goods have been clearly identified as the contract goods; and

c) where applicable, all duties, taxes and other charges, as well as the costs of carrying out customs formalities payable upon import of the goods and the costs for their transport through any country.

Comments   Under FAS the seller fulfils his delivery obligation according to A4 by placing the goods alongside the vessel. The buyer must pay the freight and other costs occurring subsequently.

Since under FAS the buyer has to contract for carriage and nominate the ship, he also has to pay any additional costs incurred because the vessel named by him has failed to arrive on time, or will be unable to take the goods, or will close for cargo earlier than the notified time (see the corresponding rule for the premature passing of the risk in the comments to B5).

The failure of the buyer to notify the seller according to B7 will not only cause the risk of loss of or damage to the goods to pass prematurely, but will also make the buyer liable to pay any additional costs caused thereby, for example, extra costs for storage and insurance.

For the buyer to be liable for additional costs according to B6, the goods to which these costs relate must be identifiable as the contract goods (see the comments on "identification" under B5).

FAS

B7   Notices to the seller

The buyer must give the seller sufficient notice of the vessel name, loading point and, where necessary, the selected delivery time within the agreed period.

Comments   As discussed in the comments to B5 and B6, the failure of the buyer to notify the seller of the name of the vessel, the loading place and the required delivery time may cause the risk of the loss of or damage to the goods to pass before the goods have been delivered according to A4, and also make the buyer liable to pay any additional costs the seller incurs as a result of the buyer's failure.

B8   Proof of delivery

The buyer must accept the proof of delivery provided as envisaged in A8.

Comments   The buyer must accept the seller's proof of delivery if the proof is adequate. If the buyer nevertheless rejects it (for example, by instructions to a bank not to pay the seller under a documentary credit), he commits a breach of contract which will give the seller remedies for the breach available under the contract of sale (for example, a right to cancel the contract or to claim damages for breach). However, the buyer is not obliged to accept a document which does not provide adequate proof of delivery. If there are notations on the document showing that the goods are defective or that they have been provided in less than the agreed quantity, the document is then considered to be "unclean".

B9   Inspection of goods

The buyer must pay the costs of any mandatory pre-shipment inspection, except when such inspection is mandated by the authorities of the country of export.

Comments   As noted in the comments to A9, the buyer has to pay for any costs of checking the goods, unless the contract determines that these costs should be wholly or partly borne by the seller. In some cases, the contract may provide that the costs should be borne by the seller if the inspection reveals that the goods do not conform with the contract.

FAS

In some countries, where import licences or permission to obtain foreign currency for the payment of the price may be required, the authorities may demand an inspection of the goods before shipment to ensure that the goods are in conformity with the contract. (This is usually called pre-shipment inspection, PSI.) If this is the case, the inspection is normally arranged by instructions from the authorities to an inspection company, which they appoint.

The costs following from this inspection have to be paid by the authorities. Any reimbursement to the authorities for the inspection costs, however, must be made by the buyer, unless the inspection has been mandated by the authorities of the contract of export or otherwise specifically agreed between the buyer and the seller.

B10 Assistance with information and related costs

The buyer must, in a timely manner, advise the seller of any security information requirements so that the seller may comply with A10.

The buyer must reimburse the seller for all costs and charges incurred by the seller in providing or rendering assistance in obtaining documents and information as envisaged in A10.

The buyer must, where applicable, in a timely manner, provide to or render assistance in obtaining for the seller, at the seller's request, risk and expense, any documents and information, including security-related information, that the seller needs for the transport and export of the goods and for their transport through any country.

Comments As discussed in the comments to A10, the seller has to render the buyer assistance in obtaining the documents or electronic messages and information which may be required for the transit, import and security-related clearance of the goods. However, this assistance is rendered at the buyer's risk and expense. Therefore, B10 stipulates that the buyer must pay all costs and charges incurred in obtaining these documents or electronic messages. He will also have to reimburse the seller for the seller's costs in rendering his assistance in these matters.

FREE ON BOARD
FOB (insert named port of shipment) the Incoterms® 2010 rules

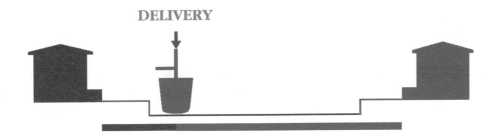

DELIVERY

GUIDANCE NOTE

This rule is to be used only for sea or inland waterway transport.

"Free on Board" means that the seller delivers the goods on board the vessel nominated by the buyer at the named port of shipment or procures the goods already so delivered. The risk of loss of or damage to the goods passes when the goods are on board the vessel, and the buyer bears all costs from that moment onwards.

The seller is required either to deliver the goods on board the vessel or to procure goods already so delivered for shipment. The reference to "procure" here caters for multiple sales down a chain ('string sales'), particularly common in the commodity trades.

FOB may not be appropriate where goods are handed over to the carrier before they are on board the vessel, for example goods in containers, which are typically delivered at a terminal. In such situations, the FCA rule should be used.

FOB requires the seller to clear the goods for export, where applicable. However, the seller has no obligation to clear the goods for import, pay any import duty or carry out any import customs formalities.

FOB

A   THE SELLER'S OBLIGATIONS

A1   General obligations of the seller

The seller must provide the goods and the commercial invoice in conformity with the contract of sale and any other evidence of conformity that may be required by the contract.

Any document referred to in A1-A10 may be an equivalent electronic record or procedure if agreed between the parties or customary.

Comments   The seller must provide the goods in conformity with the contract. It is also usual practice that the seller, in order to be paid, has to invoice the buyer. In addition, the seller must submit any other evidence stipulated in the contract itself that the goods conform with the contract.

This text only serves as a reminder of the seller's main obligation under the contract of sale.

A2   Licences, authorizations, security clearances and other formalities

Where applicable, the seller must obtain, at its own risk and expense, any export licence or other official authorization and carry out all customs formalities necessary for the export of the goods.

Comments   The seller has to clear the goods for export and assume any risk or expense which this involves. Consequently, if there is an export prohibition or if there are particular taxes on the export of the goods – and if there are other government-imposed requirements which may render the export of the goods more expensive than contemplated – all of these risks and costs must be borne by the seller. However, contracts of sale usually contain particular provisions which the seller may invoke to protect himself in the event of these contingencies. Under CISG and corresponding provisions in various national Sale of Goods Acts, unforeseen or reasonably unforeseeable export prohibitions may relieve the seller from his obligations under the contract of sale.

A3   Contracts of carriage and insurance

a)   Contract of carriage
The seller has no obligation to the buyer to make a contract of carriage. However, if requested by the buyer or if it is commercial practice and the buyer does not give an instruction to the contrary in due time, the seller may contract for carriage on usual terms at the buyer's risk and expense. In either case, the seller may decline to make the contract of carriage and, if it does, shall promptly notify the buyer.

b)   Contract of insurance
The seller has no obligation to the buyer to make a contract of insurance. However, the seller must provide the buyer, at the buyer's request, risk, and expense (if any), with information that the buyer needs for obtaining insurance.

Comments   The seller has no obligation to contract for carriage and would not be requested to do so if the FOB term is used for the carriage of full ship loads of bulk commodities. Nevertheless, the seller may contract for carriage at the buyer's risk and expense if it is commercial practice or if he is requested by the buyer to do so (compare the same stipulation in FCA A 3 (a)).

A4   Delivery

The seller must deliver the goods either by placing them on board the vessel nominated by the buyer at the loading point, if any, indicated by the buyer at the named port of shipment or by procuring the goods so delivered. In either case, the seller must deliver the goods on the agreed date or within the agreed period and in the manner customary at the port.

If no specific loading point has been indicated by the buyer, the seller may select the point within the named port of shipment that best suits its purpose.

Comments   The seller's obligation to place the goods onboard the ship in due time is the essence of the FOB term. Through the centuries the ship's rail has assumed an inordinate importance as an imaginary border between the seller's and the buyer's territory. But using the ship's rail as a point for the division of functions, costs and risks between the parties is not, and never has been, quite appropriate. To divide the functions between the parties while the goods are swinging across the ship's rail seems impracticable. In the words of an often-cited English court decision: "Only the most enthusiastic lawyer could watch with satisfaction the spectacle of liabilities shifting uneasily as the cargo sways at the end of a derrick across a notional perpendicular projecting from the ship's rail." (Pyrene v. Scindia Navigation [1954] 2 Q.B. 402 at p. 419).

The reference in FOB A4 to "the manner customary at the port" highlights the problem of using the passing of the ship's rail as the guiding factor in practice. The parties in these circumstances will have to follow the custom of the port regarding the actual measures to be taken in delivering the goods onboard. Usually the task is performed by stevedoring companies, and the practical problem normally lies in deciding who should bear the costs of their services.

The seller's obligation to place the goods on board may be extended by a phrase added to FOB, for example "FOB stowed" or "FOB stowed and trimmed". Though these additional words are primarily intended to make sure the seller has to pay all of the loading costs, it is doubtful whether they are also intended to move the "delivery point" to the extent that the seller would be considered to have failed to fulfil his delivery obligation until the loading, stowing and trimming have been completed (see Understanding the Incoterms rules page 15) and comments to FOB A5, A6 and FOB B5, B6).

When the goods are sold in transit, further sellers would not physically deliver the goods on board but would sell them procured delivered on board by the first seller.

FOB

A5   Transfer of risks

The seller bears all risks of loss of or damage to the goods until they have been delivered in accordance with A4 with the exception of loss or damage in the circumstances described in B5.

Comments   All of the Incoterms rules are based on the same principle that the risk of loss of or damage to the goods is transferred from the seller to the buyer when the seller has fulfilled his delivery obligation according to A4.

All of the Incoterms rules, in conformity with the general principle of CISG, connect the transfer of the risk with the delivery of the goods and not with other circumstances, such as the passing of ownership or the time of the conclusion of the contract. Neither the Incoterms rules nor CISG deals with transfer of title to the goods or other property rights with respect to the goods.

The passing of risk for loss of or damage to the goods concerns the risk of fortuitous events (accidents) and does not include loss or damage caused by the seller or the buyer, for example through inadequate packing or marking of the goods. Therefore, even if damage occurs subsequent to the transfer of the risk, the seller may still be responsible if the damage could be attributed to the fact that the goods were not delivered in conformity with the contract (see A1 and the comments to A9).

A5 of all of the Incoterms rules contain the phrase "with the exception of loss or damage in circumstances described in B5". This means that there are exceptions to the main rule in the circumstances described in B5 which may result in a premature passing of the risk because of the buyer's failure properly to fulfil his obligations (see the comments to B5).

A6   Allocation of costs

The seller must pay
a)   all costs relating to the goods until they have been delivered in accordance with A4, other than those payable by the buyer as envisaged in B6; and

b)   where applicable, the costs of customs formalities necessary for export, as well as all duties, taxes and other charges payable upon export.

Comments   As is the case with the transfer of the risk of loss of or damage to the goods, all of the Incoterms rules follow the same rule, that the division of costs occurs at the delivery point. All costs occurring before the seller has fulfilled his obligation to deliver according to A4 are for his account, while further costs are for the account of the buyer (see the comments to B6). This rule is made subject to the provisions of B6, which indicates that the buyer may have to bear additional costs incurred by his failure to nominate a carrier that takes the goods into his charge or to give appropriate notice to the seller.

FOB

The seller must pay the costs of customs formalities necessary for export as well as all duties, taxes and other official charges payable upon export.

A7 Notices to the buyer

The seller must, at the buyer's risk and expense, give the buyer sufficient notice either that the goods have been delivered in accordance with A4 or that the vessel has failed to take the goods within the time agreed.

Comments The seller must give the buyer sufficient notice concerning when the goods have been delivered on board or if the carrier nominated by the buyer fails to take the goods into its charge. There is no stipulation in the Incoterms rules spelling out the consequences of the seller's failure to give this notice. But it follows from the Incoterms rules that the seller's failure constitutes a breach of contract. This means that the seller could be held responsible for the breach according to the law applicable to the contract of sale.

A8 Delivery document

The seller must provide the buyer, at the seller's expense, with the usual proof that the goods have been delivered in accordance with A4.

Unless such proof is a transport document, the seller must provide assistance to the buyer, at the buyer's request, risk and expense, in obtaining a transport document.

Comments Since the seller has to hand over the goods for carriage, the carrier normally gives him a receipt which is usually identical to the transport document. If so, that document serves not only as evidence of the contract of carriage – which under F-terms is made by or on behalf of the buyer – but also as evidence of the delivery of the goods to the carrier.

If, however, the seller receives a document other than the transport document – for example, a so-called mate's receipt when the goods have been loaded on board a ship chartered by the buyer – he should, upon the buyer's request, assist the buyer to obtain the transport document. This assistance is rendered at the buyer's risk and expense.

A9 Checking – packaging – marking

The seller must pay the costs of those checking operations (such as checking quality, measuring, weighing, counting) that are necessary for the purpose of delivering the goods in accordance with A4, as well as the costs of any pre-shipment inspection mandated by the authority of the country of export.

The seller must, at its own expense, package the goods, unless it is usual for the particular trade to transport the type of goods sold unpackaged. The seller may package the goods in the manner appropriate for their transport, unless the buyer has notified the seller of specific packaging requirements before the contract of sale is concluded. Packaging is to be marked appropriately.

FOB

Comments   The goods must also be adequately packed. But the seller may not know the buyer's intentions with respect to the ultimate destination. There is a considerable difference between a short journey to an adjoining country and an intercontinental carriage by sea, which may expose the goods to the risk of breakage or corrosion from humidity and condensation.

A10   Assistance with information and related costs

The seller must, where applicable, in a timely manner, provide to or render assistance in obtaining for the buyer, at the buyer's request, risk and expense, any documents and information, including security-related information, that the buyer needs for the import of the goods and/or for their transport to the final destination.

The seller must reimburse the buyer for all costs and charges incurred by the buyer in providing or rendering assistance in obtaining documents and information as envisaged in B10.

Comments   It is for the buyer to do whatever is necessary with respect to transit and import clearance. He may also need the seller's assistance to obtain documents (for example, a certificate of origin, a health certificate, a clean report of finding, an import licence) issued or transmitted in the country of shipment and/or origin. But any cost incurred by the seller in rendering this assistance must be reimbursed to him by the buyer, according to B10. Similarly, the seller must reimburse the buyer for any assistance provided by him according to B10.

Also, the seller may be requested to provide the buyer with information relating to the goods which the buyer may require for security-clearance.

FOB

B THE BUYER'S OBLIGATIONS

B1 General obligations of the buyer

The buyer must pay the price of the goods as provided in the contract of sale.

Any document referred to in B1-B10 may be an equivalent electronic record or procedure if agreed between the parties or customary.

Comments The buyer must pay the price agreed in the contract of sale. B1 constitutes a reminder of this main obligation, which corresponds with the seller's obligation to provide the goods in conformity with the contract of sale, as stipulated in A1.

B2 Licences, authorizations, security clearances and other formalities

Where applicable, it is up to the buyer to obtain, at its own risk and expense, any import licence or other official authorization and carry out all customs formalities for the import of the goods and for their transport through any country.

Comments The buyer must take care of the import and security clearance and bear any costs and risks in connection with it. Therefore, an import prohibition will not relieve the buyer of his obligation to pay for the goods, unless there is a particular "relief clause" in the contract of sale which he invokes to obtain this relief. Such clauses may provide for the extension of time or the right to avoid the contract under the applicable law (see the comments to A2).

B3 Contracts of carriage and insurance

a) Contract of carriage
The buyer must contract, at its own expense for the carriage of the goods from the named port of shipment, except where the contract of carriage is made by the seller as provided for in A3 a).

b) Contract of insurance
The buyer has no obligation to the seller to make a contract of insurance.

Comments The buyer has to contract for carriage so that the goods can be placed on board. However, the seller – as in FCA A3 – may assist the buyer in contracting for carriage (see the comments to A3). If so, the assistance is rendered at the buyer's risk and expense.

B4 Taking delivery

The buyer must take delivery of the goods when they have been delivered as envisaged in A4.

FOB

Comments   The buyer must take delivery of the goods when they have been placed on board the vessel named by the buyer at the named port of shipment. His failure to do so will not relieve him of his obligation to pay the price and could further result in a premature passing of the risk of loss of or damage to the goods, or make him liable to pay additional costs according to B5 and B6.

B5   Transfer of risk

The buyer bears all risks of loss of or damage to the goods from the time they have been delivered as envisaged in A4.

If

a)   the buyer fails to notify the nomination of a vessel in accordance with B7; or

b)   the vessel nominated by the buyer fails to arrive on time to enable the seller to comply with A4, is unable to take the goods, or closes for cargo earlier than the time notified in accordance with B7;

then, the buyer bears all risks of loss of or damage to the goods:
(i)   from the agreed date, or in the absence of an agreed date,

(ii)   from the date notified by the seller under A7 within the agreed period, or, if no such date has been notified,

(iii)   from the expiry date of any agreed period for delivery,

provided that the goods have been clearly identified as the contract goods.

Comments   According to the main rule, while the seller under A5 bears the risk of loss of or damage to the goods until the delivery point, the buyer has to bear the risk thereafter. The delivery point is different under the different terms. In EXW and all D-terms, the goods are simply placed "at the disposal of the buyer" at the relevant point, while under the F- and C-terms the delivery point is related to the handing over of the goods to the carrier in the country of dispatch or shipment (see the comments to A4 of these terms). In the terms used for goods intended to be carried by sea, reference is made to delivery alongside the named vessel (FAS) or delivery onboard the vessel (FOB, CFR, CIF).

Premature passing of risk

The buyer's failure to notify the seller of the vessel name, loading place and required delivery time may result in a premature passing of the risk, as it cannot be accepted that the buyer should be able to delay the delivery and passing of the risk longer than contemplated when the contract of sale was made. Thus, his failure to notify according to B7 will cause the risk to pass from the agreed date or the expiry date of any agreed period stipulated for delivery.

FOB

A further problem could arise if the vessel is not named or if it fails to arrive in time, since then the goods cannot be placed onboard as contemplated. Moreover, a premature passing of the risk could occur in these circumstances. B5 also stipulates that the same could result if the vessel is "unable to take the goods, or closes for cargo earlier than the time notified in accordance with B7".

For risk to pass prematurely, it is required that the goods be identified as the contract goods. When the goods have been prepared for dispatch they have also usually been identified as the contract goods. But a failure of the buyer to give sufficient notice of the date or period of shipment according to B7 causes the seller to defer his preparations. If so, it may not be possible to identify some goods stored at the seller's premises, in an independent cargo terminal, or on the quay as the contract goods on the agreed date or the expiry date of any agreed period stipulated for delivery. The risk would then not pass until the identification has been made.

B6   Allocation of costs

The buyer must pay
a)   all costs relating to the goods from the time they have been delivered as envisaged in A4, except, where applicable, the costs of customs formalities necessary for export, as well as all duties, taxes and other charges payable upon export as referred to in A6 b);

b)   any additional costs incurred, either because:
   (i)   the buyer has failed to give appropriate notice in accordance with B7, or
   (ii) the vessel nominated by the buyer fails to arrive on time, is unable to take the goods, or closes for cargo earlier than the time notified in accordance with B7,

provided that the goods have been clearly identified as the contract goods; and

c)   where applicable, all duties, taxes and other charges, as well as the costs of carrying out customs formalities payable upon import of the goods and the costs for their transport through any country.

Comments   Under FOB the seller fulfils his delivery obligation according to A4 by placing the goods onboard the vessel at the loading place.

Since under FOB the buyer has to contract for carriage and nominate the ship, he also has to pay any additional costs incurred because the vessel named by him has failed to arrive on time, or will be unable to take the goods, or will close for cargo earlier than the notified time (see the corresponding rule for the premature passing of the risk in the comments to B5).

The failure of the buyer to notify the seller according to B7 would not only cause the risk of loss of or damage to the goods to pass prematurely but would also make the buyer liable to pay any additional costs caused thereby, for example, extra costs for storage and insurance.

FOB

For the buyer to be liable for additional costs according to B6, the goods to which these costs relate must be identifiable as the contract goods (see the comments on "identification" under B5).

Under FOB, because the buyer has to clear the goods for import, he has to pay "all duties, taxes and other official charges as well as the costs of carrying out customs formalities" and to reimburse the seller for any assistance the seller renders him in this regard.

B7   Notices to the seller

The buyer must give the seller sufficient notice of the vessel name, loading point and, where necessary, the selected delivery time within the agreed period.

Comments   As discussed in the comments to B5 and B6, the failure of the buyer to notify the seller of the name of the vessel, the loading place and the required delivery time may cause the risk of the loss of or damage to the goods to pass before the goods have been delivered according to A4 and also make the buyer liable to pay any additional costs the seller incurs as a result of the buyer's failure.

B8   Proof of delivery

The buyer must accept the proof of delivery provided as envisaged in A8.

Comments   The buyer must accept the seller's proof of delivery if the proof is adequate. If the buyer nevertheless rejects it (for example, by instructions to a bank not to pay the seller under a documentary credit), he commits a breach of contract which will give the seller remedies for the breach available under the contract of sale (for example, a right to cancel the contract or to claim damages for breach). However, the buyer is not obliged to accept a document which does not provide adequate proof of delivery. If there are notations on the document showing that the goods are defective or that they have been provided in less than the agreed quantity, the document is then considered to be "unclean".

FOB

B9   Inspection of goods

The buyer must pay the costs of any mandatory pre-shipment inspection, except when such inspection is mandated by the authorities of the country of export.

Comments   As noted in the comments to A9, the buyer has to pay for any costs of checking the goods, unless the contract determines that these costs should be wholly or partly borne by the seller. In some cases, the contract may provide that the costs should be borne by the seller if the inspection reveals that the goods do not conform with the contract. In some countries, where import licences or permission to obtain foreign currency for the payment of the price may be required, the authorities may demand an inspection of the goods before shipment, to ensure that the goods are in conformity with the contract. (This is usually called pre-shipment inspection, PSI.) If this is the case, the inspection is normally arranged by instructions from the authorities to an inspection company, which they appoint. The costs following from this inspection have to be paid by the authorities.

Any reimbursement to the authorities for the inspection costs, however, must be made by the buyer, unless the inspection has been mandated by the authorities in the country of export or specifically agreed between the buyer and the seller.

B10   Assistance with information and related costs

The buyer must, in a timely manner, advise the seller of any security information requirements so that the seller may comply with A10.

The buyer must reimburse the seller for all costs and charges incurred by the seller in providing or rendering assistance in obtaining documents and information as envisaged in A10.

The buyer must, where applicable, in a timely manner, provide to or render assistance in obtaining for the seller, at the seller's request, risk and expense, any documents and information, including security-related information, that the seller needs for the transport and export of the goods and for their transport through any country.

Comments   As discussed in the comments to A10, the seller has to render the buyer assistance in obtaining the documents or electronic messages and information which may be required for the transit, import and security-related clearance of the goods. However, this assistance is rendered at the buyer's risk and expense. Therefore, B10 stipulates that the buyer must pay all costs and charges incurred in obtaining these documents or electronic messages. He will also have to reimburse the seller for the seller's costs in rendering his assistance.

COST AND FREIGHT
CFR (insert named port of destination) the Incoterms® 2010 rules

DELIVERY

GUIDANCE NOTE

This rule is to be used only for sea or inland waterway transport.

"Cost and Freight" means that the seller delivers the goods on board the vessel or procures the goods already so delivered. The risk of loss of or damage to the goods passes when the goods are on board the vessel. The seller must contract for and pay the costs and freight necessary to bring the goods to the named port of destination.

When CPT, CIP, CFR or CIF are used, the seller fulfils its obligation to deliver when it hands the goods over to the carrier in the manner specified in the chosen rule and not when the goods reach the place of destination.

This rule has two critical points, because risk passes and costs are transferred at different places. While the contract will always specify a destination port, it might not specify the port of shipment, which is where risk passes to the buyer. If the shipment port is of particular interest to the buyer, the parties are well advised to identify it as precisely as possible in the contract.

The parties are well advised to identify as precisely as possible the point at the agreed port of destination, as the costs to that point are for the account of the seller. The seller is advised to procure contracts of carriage that match this choice precisely. If the seller incurs costs under its contract of carriage related to unloading at the specified point at the port of destination, the seller is not entitled to recover such costs from the buyer unless otherwise agreed between the parties.

The seller is required either to deliver the goods on board the vessel or to procure goods already so delivered for shipment to the destination. In addition, the seller is required either to make a contract of carriage or to procure such a contract. The reference to "procure" here caters for multiple sales down a chain ('string sales'), particularly common in the commodity trades.

CFR may not be appropriate where goods are handed over to the carrier before they are on board the vessel, for example goods in containers, which are typically delivered at a terminal. In such circumstances, the CPT rule should be used.

CFR requires the seller to clear the goods for export, where applicable. However, the seller has no obligation to clear the goods for import, pay any import duty or carry out any import customs formalities.

CFR

A   THE SELLER'S OBLIGATIONS

A1   General obligations of the seller

The seller must provide the goods and the commercial invoice in conformity with the contract of sale and any other evidence of conformity that may be required by the contract.

Any document referred to in A1-A10 may be an equivalent electronic record or procedure if agreed between the parties or customary.

Comments   The seller must provide the goods in conformity with the contract. It is also usual practice that the seller, in order to be paid, has to invoice the buyer. In addition, the seller must submit any other evidence stipulated in the contract itself that the goods conform with that contract.

This text only serves as a reminder of the seller's main obligation under the contract of sale.

A2   Licences, authorizations, security clearances and other formalities

Where applicable, the seller must obtain, at its own risk and expense, any export licence or other official authorization and carry out all customs formalities necessary for the export of the goods.

Comments   The seller has to clear the goods for export and assume any risk or expense which this involves. Consequently, if there is an export prohibition or if there are particular taxes on the export of the goods – and if there are other government-imposed requirements which may render the export of the goods more expensive than contemplated – all of these risks and costs must be borne by the seller. However, contracts of sale usually contain particular provisions which the seller may invoke to protect himself in the event of these contingencies. Under CISG and corresponding provisions in various national Sale of Goods Acts, unforeseen or reasonably unforeseeable export prohibitions may relieve the seller from his obligations under the contract of sale.

A3   Contracts of carriage and insurance

a)   Contract of carriage
The seller must contract or procure a contract for the carriage of the goods from the agreed point of delivery, if any, at the place of delivery to the named port of destination or, if agreed, any point at that port. The contract of carriage must be made on usual terms at the seller's expense and provide for carriage by the usual route in a vessel of the type normally used for the transport of the type of goods sold.

b)   Contract of insurance
The seller has no obligation to the buyer to make a contract of insurance. However, the seller must provide the buyer, at the buyer's request, risk, and expense (if any), with information that the buyer needs for obtaining insurance.

Comments   Although the CFR seller fulfils his obligations by shipping the goods (see section A4 below), he has to arrange and pay for the contract of carriage to the named port of destination. Unless the contract contains specific stipulations as to the nature of the contract of carriage, the seller may contract "on usual terms" and for carriage "by the usual route".

The CFR term can be used only for sea and inland waterway transport.

The vessel should be of a kind normally used for the transport of the goods of the contract description. It may be unacceptable, for example, to arrange for the carriage of containerized cargo on deck if the ship is not designed for carriage of containers, since the carriage may then expose the cargo to additional risks and even render the insurance cover ineffective.

Differences between goods carried in liner trade and bulk cargoes carried in chartered ships

There is a considerable difference between goods normally carried in so-called liner trade and bulk cargoes, which are normally carried in chartered ships. In most cases, it should be clear what kind of carriage the seller should arrange, since break bulk cargo now is normally containerized or otherwise carried by regular transport in transportation units (flats, pallets, etc.) from port to port.

In these cases, the carrier frequently undertakes to carry the goods, not only from port to port but from an interior point in the country of shipment to an interior point in the country of destination. It is then inappropriate to use the CFR term, and the parties are advised to use the CPT term instead (see the comments on CPT).

When it is uncertain whether the goods should be carried by regular shipping lines or by chartered ships, it is advisable that the matter be specifically dealt with in the contract of sale. It often happens that carriage by chartered ships is permitted, but that the carriage must nevertheless be contracted for on "liner terms". If so, the freight costs would ordinarily include loading and unloading costs. A charter party, however, may well provide that these costs should be "free" to the carrier. This is the so-called FIO-clause – which stands for "Free In" and "Free Out".

In any case, the expression "liner terms" is vague and ambiguous, and it is recommended that the parties specifically deal with the conditions of the contract of carriage in the contract of sale when carriage is not to be arranged by regular, well-known shipping lines.

A4   Delivery

The seller must deliver the goods either by placing them on board the vessel or by procuring the goods so delivered. In either case, the seller must deliver the goods on the agreed date or within the agreed period and in the manner customary at the port.

CFR

Comments   As noted above, delivery under the CFR term occurs at the moment the goods are placed on board the vessel at the port of shipment. Thus, the CFR term, like the FOB term, is evidence of a shipment contract. Since the port of destination is mentioned after CFR, for example "CFR London" by a seller in New York, the legal nature of a CFR contract is frequently misunderstood by traders. This is quite understandable, because the critical point where the seller fulfils his obligation is usually omitted. CFR contracts do not usually provide that shipment shall take place at a particular port, for example "CFR London shipment from New York", since this would restrict the seller's options to ship the goods from alternative ports of shipment.

It must be emphasized that the CFR term, as distinguished from the FOB term, contains two critical points. The first represents the point at which delivery takes place upon shipment according to A4, namely when the goods are placed on board the vessel. The second represents the point at destination, up to which the seller shall arrange for carriage of the goods.

Avoid stipulating date of delivery at destination

One essential point of the CFR term is sometimes ignored in commercial practice. When, for example, the contract stipulates that delivery should take place not later than a specified date at destination (for example "arrival London not later than ..."), this kind of stipulation defeats the object of the CFR term and leaves room for different interpretations of the contract.

One option would be to interpret this stipulation to mean that the parties have agreed on an arrival contract rather than a shipment contract. If that is the case, the seller is not considered to have fulfilled the contract until the goods have actually arrived at destination. If in such a case the goods are delayed because of casualties after shipment or are even lost, the seller would not be free from his obligations under the contract of sale unless, of course, he has the protection of a particular relief clause or force majeure clause in the contract of sale. Such a contract is, of course, different from a CFR contract under which the seller fulfils the contract in the port of shipment.

The other option would be to interpret the stipulation in a way which would allow the basic nature of the CFR contract to supersede the particular wording the parties use, even in cases when the parties have stipulated that the goods should arrive before a particular date at destination. If that is done, the contract would be interpreted to mean that the goods must be placed onboard the ship at such time as would normally suffice for its arrival at destination at the stipulated date.

Since it is uncertain which of these options will be used to interpret CFR with this or similar language added, the parties are strongly advised to abstain from using such additions.

When the goods are sold in transit, further sellers would not physically deliver the goods on board but would sell them procured delivered on board by the first seller.

CFR

A5   Transfer of risks

The seller bears all risks of loss of or damage to the goods until they have been delivered in accordance with A4, with the exception of loss or damage in the circumstances described in B5.

Comments   All of the Incoterms rules are based on the same principle that the risk of loss of or damage to the goods is transferred from the seller to the buyer when the seller has fulfilled his delivery obligation according to A4.

All of the Incoterms rules, in conformity with the general principle of CISG, connect the transfer of the risk with the delivery of the goods and not with other circumstances, such as the passing of ownership or the time of the conclusion of the contract. As noted, neither the Incoterms rules nor CISG deals with transfer of title to the goods or other property rights with respect to the goods.

The passing of risk of loss of or damage to the goods concerns the risk of fortuitous events (accidents) and does not include loss or damage caused by the seller or the buyer, for example, inadequate packing or marking of the goods. Therefore, even if damage occurs subsequent to the transfer of the risk, the seller may still be responsible if the damage could be attributed to the fact that the goods were not delivered in conformity with the contract (see A1 and the comments to A9).

A5 of all of the Incoterms rules contain the phrase "with the exception of loss or damage in the circumstances described in B5". This means that there are exceptions to the main rule concerning the passing of risk under the circumstances mentioned in B5, which may result in a premature passing of the risk because of the buyer's failure properly to fulfil his obligations (see the comments to B5).

A6   Allocation of costs

The seller must pay

a)   all costs relating to the goods until they have been delivered in accordance with A4, other than those payable by the buyer as envisaged in B6;

b)   the freight and all other costs resulting from A3 a), including the costs of loading the goods on board and any charges for unloading at the agreed port of discharge that were for the seller's account under the contract of carriage; and

c)   where applicable, the costs of customs formalities necessary for export as well as all duties, taxes and other charges payable upon export, and the costs for their transport through any country that were for the seller's account under the contract of carriage.

Comments   As is the case with the transfer of the risk of loss of or damage to the goods, all of the Incoterms rules follow the same rule, that the division of costs occurs at the delivery point. All costs occurring before the seller has fulfilled his obligation to deliver according to A4

CFR

are for his account, while further costs are for the account of the buyer (see the comments to B6). This rule is made subject to the provisions of B6, which indicates that the buyer may have to bear additional costs incurred by his failure to give appropriate notice to the seller.

A7 Notices to the buyer

The seller must give the buyer any notice needed in order to allow the buyer to take measures that are normally necessary to enable the buyer to take the goods.

Comments The seller must give the buyer sufficient notice that the goods have been delivered onboard the vessel, as well as other relevant information, so that the buyer can make preparations in time to take delivery according to B4. There is no stipulation in the Incoterms rules spelling out the consequences of the seller's failure to give such notice. But it follows from the Incoterms rules that the seller's failure constitutes a breach of contract. This means that the seller could be held responsible for the breach according to the law applicable to the contract of sale.

A8 Delivery document

The seller must, at its own expense, provide the buyer without delay with the usual transport document for the agreed port of destination.

This transport document must cover the contract goods, be dated within the period agreed for shipment, enable the buyer to claim the goods from the carrier at the port of destination and, unless otherwise agreed, enable the buyer to sell the goods in transit by the transfer of the document to a subsequent buyer or by notification to the carrier.

When such a transport document is issued in negotiable form and in several originals, a full set of originals must be presented to the buyer.

Comments It is of vital importance for the buyer to know that the seller has fulfilled his obligation to deliver the goods onboard the ship. The transport document usually constitutes proof of such delivery.

Non-negotiable transport documents

Generally, it suffices for the parties to refer to the "usual transport document" obtained from the carrier when the goods are handed over to him. But in maritime carriage different documents can be used. While, traditionally, negotiable bills of lading were used for carriage of goods by sea, other documents have appeared in recent years, for example transport documents which are non-negotiable and similar to those used for other modes of transport. These alternative documents have different names – "liner waybills", "ocean waybills", "cargo quay receipts", "data freight receipts" or "sea waybills". The term "sea waybill" is frequently used to include all of the various non-negotiable transport documents used for carriage of goods by sea.

CFR

Unfortunately, international conventions and most national laws do not yet provide specific regulations for these non-negotiable transport documents. (The exception is in the United States, where a non-negotiable bill of lading is recognized; this is the "straight bill of lading".) For this reason, the Comité Maritime International (CMI) in June 1990 adopted Uniform Rules for Sea Waybills. The parties should refer to these Rules in the contract of carriage to avoid any legal uncertainties stemming from the use of non-negotiable documents (see Annex 1).

Sale of goods in transit

In most cases, goods intended for carriage by regular shipping lines will not be the subject of a further sale in transit. But with respect to goods intended to be carried in chartered ships, the situation is frequently quite different. For example, when commodities are sold on the spot market, they are often sold many times before they reach destination. In these cases the negotiable bill of lading has traditionally been very important, since the possession of the paper document enables the subsequent buyer to claim the goods from the carrier at destination. He does this by surrendering the original bill of lading to the carrier in exchange for the goods.

However, when no sale of the goods in transit is intended, there is no need to use a bill of lading if the buyer's right to claim the goods from the carrier at destination is ensured by other means, such as by reference in the contract to the CMI Uniform Rules for Sea Waybills.

A buyer intending to sell the goods in transit to a subsequent buyer has the right under CFR and CIF terms to claim from his seller a document controlling the disposition of the goods, such as a negotiable bill of lading. This sale in transit can also be arranged, however, without a bill of lading. It can occur if the parties involved use a system which calls upon the carrier to follow instructions to hold the goods at the disposition of subsequent buyer(s).

EDI and the bill of lading

Section A1 takes into account that the parties may wish to engage in "paperless trading". If the parties have agreed to communicate electronically, the requirement that a paper document be presented is no longer compulsory.

The traditional bill of lading is out of step with the modern development towards paperless trading. For this reason, the CMI in June 1990 designed the "Uniform Rules for Electronic Bills of Lading", which cover situations in which EDI messages between the parties involved are intended to replace the need for the traditional paper bill of lading.

These Uniform Rules are based on EDI messages to the carrier which serve the same purpose as the words "notification to the carrier" in A8. Parties who have not agreed to use the "Uniform Rules for Electronic Bills of Lading", however, have to continue the traditional practice of requiring negotiable bills of lading. Systems – such as BOLERO –

CFR

are now being developed for EDI messages not only among the shipper, the carrier and the consignee but also among other parties such as banks, insurers, freight forwarders and customs authorities.

Risk of maritime fraud when issuing several original bills of lading

Unfortunately, the malpractice of issuing bills of lading in several originals has persisted despite the fact that it creates a considerable risk of maritime fraud. A buyer paying for the goods directly or through a bank must therefore ensure that he receives all originals of the bill of lading, if several originals have been issued.

Bills of lading issued upon request of a charterer

When bills of lading are issued upon the request of a charterer by the owner of a chartered ship, the bill of lading may refer to the terms of the charter party (for example, "all other terms as per charter party"). For these cases, the Incoterms 1990 rules stipulated that the seller must also provide a copy of the charter party. This stipulation was deleted in the Incoterms 2000 rules and does not appear in the Incoterms® 2010 rules.

A9   Checking – packaging – marking

The seller must pay the costs of those checking operations (such as checking quality, measuring, weighing, counting) that are necessary for the purpose of delivering the goods in accordance with A4, as well as the costs of any pre-shipment inspection mandated by the authority of the country of export.

The seller must, at its own expense, package the goods, unless it is usual for the particular trade to transport the type of goods sold unpackaged. The seller may package the goods in the manner appropriate for their transport, unless the buyer has notified the seller of specific packaging requirements before the contract of sale is concluded. Packaging is to be marked appropriately.

Comments It is necessary for the buyer to ensure that the seller has duly fulfilled his obligation with respect to the condition of the goods. This is particularly important if the buyer is called upon to pay for the goods before he has received and checked them. However, the seller has no duty to arrange and pay for inspection of the goods before shipment, unless this is mandated by the authorites in the country of export or has been specifically agreed in the contract of sale.

The goods must also be adequately packed. Since the seller arranges the carriage, he is in a good position to decide the packing required for the transport of the goods. However, if he knows the ultimate destination and circumstances relating to oncarriage he may be required to pack the goods accordingly. The goods should also be marked in accordance with applicable standards and regulations.

CFR

A10   Assistance with information and related costs

The seller must, where applicable, in a timely manner, provide to or render assistance in obtaining for the buyer, at the buyer's request, risk and expense, any documents and information, including security-related information, that the buyer needs for the import of the goods and/or for their transport to the final destination.

The seller must reimburse the buyer for all costs and charges incurred by the buyer in providing or rendering assistance in obtaining documents and information as envisaged in B10.

Comments   The seller has the obligation to clear the goods for export, but he has no obligation after shipment to bear any costs or risks connected either with the transit through another country or with import clearance of the goods at destination. However, he has the duty to render assistance to the buyer in obtaining any documents (for example, a certificate of origin, a health certificate, a clean report of findings, an import licence) or equivalent electronic messages and information which may be required for these purposes. The buyer, however, must reimburse the seller for any expenses which the seller might have incurred in connection with this assistance. Moreover, if something goes wrong, the buyer will have to assume the risk.

Also, the seller may be requested to provide the buyer with such information relating to the goods as the buyer may require for security-related clearance of the goods.

CFR

B   THE BUYER'S OBLIGATIONS

B1   General obligations of the buyer

The buyer must pay the price of the goods as provided in the contract of sale.

Any document referred to in B1-B10 may be an equivalent electronic record or procedure if agreed between the parties or customary.

Comments   The buyer must pay the price agreed in the contract of sale. B1 constitutes a reminder of this main obligation, which corresponds with the seller's obligation to provide the goods in conformity with the contract of sale, as stipulated in A1.

B2   Licences, authorizations, security clearances and other formalities

Where applicable, it is up to the buyer to obtain, at its own risk and expense, any import licence or other official authorization and carry out all customs formalities for the import of the goods and for their transport through any country.

Comments   The buyer must take care of the import and security clearance and bear any costs and risks in connection with it. Therefore, an import prohibition will not relieve the buyer of his obligation to pay for the goods, unless there is a particular "relief clause" in the contract of sale which he invokes to obtain this relief. Such clauses may provide for the extension of time or the right to avoid the contract under the applicable law (see the comments to A2).

The buyer must also do whatever may be needed to pass the goods through a third country after they have been shipped (dispatched) from the seller's country, unless this obligation is for the seller's account under the contract of carriage.

B3   Contracts of carriage and insurance

a)   Contract of carriage
The buyer has no obligation to the seller to make a contract of carriage.

b)   Contract of insurance
The buyer has no obligation to the seller to make a contract of insurance. However, the buyer must provide the seller, upon request, with the necessary information for obtaining insurance.

Comments   Although B3(a) merely stipulates "No obligation" for the buyer, on-carriage from the port of destination is necessary in most cases, and it is the buyer's responsibility to do whatever is required for this purpose. But the seller is not concerned with the further carriage of the goods, and the buyer has no obligation to the seller in this respect. Whatever the buyer does is in his own interest and is not covered by the contract of sale.

CFR

B4   Taking delivery

The buyer must take delivery of the goods when they have been delivered as envisaged in A4 and receive them from the carrier at the named port of destination.

Comments   Here, the two critical points under a CFR sale appear again. Since the seller fulfils his obligation by delivering the goods on board the vessel at the port of shipment (A4), it is for the buyer to accept such delivery under B4. But the buyer also has a further obligation to receive the goods from the carrier at the named port of destination. This is not something he does only in his own interest (as in B3) but is an obligation to the seller, who has concluded the contract of carriage with the carrier.

Unless the buyer frees the goods from the ship when they duly arrive, the seller may incur additional costs debited to him by the carrier. These costs must be borne by the buyer if he is in breach of his obligation to receive the goods from the carrier.

That the buyer must take delivery of the goods when they have been delivered in accordance with A4 does not, of course, preclude him from raising claims against the seller if the goods do not conform with the contract.

Charter party loading and discharge

In the charter party trade, problems frequently arise in ports of loading as well as in ports of discharge when the time for loading and discharging the cargo exceeds the "free" time according to the charter party terms (the "lay-time"). In these cases, the charterer has to pay particular compensation ("demurrage") to the owner.

Needless to say, it is vital for sellers and buyers to agree, not only in the charter party but also in the contract of sale, how much time should be available for loading and discharge respectively, and which of the parties should bear the costs of any demurrage charged by the shipowner. Charter parties may also provide that the shipowner should pay compensation if the time of loading and/or discharge is less than a certain stipulated time. This is so-called dispatch, or despatch, money. In this case, it is also important to stipulate in the contract of sale which of the parties should be entitled to this compensation.

B5   Transfer of risks

The buyer bears all risks of loss of or damage to the goods from the time they have been delivered as envisaged in A4.

If the buyer fails to give notice in accordance with B7, then it bears all risks of loss of or damage to the goods from the agreed date or the expiry date of the agreed period for shipment, provided that the goods have been clearly identified as the contract goods.

Comments   According to the main rule, while the seller under A5 bears the risk of loss of or damage to the goods until the delivery point, the buyer has to bear the risk thereafter. The delivery point is different under the different terms. In EXW and all D-terms, the goods are simply placed "at the disposal of the buyer" at the relevant point, while under the F- and C-terms the delivery point is related to the handing over of the goods to the carrier in the country of dispatch or shipment (see the comments to A4 of these terms). In the terms used for goods intended to be carried by sea, reference is made to delivery alongside the named vessel (FAS) or delivery on board the vessel (FOB, CFR, CIF).

Since the seller is relieved from any further risk of loss of or damage to the goods when they have placed on board, it follows that the buyer has to assume these risks subsequent to the passing of that critical point. According to the terms of the contract of sale, the buyer may be given the option to determine the time for shipping the goods. This option may also include the right to later name the port to which the goods should be shipped. In these cases, it is necessary that the seller be given timely and sufficient notice (see comments to B7).

Premature transfer of risk

If the buyer fails to give appropriate notice to the seller, he could be exposed to additional costs and risks if the goods have to be stored in the port of loading, pending shipping instructions. B5 stipulates that in these cases the risk may be transferred from the seller to the buyer before the time when the goods have placed on board. This is an important exception to the main rule.

This premature transfer of the risks could occur at one of two points: (1) when, as a result of the buyer's failure to give sufficient notice, the goods cannot be shipped at an agreed date or (2) on the expiry date, in cases when the buyer has been given a period during which to determine the time for shipment.

In accordance with the general principle of the Incoterms rules, this premature transfer of the risks will never occur until the goods have been identified as the contract goods.

B6   Allocation of costs

The buyer must, subject to the provisions of A3 a), pay

a)   all costs relating to the goods from the time they have been delivered as envisaged in A4, except, where applicable, the costs of customs formalities necessary for export as well as all duties, taxes, and other charges payable upon export as referred to in A6 c);

b)   all costs and charges relating to the goods while in transit until their arrival at the port of destination, unless such costs and charges were for the seller's account under the contract of carriage;

c)   unloading costs including lighterage and wharfage charges, unless such costs and charges were for the seller's account under the contract of carriage;

d)   any additional costs incurred if it fails to give notice in accordance with B7, from the agreed date or the expiry date of the agreed period for shipment, provided that the goods have been clearly identified as the contract goods; and

e)   where applicable, all duties, taxes and other charges, as well as the costs of carrying out customs formalities payable upon import of the goods and the costs for their transport through any country unless included within the cost of the contract of carriage.

CFR

Comments   While the seller has to pay all costs required to bring the goods to the port of shipment and to deliver the goods onboard the vessel (as well as unloading charges at the port of discharge, provided they have been included in the freight), the buyer has to pay any further costs which may arise after the seller has delivered the goods on board the vessel. In this sense, the transfer of the risk also determines the division of costs. If something occurs as a result of contingencies after shipment – such as strandings, collisions, strikes, government directions, hindrances because of ice or other weather conditions – any additional costs charged by the carrier as a result of these contingencies, or otherwise occurring, will be for the account of the buyer.

The buyer is free from paying the further costs only if these costs "were for the seller's account under the contract of carriage". This does not mean, however, that the buyer must pay for costs and charges payable under the contract of carriage in the ordinary course of events (for example, when the shipper has been given credit by the carrier, i.e., "collect freight").

Failure to give notice and premature passing of risk

The failure to give appropriate notice in accordance with B7 not only results in a premature transfer of the risks (see comments to B5) but also imposes on the buyer the responsibility to pay any additional costs as a consequence. In this case, the obligation to pay these additional costs occurs only if the goods have been identified as the contract goods (as discussed in the comments to B5).

Buyer's duties in clearing goods for import

As noted in the comments to B2, the buyer has the duty to clear the goods for import; it is then established in B6 that he has to pay the costs arising from the clearance ("duties, taxes and other charges as well as the costs of carrying out customs formalities"). The buyer also has to pay any duties, taxes and other charges arising in connection with the transit of the goods through another country after they have been delivered by the seller in accordance with A4 unless these costs were for the seller's account under the contract of carriage.

B7   Notices to the seller

The buyer must, whenever it is entitled to determine the time for shipping the goods and/or the point of receiving the goods within the named port of destination, give the seller sufficient notice thereof.

Comments   As discussed in the comments to B5 and B6, the failure of the buyer to notify the seller of the time for dispatching the goods and/or the named place of destination or the point of receiving the goods within that place – when the buyer in the contract of sale has been given the option to determine these matters – may cause the risk of the loss of or damage to the goods to pass before the goods have been delivered according to A4. In addition, it can make the buyer liable to pay any additional costs incurred by the seller as a result of the buyer's failure.

CFR

B8   Proof of delivery

The buyer must accept the transport document provided as envisaged in A8 if it is in conformity with the contract.

Comments   The buyer has to accept the transport document if it conforms with the contract and with the requirements of A8 (see the comments to A8). If the buyer rejects a conforming transport document (for example, by instructions to a bank not to pay the seller under a documentary credit), he commits a breach of contract, which would give the seller remedies available for such a breach under the contract of sale.

These remedies could include, for example, a right to cancel the contract or to claim damages for breach. However, the buyer is not obliged to accept a document which does not provide adequate proof of delivery, for example, one which has notations on it showing that the goods are defective or that they have been provided in less than the agreed quantity. In these cases, the document is termed "unclean".

B9   Inspection of goods

The buyer must pay the costs of any mandatory pre-shipment inspection, except when such inspection is mandated by the authorities of the country of export.

Comments   As discussed in the comments to A9, the buyer has to pay for any costs of checking the goods unless the contract states that these costs should be borne wholly or partly by the seller. In some cases, the contract may provide that the costs should be borne by the seller if the inspection reveals that the goods do not conform with the contract.

In some countries, where import licences or permission to obtain foreign currency for the payment of the price may be required, the authorities may demand an inspection of the goods before shipment, to ensure that the goods are in conformity with the contract. (This is usually called pre-shipment inspection, PSI.) If this is the case, the inspection is normally arranged by instructions from the authorities to an inspection company, which they appoint. The costs following from this inspection have to be paid by the authorities. Any reimbursement to the authorities for the inspection costs, however, must be made by the buyer, unless mandated by the authorities of the country of export or specifically agreed between the buyer and the seller.

B10   Assistance with information and related costs

The buyer must, in a timely manner, advise the seller of any security information requirements so that the seller may comply with A10.

The buyer must reimburse the seller for all costs and charges incurred by the seller in providing or rendering assistance in obtaining documents and information as envisaged in A10.

The buyer must, where applicable, in a timely manner, provide to or render assistance in obtaining for the seller, at the seller's request, risk and expense, any documents and information, including security-related information, that the seller needs for the transport and export of the goods and for their transport through any country.

CFR

Comments   As discussed in the comments to A10, the seller has to render the buyer assistance in obtaining the documents or electronic messages and information which may be required for the transit and import and security-clearance of the goods. However, this assistance is rendered at the buyer's risk and expense. Therefore, B10 stipulates that the buyer must pay all costs and charges incurred in obtaining these documents or electronic messages. He will also have to reimburse the seller for the seller's costs in rendering his assistance in these matters.

COST INSURANCE AND FREIGHT
CIF (insert named port of destination) the Incoterms® 2010 rules

DELIVERY

GUIDANCE NOTE

This rule is to be used only for sea or inland waterway transport.

"Cost, Insurance and Freight" means that the seller delivers the goods on board the vessel or procures the goods already so delivered. The risk of loss of or damage to the goods passes when the goods are on board the vessel. The seller must contract for and pay the costs and freight necessary to bring the goods to the named port of destination.

The seller also contracts for insurance cover against the buyer's risk of loss of or damage to the goods during the carriage. The buyer should note that under CIF the seller is required to obtain insurance only on minimum cover. Should the buyer wish to have more insurance protection, it will need either to agree as much expressly with the seller or to make its own extra insurance arrangements.

When CPT, CIP, CFR, or CIF are used, the seller fulfils its obligation to deliver when it hands the goods over to the carrier in the manner specified in the chosen rule and not when the goods reach the place of destination.

This rule has two critical points, because risk passes and costs are transferred at different places. While the contract will always specify a destination port, it might not specify the port of shipment, which is where risk passes to the buyer. If the shipment port is of particular interest to the buyer, the parties are well advised to identify it as precisely as possible in the contract.

The parties are well advised to identify as precisely as possible the point at the agreed port of destination, as the costs to that point are for the account of the seller. The seller is advised to procure contracts of carriage that match this choice precisely. If the seller incurs costs under its contract of carriage related to unloading at the specified point at the port of destination, the seller is not entitled to recover such costs from the buyer unless otherwise agreed between the parties.

The seller is required either to deliver the goods on board the vessel or to procure goods already so delivered for shipment to the destination. In addition the seller is required either to make a contract of carriage or to procure such a contract. The reference to "procure" here caters for multiple sales down a chain ('string sales'), particularly common in the commodity trades.

CIF may not be appropriate where goods are handed over to the carrier before they are on board the vessel, for example goods in containers, which are typically delivered at a terminal. In such circumstances, the CIP rule should be used.

CIF requires the seller to clear the goods for export, where applicable. However, the seller has no obligation to clear the goods for import, pay any import duty or carry out any import customs formalities.

CIF

A   THE SELLER'S OBLIGATIONS

A1, A2, A3(a), A4 to A10

See the comments to CFR A1, A2, A3 (a), A4 to A10.

A3 (b)   Contracts of insurance

b)   Contract of insurance
The seller must obtain, at its own expense, cargo insurance complying at least with the minimum cover provided by Clauses (C) of the Institute Cargo Clauses (LMA/IUA) or any similar clauses. The insurance shall be contracted with underwriters or an insurance company of good repute and entitle the buyer, or any other person having an insurable interest in the goods, to claim directly from the insurer.

When required by the buyer, the seller shall, subject to the buyer providing any necessary information requested by the seller, provide at the buyer's expense any additional cover, if procurable, such as cover as provided by Clauses (A) or (B) of the Institute Cargo Clauses (LMA/IUA) or any similar clauses and/or cover complying with the Institute War Clauses and/or Institute Strikes Clauses (LMA/IUA) or any similar clauses.

The insurance shall cover, at a minimum, the price provided in the contract plus 10% (i.e., 110%) and shall be in the currency of the contract.

The insurance shall cover the goods from the point of delivery set out in A4 and A5 to at least the named port of destination.

The seller must provide the buyer with the insurance policy or other evidence of insurance cover.

Moreover, the seller must provide the buyer, at the buyer's request, risk, and expense (if any), with information that the buyer needs to procure any additional insurance.

Comments   The only difference between the CFR and the CIF term is that the latter requires the seller also to obtain and pay for cargo insurance. This is particularly important for the buyer, since under CIF the risk for loss of or damage to the goods will pass from the seller to the buyer when the goods are loaded on board at the port of shipment (see A5 under CFR).

In addition, it is vital for the buyer to be given the right to claim against the insurer independently of the seller. For this purpose it may be necessary to provide the buyer with the insurance policy under which the insurer makes his undertaking directly to the buyer.

Seller need only provide "minimum cover"
It is important to note that the seller only has to provide for "minimum cover". Such limited cover is suitable only for bulk cargoes, which normally do not suffer loss or damage in transit unless something happens to the ship as well as to the cargo (strandings, collisions, fire, etc.). The buyer and seller are therefore advised to agree that the seller should provide a more suitable insurance cover. The buyer should then specify the extended cover he prefers.

CIF

The insurance cover according to the so-called Institute Cargo Clauses is available in different categories. However, even the most extended cover in A does not provide for what is misleadingly called "all-risk insurance". Furthermore, there are other important exceptions which category A insurance does not cover, for example, cases when the loss of the goods has been caused by insolvency or fraud, or when financial loss has been incurred by delay in delivery.

Duration of insurance cover

The duration of the insurance cover must coincide with the carriage and must protect the buyer from the moment he has to bear the risk of loss of or damage to the goods (i.e., from the moment the goods are loaded on board at the port of shipment). It must extend until the goods arrive at the agreed port of destination.

Some risks require additional cover

Some particular risks require additional insurance, and if the buyer requests it, the seller must arrange this additional cover at the buyer's expense – for example, insurance against the risks of war, strikes, riots and civil commotion – if this cover can possibly be arranged.

Amount of the insurance cover

The amount of the insurance should correspond to the price provided in the contract, plus 10 per cent. The additional 10 per cent is intended to cover the average profit that buyers of goods expect from the sale. The insurance should be provided in the same currency as stipulated in the contract for the price of the goods. Consequently, if the price of the goods is to be paid in convertible currency, the seller may not provide insurance in other than convertible currency.

B THE BUYER'S OBLIGATIONS

B1 to B2, B3(a) and B4 to B10

See the comments to CFR B1,B2, B3(a) and B4 to B10.

B3(b) Contract of insurance

b)   Contract of insurance
The buyer has no obligation to the seller to make a contract of insurance. However, the buyer must provide the seller, upon request, with any information necessary for the seller to procure any additional insurance requested by the buyer as envisaged in A3 (b).

Comments   It is vital for the buyer to understand that the seller only has to take out minimum insurance cover. This cover in most cases is insufficient when manufactured goods are involved. In the contract of sale, therefore, the buyer should require the seller to take out additional cover, usually according to the Institute Clauses A or a corresponding cover. If, however, the contract does not deal with this matter at all, the seller's obligation is limited as stipulated in A3(b), and the buyer has to arrange and pay for any additional insurance cover required.

In most cases the seller will know how to arrange the insurance from the contract of sale (from the invoice value of the goods, their destination, etc.). But if this is not the case, the buyer has to provide the seller, upon the latter's request, with any additional necessary information.

Role of the Incoterms rules in an international contract of sale

1. Choice of trade terms

2. The Incoterms rules in conjunction with other terms in the contract sale

3. The Incoterms rules in conjunction with CISG

4. Transfer of risk and cost

1. CHOICE OF TRADE TERMS

GROUP I: ANY MODE OR MODES OF TRANSPORT

EXW FCA CPT CIP DAP DAT DDP: may be chosen for maritime transport and should be chosen for wholly or partly non-maritime transport

GROUP II: SEA AND INLAND WATERWAY TRANSPORT

FAS FOB CFR CIF: should only be chosen for maritime transport

CHOICE WITHIN GROUP I

EXW   Seller wants to restrict its obligation merely to place the goods at the buyer's disposal at the seller's premises or another named place

FCA   Seller willing to make the goods available for the buyer at the carrier's named reception point and to clear the goods for export

CPT   Seller, in addition to obligations under FCA, is also willing to provide and pay for a contract of carriage to a named destination

CIP   Seller, in addition to obligations under CPT, is also willing to provide and pay for insurance

DAP   Seller willing to deliver at a named place and to assume all costs and risks until the goods arrive there

DAT   Seller, in addition to obligations under DAP, is also willing to unload the goods from the means of transport upon arrival at the named place or point

DDP   Seller, in addition to obligations under DAP, is also willing to clear the goods for import and pay the duty

CHOICE WITHIN GROUP II

FAS   Seller willing to deliver, or procure the goods delivered alongside the ship

FOB   Seller willing to deliver, or procure the goods delivered on board the ship

CFR   Seller, in addition to obligations under FOB, is also willing to provide and pay for a contract of carriage to the named destination

CIF   Seller, in addition to obligations under CFR, is also willing to provide and pay for insurance

2.   THE INCOTERMS RULES IN CONJUNCTION WITH OTHER TERMS OF THE CONTRACT AS SET FORTH IN THE ICC SALE FORM

What happens if:

EXW   Seller fails to place conforming goods at the buyer's disposal in time?

FCA   Seller fails to timely deliver conforming goods at the carrier's reception point and/or to clear the goods for export?

CPT   Seller fails to timely deliver conforming goods at the carrier's reception point and/or to clear the goods for export or to provide and pay for the contract of carriage?

CIP   Seller, in addition to any non-performance of obligations under CPT, fails to provide and pay for insurance?

DAP   Seller fails to timely deliver conforming goods at the agreed place and/or to clear the goods for export?

DAT   Seller, in addition to any non-performance of obligations under DAP, fails to properly unload the goods from the arriving means of transport?

DDP   Seller fails to timely deliver conforming goods at the agreed place and/or to clear the goods for export and import?

Under all terms   Buyer fails to pay or take the goods?

Answer:

Seller incurs liability for the consequences following from non-conformity and delay but subject to the seller's right to cure any non-conformity by providing substitute goods and the right to avoid further liability by payment of fixed amounts for period(s) of delay and for the buyer's loss in the event of its termination of the contract due to the seller's breach.

If, under CIP or CIF, the seller fails to fulfill his obligation to provide and pay for insurance, the buyer is entitled to get the same amount from the seller as the buyer could have recovered from the insurer in case the seller had fulfilled its insurance obligation.

Buyer incurs liability for his failure to pay or take the goods, which may result in a liability to pay default interest (2% above the average bank short- term lending rate; clause 6.2) and/or damages. If the buyer's breach is fundamental, the seller may be entitled to terminate the contract.

Relief from liability may be obtained in some cases of so-called force majeure events.

3. THE INCOTERMS RULES IN CONJUNCTION WITH CISG

What happens if:

FAS Seller fails to timely place conforming goods alongside the ship in the port of shipment and/or to clear the goods for export?

FOB Seller fails to timely place conforming goods on board the ship in the port of shipment and to clear the goods for export?

CFR Seller fails to timely place conforming goods on board the ship in the port of shipment and/or to clear the goods for export or to arrange and pay for the usual contract of carriage?

CIF Seller, in addition to non-performance of obligations under CFR, fails to arrange and pay for insurance?

Under all terms Buyer fails to pay or take the goods?

Answer:

The seller's and the buyer's obligations are strict and, in the sale of commodities, time is of essence. The possibility to obtain relief by invoking "impediments beyond control" according to article 79 CISG is limited and any non-performance may work to the detriment of the other party in such a manner that it is entitled to terminate the contract according to articles 47,49 (buyer for seller's breach) and articles 63,64 (seller for buyer's breach) compared with article 25 CISG. Also, when documents are tendered by the seller under documentary credits, any discrepancy may cause the bank to reject non-compliant document(s). Hence, the seller or the buyer may not only risk the loss of a profitable bargain but also a liability in damages for all consequences of the breach, except where, at the time of the conclusion of the contract, it was impossible to foresee such consequences of the breach.

If, under CIF, the seller fails to provide and pay for insurance, the buyer is entitled to get from the seller the same amount as he could have received from the insurer if the seller had fulfilled his insurance obligation. The seller's failure to provide a document evidencing insurance will prevent him from obtaining payment under a documentary credit and may entitle the buyer to terminate the contract.

4. TRANSFER OF RISK AND COST

Buyer, under all terms, has to pay the agreed price even if the goods have become lost or damaged and bear any additional costs, provided the goods have been delivered as defined in articles A4.

Buyer, under FAS and FOB , has to bear the risk and cost if he fails to give appropriate notice or the nominated ship fails to arrive in time or is unable to take the goods, provided the goods have been identified as the contract goods.

ANNEXES

1/ CMI Uniform Rules for SEA WAYBILLS

Comité Maritime International – Paris, June 29, 1990

1.   Scope of Application

(i) These Rules shall be called the "CMI Uniform Rules for Sea Waybills".

(ii) They shall apply when adopted by a contract of carriage which is not covered by a bill of lading or similar document of title, whether the contract be in writing or not.

2.   Definitions

In these Rules:

"Contract of carriage" shall mean any contract of carriage subject to these Rules which is to be performed wholly or partly by sea.

"Goods" shall mean any goods carried or received for carriage under a contract of carriage.

"Carrier" and "Shipper" shall mean the parties named in or identifiable as such from the contract of carriage.

"Consignee" shall mean the party named in or identifiable as such from the contract of carriage, or any person substituted as consignee in accordance with rule 6(i).

"Right of Control" shall mean the rights and obligations referred to in rule 6.

3.   Agency

(i) The shipper on entering into the contract of carriage does so not only on his own behalf but also as agent for and on behalf of the consignee, and warrants to the carrier that he has authority so to do.

(ii) This rule shall apply if, and only if, it be necessary by the law applicable to the contract of carriage so as to enable the consignee to sue and be sued thereon. The consignee shall be under no greater liability than he would have been had the contract of carriage been covered by a bill of lading or similar document of title.

4.   Rights and Responsibilities

(i) The contract of carriage shall be subject to any International Convention or National Law which is, or if the contract of carriage had been covered by a bill of lading or similar document of title would have been, compulsorily applicable thereto. Such convention or law shall apply notwithstanding anything inconsistent therewith in the contract of carriage.

(ii) Subject always to subrule (i), the contract of carriage is governed by:

    (a) these Rules;

    (b) unless otherwise agreed by the parties, the carrier's standard terms and conditions for the trade, if any, including any terms and conditions relating to the non-sea part of the carriage;

    (c) any other terms and conditions agreed by the parties.

(iii) In the event of any inconsistency between the terms and conditions mentioned under subrule (ii)(b) or (c) and these Rules, these Rules shall prevail.

5.   Description of the Goods

(i) The shipper warrants the accuracy of the particulars furnished by him relating to the goods, and shall indemnify the carrier against any loss, damage or expense resulting from any inaccuracy.

(ii) In the absence of reservation by the carrier, any statement in a sea waybill or similar document as to the quantity or condition of the goods shall

(a) as between the carrier and the shipper be prima facie evidence of receipt of the goods as so stated;

(b) as between the carrier and the consignee be conclusive evidence of receipt of the goods as so stated, and proof to the contrary shall not be permitted, provided always that the consignee has acted in good faith.

6. Right of Control

(i) Unless the shipper has exercised his option under subrule (ii) below, he shall be the only party entitled to give the carrier instructions in relation to the contract of carriage. Unless prohibited by the applicable law, he shall be entitled to change the name of the consignee at any time up to the consignee claiming delivery of the goods after their arrival at destination, provided he gives the carrier reasonable notice in writing, or by some other means acceptable to the carrier, and thereby undertaking to indemnify the carrier against any additional expense caused thereby.

(ii) The shipper shall have the option, to be exercised not later than the receipt of the goods by the carrier, to transfer the right of control to the consignee. The exercise of this option must be noted on the sea waybill or similar document, if any. Where the option has been exercised the consignee shall have such rights as are referred to in subrule (i) above and the shipper shall cease to have such rights.

7. Delivery

(i) The carrier shall deliver the goods to the consignee upon production of proper identification.

(ii) The carrier shall be under no liability for wrong delivery if he can prove that he has exercised reasonable care to ascertain that the party claiming to be the consignee is in fact that party.

8. Validity

In the event of anything contained in these Rules or any such provisions as are incorporated into the contract of carriage by virtue of Rule 4, being inconsistent with the provisions of any International Convention or National Law compulsorily applicable to the contract of carriage, such Rules and provisions shall to that extent but no further be null and void.

2/CMI Rules for ELECTRONIC BILLS of LADING

Comité Maritime International – Paris, June 29, 1990

1. Scope of Application

These rules shall apply whenever the parties so agree.

2. Definitions

a. "Contract of Carriage" means any agreement to carry goods wholly or partly by sea.

b. "EDI" means Electronic Data Interchange, i.e. the interchange of trade data effected by teletransmission.

c. "UN/EDIFACT" means the United Nations Rules for Electronic Data Interchange for Administration, Commerce and Transport.

d. "Transmission" means one or more messages electronically sent together as one unit of dispatch which includes heading and terminating data.

e. "Confirmation" means a Transmission which advises that the content of a Transmission appears to be complete and correct, without prejudice to any subsequent consideration or action that the content may warrant.

f. "Private Key" means any technically appropriate form, such as a combination of numbers and/or letters, which the parties may agree for securing the authenticity and integrity of a Transmission.

g. "Holder" means the party who is entitled to the rights described in Article 7(a) by virtue of its possession of a valid Private Key.

h. "Electronic Monitoring System" means the device by which a computer system can be examined for the transactions that it recorded, such as a Trade Data Log or an Audit Trail.

i. "Electronic Storage" means any temporary, intermediate or permanent storage of electronic data including the primary and the back-up storage of such data.

3. Rules of Procedure

a. When not in conflict with these Rules, the Uniform Rules of Conduct for Interchange of Trade Data by Teletransmission, 1987 (UNCID) shall govern the conduct between the parties.

b. The EDI under these Rules should conform with the relevant UN/EDIFACT standards. However, the parties may use any other method of trade data interchange acceptable to all of the users.

c. Unless otherwise agreed, the document format for the Contract of Carriage shall conform to the UN Layout Key of compatible national standard for bills of lading.

d. Unless otherwise agreed, a recipient of a Transmission is not authorized to act on a Transmission unless he has sent a Confirmation.

e. In the event of a dispute arising between the parties as to the data actually transmitted, an Electronic Monitoring System may be used to verify the data received. Data concerning other transactions not related to the data in dispute are to be considered as trade secrets and thus not available for examination. If such data are unavoidably revealed as part of the examination of the Electronic Monitoring System, they must be treated as confidential and not released to any outside party or used for any other purpose.

f. Any transfer of rights to the goods shall be considered to be private information, and shall not be released to any outside party not connected to the transport or clearance of the goods.

4. Form and Content of the Receipt Message

a. The carrier, upon receiving the goods from the shipper, shall give notice of the receipt of the goods to the shipper by a message at the electronic address specified by the shipper.

b. This receipt message shall include:

   i. the name of the shipper;

   ii. the description of the goods, with any representations and reservations, in the same tenor as would be required if a paper bill of lading were issued;

   iii. the date and place of the receipt of the goods;

   iv. a reference to the carrier's terms and conditions of carriage; and

   v. the Private Key to be used in subsequent Transmissions.

   The shipper must confirm this receipt message to the carrier, upon which Confirmation the shipper shall be the Holder.

c. Upon demand of the Holder, the receipt message shall be updated with the date and place of shipment as soon as the goods have been loaded on board.

d. The information contained in (ii), (iii) and (iv) of paragraph (b) above, including the date and place of shipment if updated in accordance with paragraph (c) of this Rule, shall have the same force and effect as if the receipt message were contained in a paper bill of lading.

5. **Terms and Conditions of the Contract of Carriage**

   a. It is agreed and understood that whenever the carrier makes a reference to its terms and conditions of carriage, these terms and conditions shall form part of the Contract of Carriage.

   b. Such terms and conditions must be readily available to the parties to the Contract of Carriage.

   c. In the event of any conflict or inconsistency between such terms and conditions and these Rules, these Rules shall prevail.

6. **Applicable Law**

   The Contract of Carriage shall be subject to any international convention or national law which would have been compulsorily applicable if a paper bill of lading had been issued.

7. **Right of Control and Transfer**

   a. The Holder is the only party who may, as against the carrier:

      (1) claim delivery of the goods;

      (2) nominate the consignee or substitute a nominated consignee for any other party, including itself;

      (3) transfer the Right of Control and Transfer to another party;

      (4) instruct the carrier on any other subject concerning the goods, in accordance with the terms and conditions of the Contract of Carriage, as if he were the holder of a paper bill of lading.

   b. A transfer of the Right of Control and Transfer shall be effected: (i) by notification of the current Holder to the carrier of its intention to transfer its Right of Control and Transfer to a proposed new Holder, and (ii) Confirmation by the carrier of such notification message, whereupon (iii) the carrier shall transmit the information as referred to in article 4 [except for the Private Key] to the proposed new Holder, whereafter (iv) the proposed new Holder shall advise the carrier of its acceptance of the Right of Control and Transfer, whereupon (v) the carrier shall cancel the current Private Key and issue a new Private Key to the new Holder.

   c. If the proposed new Holder advises the carrier that it does not accept the Right of Control and Transfer or fails to advise the carrier of such acceptance within a reasonable time, the proposed transfer of the Right of Control and Transfer shall not take place. The carrier shall notify the current Holder accordingly and the current Private Key shall retain its validity.

   d. The transfer of the Right of Control and Transfer in the manner described above shall have the same effect as the transfer of such rights under a paper bill of lading.

8. **The Private Key**

   a. The Private Key is unique to each successive Holder. It is not transferable by the Holder. The carrier and the Holder shall each maintain the security of the Private Key.

   b. The carrier shall only be obliged to send a Confirmation of an electronic message to the last Holder to whom it issued a Private Key, when such Holder secures the Transmission containing such electronic message by the use of the Private Key.

   c. The Private Key must be separate and distinct from any means used to identify the Contract of Carriage, and any security password or identification used to access the computer network.

9. **Delivery**

   a. The carrier shall notify the Holder of the place and date of intended delivery of the goods. Upon such notification the Holder has a duty to nominate a consignee and to give adequate delivery instructions to the carrier with verification by the Private Key. In the absence of such nomination, the Holder will be deemed to be the consignee.

    b.   The carrier shall deliver the goods to the consignee upon production of proper identification in accordance with the delivery instructions specified in paragraph (a) above; such delivery shall automatically cancel the Private Key.

    c.   The carrier shall be under no liability for misdelivery if it can prove that it exercised reasonable care to ascertain that the party who claimed to be the consignee was in fact that party.

10.   Option to Receive a Paper Document

    a.   The Holder has the option at any time prior to delivery of the goods to demand from the carrier a paper bill of lading. Such document shall be made available at a location to be determined by the Holder, provided that no carrier shall be obliged to make such document available at a place where it has no facilities and in such instance the carrier shall only be obliged to make the document available at the facility nearest to the location determined by the Holder. The carrier shall not be responsible for delays in delivering the goods resulting from the Holder exercising the above option.

    b.   The carrier has the option at any time prior to delivery of the goods to issue to the Holder a paper bill of lading unless the exercise of such option could result in undue delay or disrupts the delivery of the goods.

    c.   A bill of lading issued under Rules 10(a) or (b) shall include: (i) the information set out in the receipt message referred to in Rule 4 (except for the Private Key); and (ii) a statement to the effect that the bill of lading has been issued upon termination of the procedures for EDI under the CMI Rules for Electronic Bills of Lading. The aforementioned bill of lading shall be issued at the option of the Holder either to the order of the Holder < whose name for this purpose shall then be inserted in the bill of lading > or to bearer.

    d.   The issuance of a paper bill of lading under Rule 10(a) or (b) shall cancel the Private Key and terminate the procedures for EDI under these Rules. Termination of these procedures by the Holder or the carrier will not relieve any of the parties to the Contract of Carriage of their rights, obligations or liabilities while performing under the present Rules nor of their rights, obligations or liabilities under the Contract of Carriage.

    e.   The Holder may demand at any time the issuance of a print-out of the receipt message referred to in Rule 4 (except for the Private Key) marked as ``non-negotiable copy." The issuance of such a print-out shall not cancel the Private Key nor terminate the procedures for EDI.

11.   Electronic Data is Equivalent to Writing

The carrier and the shipper and all subsequent parties utilizing these procedures agree that any national or local law, custom or practice requiring the Contract of Carriage to be evidenced in writing and signed, is satisfied by the transmitted and confirmed electronic data residing on computer data storage media displayable in human language on a video screen or as printed out by a computer. In agreeing to adopt these Rules, the parties shall be taken to have agreed not to raise the defense that this contract is not in writing.

Synopsis of usages rules
for the trademark " Incoterms"

"Incoterms" is a trademark of the International Chamber of Commerce.

Although ICC encourages and promotes the use of the Incoterms® rules by third parties in sales contracts in compliance with ICC's copyright policy, "Incoterms" is not a generic term that may be used to designate any trade terms, but is a trademark used to designate only the terms devised by ICC and products and services from ICC.

Below are some rules on the correct usage of the " Incoterms " trademark:

- Use the trademark " Incoterms" to refer only to ICC's Incoterms® rules and other Incoterms® products and services from ICC.

- In text, use " Incoterms" as an adjective, not a noun.

- Do not use " Incoterms" without the initial letter as a capital letter.

- Do not use " Incoterms" (without the final "s"). An individual term from the the Incoterms should be referred to as an Incoterms® rule, and never as an " Incoterms ".

- Use the registered trademark symbol ® next to the trademark " Incoterms ".

- Any use of the trademark " Incoterms" in association with products and services not from ICC requires a licence from ICC.

More information on the correct usage of ICC's " Incoterms" trademark can be found on ICC's website on the Incoterms® rules at www.incoterms.org

Now available on www.iccbooks.com

The Incoterms rules® 2010
ICC Pub. No.715E, 2010 edition
ISBN: 978-92-842-0080-1

For more than 70 years, ICC's Incoterms® rules have helped traders to avoid costly disputes by clearly defining the responsibilities of buyers and sellers for the delivery of goods under sales contracts. This new edition now includes - Advice for the use of electronic procedures; - Information on security-related clearances for shipments; - Advice for the use of the Incoterms® 2010 rules in domestic trade; - and more.

Also available: bilingual English-French edition (715EF). Other languages are available from ICC National Committees around the world. Please visit **www.incoterms.org** or **www.iccbooks.com** for more information.

The Incoterms® 2010 rules Wall Chart
ICC Pub. No. 716L, 2010 edition
ISBN: 978-92-842-0090-0

This practical wallchart explains all 11 Incoterms® 2010 rules at a glance. The poster format is ideal to brighten up classroom and office walls or as a gift for business partners.

ICC International Court of Arbitration Bulletin
ICC Pub. No. BUL-E-VOL21-1

The Incoterms® rules in ICC arbitration: the latest issue of the ICC International Court of Arbitration Bulletin contains the first part of a special feature on the Incoterms® rules, including extracts from 23 awards rendered between 2000 and 2006. Subscriptions and individual issues available on www.icc-books.com.

Training
ICC Events runs training courses on the Incoterms® 2010 rules, as well as on international arbitration and negotiating international contracts for business people, corporate counsel, lawyers and legal practitioners involved in international trade.
www.iccwbo.org/events

In the banking sector:

Uniform Rules for Demand Guarantees (URDG)
ICC Pub. No. 758E, 2010 edition
ISBN: 978-92-842-0036-8

URDG 758, a new set of banking rules for the twenty-first century that will become the international standard for guarantee practice.

ICC's Uniform Rules for Demand Guarantees (URDG) balance the legitimate interests of all parties. Since their first adoption in 1991, these rules have gained international acceptance and official recognition by bankers, traders, industry associations and international organizations including UNCITRAL, FIDIC and the World Bank.

ICC at a glance

ICC is the world business organization, a representative body that speaks with authority on behalf of enterprises from all sectors in every part of the world.

The fundamental mission of ICC is to promote trade and investment across frontiers and help business corporations meet the challenges and opportunities of globalization. Its conviction that trade is a powerful force for peace and prosperity dates from the organization's origins early in the last century. The small group of far-sighted business leaders who founded ICC called themselves "the merchants of peace".

Because its member companies and associations are themselves engaged in international business, ICC has unrivalled authority in making rules that govern the conduct of business across borders. Although these rules are voluntary, they are observed in countless thousands of transactions every day and have become part of the fabric of international trade.

ICC also provides essential services, foremost among them the ICC International Court of Arbitration, the world's leading arbitral institution. Another service is the World Chambers Federation, ICC's worldwide network of chambers of commerce, fostering interaction and exchange of chamber best practice.

Business leaders and experts drawn from the ICC membership establish the business stance on broad issues of trade and investment policy as well as on vital technical and sectoral subjects. These include financial services, information technologies, telecommunications, marketing ethics, the environment, transportation, competition law and intellectual property.

ICC enjoys a close working relationship with the United Nations and other intergovernmental organizations, including the World Trade Organization, the G20 and the G8.

ICC was founded in 1919. Today it groups thousands of member companies and associations from over 120 countries. National committees work with their members to address the concerns of business in their countries and convey to their governments the business views formulated by ICC.

For more information, please visit www.iccwbo.org

ICC publications for global business

ICC's list of specialized publications covers a range of topics including international banking, international trade reference and rules (the Incoterms® rules), law and arbitration, counterfeiting and fraud, model commercial contracts and environmental issues.

ICC products are available from ICC national committees, which exist in over 90 countries around the world. Contact details for a national committee in your country are available at **www.iccwbo.org**

You may also order ICC products online from the ICC Business Bookstore at **www.iccbooks.com,** or purchase them at the ICC Secretariat, located at the address below.

ICC Publications

38 Cours Albert 1er
75008 Paris
France
Tel.   +33 1 49 53 29 23
Fax.   +33 1 49 53 29 02
e-mail   pub@iccwbo.org

International Chamber of Commerce
The world business organization